Siegel's

WILLS AND TRUSTS

Essay and Multiple-Choice Questions and Answers

BRIAN N. SIEGEL
J.D., Columbia Law School
and
LAZAR EMANUEL
J.D., Harvard Law School

PUBLISHERS

111 Eighth Avenue, New York, NY 10011
www.aspenpublishers.com

© 2005 Aspen Publishers, Inc.
a Wolters Kluwer business
www.aspenpublishers.com

Printed in the United States of America.
1 2 3 4 5 6 7 8 9 0
ISBN 0-7355-5694-6

This book is intended as a general review of a legal subject. It is not intended as a source of advice for the solution of legal matters or problems. For advice on legal matters, the reader should consult an attorney.

Siegel's, Emanuel, the judge logo, Law in a Flash and design, CrunchTime and design, Strategies & Tactics and design, and The Professor Series are registered trademarks of Aspen Publishers.

About Aspen Publishers

Aspen Publishers, headquartered in New York City, is a leading information provider for attorneys, business professionals, and law students. Written by preeminent authorities, our products consist of analytical and practical information covering both U.S. and international topics. We publish in the full range of formats, including updated manuals, books, periodicals, CDs, and online products.

Our proprietary content is complemented by 2,500 legal databases, containing over 11 million documents, available through our Loislaw division. Aspen Publishers also offers a wide range of topical legal and business databases linked to Loislaw's primary material. Our mission is to provide accurate, timely, and authoritative content in easily accessible formats, supported by unmatched customer care.

To order any Aspen Publishers title, go to *www.aspenpublishers.com* or call 1-800-638-8437.

To reinstate your manual update service, call 1-800-638-8437.

For more information on Loislaw products, go to *www.loislaw.com* or call 1-800-364-2512.

For Customer Care issues, e-mail *CustomerCare@aspenpublishers.com;* call 1-800-234-1660; or fax 1-800-901-9075.

Aspen Publishers
a Wolters Kluwer business

Acknowledgment

The authors gratefully acknowledge the assistance of the California Committee of Bar Examiners which provided access to questions upon which many of the questions in this book are based.

Introduction

Although law school grades are a significant factor in obtaining a summer internship or entry position at a law firm, no formalized preparation for finals is offered at most law schools. For the most part, students are expected to fend for themselves in learning how to take a law school exam. Ironically, law school exams ordinarily bear little correspondence to the teaching methods used by professors during the school year. Professors require you to spend most of your time briefing cases. Although many claim this is "great preparation" for issue-spotting on exams, it really isn't. Because, in briefing cases, you are made to focus on one or two principles of law at a time, you don't get practice in relating one issue to another or in developing a picture of an entire problem or the entire course. When exams finally come, you're forced to make an abrupt 180-degree turn. Suddenly, you are asked to recognize, define, and discuss a variety of issues buried within a single multi-issue fact pattern. In most schools, you are then asked to select among a number of possible answers, all of which look inviting but only one of which is right.

The comprehensive course outline you've created so diligently, and with such pain, means little if you're unable to apply its contents on your final exams. There is a vast difference between reading opinions in which the legal principles are clearly stated, and applying those same principles to hypothetical essay exams and multiple-choice questions.

The purpose of this book is to help you bridge the gap between memorizing a rule of law and **understanding how to use it** in an exam. After an initial overview describing the exam writing process, you see a large number of hypotheticals which test your ability to write analytical essays and to pick the right answers to multiple-choice questions. **Read them—all of them!** Then review the suggested answers which follow. You'll find that the key to superior grades lies in applying your knowledge through questions and answers, not through rote memory.

GOOD LUCK !

Table of Contents

Preparing Effectively for Essay Examinations

Essay Exam Questions

Essay Exam Answers

Multiple-Choice Questions

Multiple-Choice Answers

Tables and Index

Preparing Effectively for Essay Examinations[1]

To achieve superior scores on essay exams, a law student must (1) learn and understand "blackletter" principles and rules of law for each subject; (2) analyze how those principles of law arise within a test fact pattern; and (3) write clearly and succinctly a short discussion of each principle and how it relates to the facts. One of the most common misconceptions about law school is that you must memorize each word on every page of your casebooks or outlines to do well on exams. The reality is that you can commit an entire casebook to memory and still do poorly on an exam. Our review of hundreds of student answers has shown us that most students can recite the rules. The students who do **best** on exams are able to analyze how the rules they have memorized relate to the facts in the questions, and how to communicate their analysis to the grader. The following pages cover what you need to know to achieve superior scores on your law school essay exams.

The "ERC" Process

To study effectively for law school exams you must be able to "*ERC*" (*E*lementize, *R*ecognize, and *C*onceptualize) each legal principle covered in your casebooks and course outlines. *Elementizing* means reducing each legal theory and rule you learn to a concise, straightforward statement of its essential elements. Without knowledge of these elements, it's difficult to see all the issues as they arise.

For example, if you are asked, "What is self-defense?", it is **not** enough to say, "self-defense is permitted when, if someone is about to hit you, you can prevent him from doing it." This layperson description would leave a grader wondering if you had actually attended law school. An accurate statement of the self-defense principle would go something like this: "When one reasonably believes she is in imminent danger of an offensive touching, she may assert whatever force she reasonably believes necessary under the circumstances to prevent the offensive touching from occurring." This formulation correctly shows that there are four separate, distinct elements which must be satisfied before the defense of self-defense can be successfully asserted: (1) the actor must have a ***reasonable belief*** that (2) the touching which she seeks to prevent is ***offensive***, and that (3) the offensive touching is ***imminent***, and

---

1 To illustrate the principles of effective exam preparation, we have used examples from Torts and Constitutional Law. However, these principles apply to all subjects. One of the most difficult tasks faced by law students is learning how to apply principles from one area of the law to another. We leave it to you, the reader, to think of comparable examples for the subject-matter of this book.

(4) she must use no greater force than she *reasonably believes necessary under the circumstances* to prevent the offensive touching from occurring.

Recognizing means perceiving or anticipating which words or ideas within a legal principle are likely to be the source of issues, and how those issues are likely to arise within a given hypothetical fact pattern. With respect to the self-defense concept, there are four *potential* issues. Did the actor reasonably believe the other person was about to make an offensive contact with her? Was the contact imminent? Would the contact have been offensive? Did she use only such force as she reasonably believed necessary to prevent the imminent, offensive touching?

Conceptualizing means imagining situations in which each of the elements of a rule of law can give rise to factual issues. *Unless you can imagine or construct an application of each element of a rule, you don't truly understand the legal principles behind the rule!* In our opinion, the inability to conjure up hypothetical fact patterns or stories involving particular rules of law foretells a likelihood that you will miss issues involving those rules on an exam. It's *crucial* (1) to *recognize* that issues result from the interaction of facts with the words defining a rule of law; and (2) to develop the ability to *conceptualize* or *imagine* fact patterns using the words or concepts within the rule.

For example, a set of facts illustrating the "reasonable belief" element of the self-defense rule might be the following:

> One evening, A and B had an argument at a bar. A screamed at B, "I'm going to get a knife and stab you!" A then ran out of the bar. B, who was armed with a concealed pistol, left the bar about 15 minutes later. As B was walking home, he heard someone running toward him from behind. B drew his pistol, turned, and shot the person advancing toward him (who was only about ten feet away when the shooting occurred). When B walked over to his victim, he realized that the person he had shot was dead and was not A, but another individual who had simply decided to take an evening jog. There would certainly be an issue whether B had a reasonable belief that the person who was running behind him was A. In the subsequent wrongful-death action, the victim's estate would contend that the earlier threat by A was not enough to give B a reasonable belief that the person running behind him was A. B could contend in rebuttal that given the prior altercation at the bar, A's threat, the darkness, and the fact that the incident occurred soon after A's threat, his belief that A was about to attack him was "reasonable."

An illustration of how the word "imminent" might generate an issue is the following:

> X and Y had been feuding for some time. One afternoon, X suddenly attacked Y with a hunting knife. However, Y was able to wrest the knife

> away from X. At that point, X retreated about four feet away from Y and screamed: "You were lucky this time, but next time I'll have a gun and you'll be finished." Y, having good reason to believe that X would subsequently carry out his threats (after all, X had just attempted to kill Y), immediately thrust the knife into X's chest, killing him. While Y certainly had a reasonable belief that X would attempt to kill him the ***next time*** the two met, Y would probably ***not*** be able to assert the self-defense privilege because the element of "imminency" was absent.

A fact pattern illustrating the actor's right to use only that force which is reasonably necessary under the circumstances might be the following:

> D rolled up a newspaper and was about to strike E on the shoulder with it. As D pulled back his arm for the purpose of delivering the blow, E drew a knife and plunged it into D's chest. While E had every reason to believe that D was about to deliver an offensive impact on him, E probably could not successfully assert the self-defense privilege because the force he utilized in response was greater than reasonably necessary under the circumstances to prevent the impact. E could simply have deflected D's blow or punched D away. The use of a knife constituted a degree of force by E which was ***not*** reasonable, given the minor injury which he would have suffered from the newspaper's impact.

"Mental games" such as these must be played with every element of every rule you learn.

Issue-Spotting

One of the keys to doing well on an essay examination is issue-spotting. In fact, issue-spotting is *the* most important skill you will learn in law school. If you recognize a legal issue, you can always find the applicable rule of law (if there is any) by researching the issue. But if you fail to see the issues, you won't learn the steps that lead to success or failure on exams or, for that matter, in the practice of law. It is important to remember that (1) an issue is a question to be decided by the judge or jury; and (2) a question is "in issue" when it can be disputed or argued about at trial. The bottom line is that *if you don't spot an issue, you can't raise it or discuss it.*

The key to issue-spotting is to learn to approach a problem in the same way as an attorney does. Let's assume you've been admitted to practice and a client enters your office with a legal problem. He will recite his facts to you and give you any documents that may be pertinent. He will then want to know if he can sue (or be sued, if your client seeks to avoid liability). To answer your client's questions intelligently, you will have to decide the following: (1) what principles or rules can possibly be asserted by your client; (2) what defense or defenses can possibly be raised to these princi-ples; (3) what issues may arise if these defenses are asserted; (4) what arguments can each side make to persuade the fact-finder to resolve the issue in his favor; and (5) finally, what will the *likely* outcome of each issue be. *All the issues which can possibly arise at trial will be relevant to your answers.*

How to Discuss an Issue

Keep in mind that *rules of law are the guides to issues* (i.e., an issue arises where there is a question whether the facts do, or do not, satisfy an element of a rule); a rule of law *cannot dispose of an issue* unless the rule can reasonably be *applied to the facts*.

A good way to learn how to discuss an issue is to study the following mini-hypothetical and the two student responses which follow it.

Mini-Hypothetical

A and B were involved in making a movie which was being filmed at a local bar. The script called for A to appear to throw a bottle (which was actually a rubber prop) at B. The fluorescent lighting at the bar had been altered for the movie—the usual subdued blue lights had been replaced with rather bright white lights. The cameraperson had stationed herself just to the left of the swinging doors which served as the main entrance to the bar. As the scene was unfolding, C, a regular patron of the bar, unwit-tingly walked into it. The guard who was usually stationed immediately outside the bar had momentarily left his post to visit the restroom. As C pushed the barroom doors inward, the left door panel knocked the cam-era to the ground with a resounding crash. The first (and only) thing C saw was A (about 5 feet from C), who was getting ready to throw the bottle at B, who was at the other end of the bar (about 15 feet from A). Without hesitation, C pushed A to the ground and punched him in the face. Plastic surgery was required to restore A's profile to its Hollywood-handsome pre-altercation look.

Discuss A's right against C.

Pertinent Principles of Law:

1. Under the rule defining the prevention-of-crime privilege, if one sees that someone is about to commit what she reasonably believes to be a felony or misdemeanor involving a breach of the peace, she may exer-cise whatever degree of force is reasonably necessary under the cir-cumstances to prevent that person from committing the crime.

2. Under the defense-of-others privilege, where one reasonably believes that someone is about to cause an offensive contact upon a third party, she may use whatever force is reasonably necessary under the circumstances to prevent the contact. Some jurisdictions, however, limit this privilege to situations in which the actor and the third party are related.

First Student Answer

Did C commit an assault and battery upon A?

An assault occurs when the defendant intentionally causes the plaintiff to be reasonably in apprehension of an imminent, offensive touching. The facts state that C punched A to the ground. Thus, a battery would have occurred at this point. We are also told that C punched A in the face. It is reasonable to assume that A saw the punch being thrown at him, and therefore A felt in imminent danger of an offensive touching. Based upon the facts, C has committed an assault and battery upon A.

Were C's actions justifiable under the defense-of-others privilege?

C could successfully assert the defense-of-others and prevention-of-crime privileges. When C opened the bar doors, A appeared to be throwing the bottle at B. Although the "bottle" was actually a prop, C had no way of knowing this fact. Also, it was necessary for C to punch A in the face to assure that A could not get back up, retrieve the bottle, and again throw it at B. Although the plastic surgery required by A is unfortunate, C could not be successfully charged with assault and battery.

Second Student Answer

Assault and Battery:

C committed an assault (causing A to be reasonably in apprehension of an imminent, offensive contact) when A saw that C's punch was about to hit him, and battery (causing an offensive contact upon A) when (1) C knocked A to the ground, and (2) C punched A.

Defense-of-Others/Prevention-of-Crime Defenses:

C would undoubtedly assert the privileges of defense-of-others (when defendant reasonably believed the plaintiff was about to make an offensive contact upon a third party, he was entitled to use whatever force was reasonably necessary to prevent the contact); and prevention-of-crime defense (when one reasonably believes another is about to commit a felony or misdemeanor involving a breach of the peace, he may exercise whatever force is reasonably necessary to prevent that person from committing a crime).

A could contend that C was not reasonable in believing that A was about to cause harm to B because the enhanced lighting at the bar and camera crash should have indicated to C, a regular customer, that a movie was being filmed. However, C could probably success-fully contend in rebuttal that his belief was reasonable in light of the facts that (1) he had not seen the camera when he attacked A, and (2) instantaneous action was required (he did not have time to notice the enhanced lighting around the bar).

A might also contend that the justification was forfeited because the degree of force used by C was not reasonable, since C did not have to punch A in the face after A had already been pushed to the ground (i.e., the danger to B was no longer present). However, C could argue in rebuttal that it was necessary to incapacitate A (an individual with apparently violent propensities) while the opportu-nity existed, rather than risk a drawn-out scuffle in which A might prevail. The facts do not indicate how big A and C were; but assum-ing C was not significantly larger than A, C's contention will probably be successful. If, however, C was significantly larger than A, the punch may have been excessive (C could presumably have simply held A down).

Critique

Let's examine the First Student Answer first. It mistakenly treats as an "issue" the assault and battery committed by C upon A. While the actions creating these torts must be mentioned in the facts to provide a foundation for a discussion of the applicable privileges, there was no need to discuss them further because they were not the issue the examiners were testing for.

The structure of the initial paragraph of First Student Answer is also in-correct. After an assault is defined in the first sentence, the second sentence abruptly describes the facts necessary to constitute the commission of a battery. The third sentence then sets forth the elements of a battery. The fourth sentence completes the discussion of assault by describing the facts pertaining to that tort. The two-sentence break between the original men-tion of assault and the facts which constitute assault is confusing; the facts which call for the application of a rule should be mentioned *immediately* after the rule is stated.

A more serious error, however, occurs in the second paragraph of the First Student Answer. While there is an allusion to the correct principle of law (prevention of crime), the *rule is not stated*. As a consequence, the grader can only guess why the student thinks the facts set forth in the subsequent sentences are significant. A grader reading this answer could not be certain whether the student recognized that the issues revolved around the *reasonable belief* and *necessary force* elements of the prevention-of-crime privilege. Superior exam-writing requires that the pertinent facts be *tied* directly and clearly to the operative rule.

The Second Student Answer is very much better than the First Answer. It disposes of C's assault and battery upon A in a few words (yet tells the grader that the writer knows these torts are present). More importantly, the grader can easily see the issues which would arise if the prevention-of-crime privilege were asserted (i.e., "whether C's belief that A was about to commit a crime against B was reasonable" and "whether C used unnecessary force in punching A after A had been knocked to the ground"). Finally, it also utilizes all the facts by indicating how an attorney would assert those facts which are most advantageous to her client.

Structuring Your Answer

Graders will give high marks to a clearly written, well-structured answer. Each issue you discuss should follow a specific and consistent structure which a grader can easily follow.

The Second Student Answer basically utilizes the *I-R-A-A-O format* with respect to each issue. In this format, the *I* stands for the word *Issue*; the *R* for *Rule of law*; the initial *A* for the words *one side's Argument*; the second *A* for *the other party's rebuttal Argument*; and the *O* for your *Opinion as to how the issue would be resolved*. The *I-R-A-A-O* format emphasizes the importance of (1) discussing *both* sides of an issue, and (2) communicating to the grader that where an issue arises, an attorney can only advise her client as to the *probable* decision on that issue.

A somewhat different format for analyzing each issue is the *I-R-A-C format*. Here, the *I* stands for *Issue;* the *R* for *Rule of law;* the *A* for *Application of the facts to the rule of law;* and the *C* for *Conclusion. I-R-A-C* is a legitimate approach to the discussion of a particular issue, within the time constraints imposed by the question. The *I-R-A-C format* must be applied to each issue in the question; it is not the solution to the entire answer. If there are six issues in a question, for example, you should offer six separate, independent *I-R-A-C* analyses.

We believe that the *I-R-A-C* approach is preferable to the *I-R-A-A-O* formula. However, either can be used to analyze and organize essay exam answers. Whatever format you choose, however, you should be consistent throughout the exam and remember the following rules:

First, *analyze all of the relevant facts.* Facts have significance in a particular case *only as they come under the applicable rules of law.* The facts presented must be analyzed and examined to see if they do or do not satisfy one element or another of the applicable rules, and the essential facts and rules must be stated and argued in your analysis.

Second, you must communicate to the grader the *precise rule of law* controlling the facts. In their eagerness to commence their arguments, students sometimes fail to state the applicable rule of law first. Remember, the *R* in either format stands for *Rule of Law.* Defining the rule of law *before* an analysis of the facts is essential in order to allow the grader to follow your reasoning.

Third, it is important to treat *each side of an issue with equal detail.* If a hypothetical describes how an elderly man was killed when he ventured upon the land of a huge power company to obtain a better view of a nuclear reactor, your sympathies might understandably fall on the side of the old man. The grader will nevertheless expect you to see and make every possible argument for the other side. Don't permit your personal viewpoint to affect your answer! A good lawyer never does! When discussing an issue, always state the arguments for each side.

Finally, don't forget to *state your opinion or conclusion* on each issue. Keep in mind, however, that your opinion or conclusion is probably the *least* important part of an exam answer. Why? Because your professor knows that no attorney can tell her client exactly how a judge or jury will decide a particular issue. By definition, an issue is a legal dispute which can go either way. An attorney, therefore, can offer her client only her best opinion about the likelihood of victory or defeat on an issue. Since the decision on any issue lies with the judge or jury, no attorney can ever be absolutely certain of the resolution.

Discuss All Possible Issues

As we've noted, a student should draw *some* type of conclusion or opinion for each issue raised. Whatever your conclusion on a particular issue, it is essential to anticipate and discuss *all of the issues* which would arise if the question were actually tried in court.

Let's assume that a negligence hypothetical involves issues pertaining to duty, breach of duty, proximate causation, and contributory negligence. If the defendant prevails on any one of these issues, he will avoid liability. Nevertheless, even if you feel strongly that the defendant owed no duty to the plaintiff, you *must* go on to discuss all of the other potential issues as well (breach of duty, proximate causation, and contributory negligence). If you were to terminate your answer after a discussion of the duty element only, you'd receive an inferior grade.

Why should you have to discuss every possible issue if you are relatively certain that the outcome of a particular issue would be dispositive of the entire case? Because at the commencement of litigation, neither party can be *absolutely positive* about which issues he will prevail upon at trial. We can state with confidence that every attorney with some degree of experience has won issues he thought he would lose, and has lost issues on which victory was assured. Since one can never be absolutely certain how a factual issue will be resolved by the fact-finder, a good attorney (and exam-writer) will consider *all* possible issues.

To understand the importance of discussing all of the potential issues, you should reflect on what you will do in the actual practice of law. If you represent the defendant, for example, it is your job to raise every possible defense. If there are five potential defenses, and your pleadings only rely on three of them (because you're sure you will win on all three), and the plaintiff is somehow successful on all three issues, your client may well sue you for malpractice. Your client's contention would be that you should be liable because if you had only raised the two additional issues, you might have prevailed on at least one of them, and therefore liability would have been avoided. It is an attorney's duty to raise *all* legitimate issues. A similar philosophy should be followed when taking essay exams.

What exactly do you say when you've resolved the initial issue in favor of the defendant, and discussion of any additional issues would seem to be moot? The answer is simple. You begin the discussion of the next issue with something like, "Assuming, however, the plaintiff prevailed on the fore-going issue, the next issue would be . . ." The grader will understand and appreciate what you have done.

The corollary to the importance of raising all potential issues is that you should avoid discussion of obvious non-issues. Raising non-issues is detrimental in three ways: first, you waste a lot of precious time; second, you usually receive absolutely no points for discussing a point which the grader deems extraneous; and third, it suggests to the grader that you lack the ability to distinguish the significant from the irrelevant. The best guideline for avoiding the discussion of a non-issue is to ask yourself, "Would I, as an attorney, feel comfortable about raising that particular issue or objection in front of a judge"?

Delineate the Transition from One Issue to the Next

It's a good idea to make it easy for the grader to see the issues you've found. One way to accomplish this is to cover no more than one issue per paragraph. Another way is to underline each issue statement. Provided time permits, we recommend that you use both techniques. The essay answers in this book contain numerous illustrations of these suggestions.

One frequent student error is to write two separate paragraphs in which all of the arguments for one side are made in the initial paragraph, and all of the rebuttal arguments by the other side are made in the next paragraph. This is *a bad idea*. It obliges the grader to reconstruct the exam answer in his mind several times to determine whether all possible issues have been discussed by both sides. It will also cause you to state the same rule of law more than once. A better-organized answer presents a given argument by one side and follows that immediately in the same paragraph with the other side's rebuttal to that argument.

Understanding the "Call" of a Question

The statement *at the end of* an essay question or of the fact pattern in a multiple-choice question is sometimes referred to as the "call" of the question. It usually asks you to do something specific like "discuss," "discuss the rights of the parties," "what are X's rights?" "advise X," "the best grounds on which to find the statute unconstitutional are:," "D can be convicted of:," "how should the estate be distributed?," etc. The call of the question should be read carefully because it tells you exactly what you're expected to do. If a question asks, "what are X's rights against Y?" or "X is liable to Y for: . . ." you don't have to spend a lot of time on Y's rights against Z. You will usually receive absolutely no credit for discussing issues or facts that are not required by the call. On the other hand, if the call of an essay question is simply "discuss" or "discuss the rights of the parties," then *all* foreseeable issues must be covered by your answer.

Students are often led astray by an essay question's call. For example, if you are asked for "X's rights against Y" or to "advise X," you may think you may limit yourself to X's viewpoint with respect to the issues. This is *not correct*! You cannot resolve one party's rights against another party without considering the issues which would arise (and the arguments which the other side would assert) if litigation occurred. In short, although the call of the question may appear to focus on the rights of one of the parties to the litigation, a superior answer will cover all the issues and arguments which that person might *encounter* (not just the arguments she would *make*) in attempting to pursue her rights against the other side.

The Importance of Analyzing the Question Carefully Before Writing

The overriding *time pressure* of an essay exam is probably a major reason why many students fail to analyze a question carefully before writing. Five minutes into the allocated time for a particular question, you may notice that the person next to you is writing furiously. This thought then flashes through your mind, "Oh, my goodness, he's putting down more words on the paper than I am, and therefore he's bound to get a better grade." It can be stated **unequivocally** that there is no necessary correlation between the number of words on your exam paper and the grade you'll receive. Students who begin their answer after only five minutes of analysis have probably seen only the most obvious issues, and missed many, if not most, of the subtle ones. They are also likely to be less well-organized.

Opinions differ as to how much time you should spend analyzing and outlining a question before you actually write the answer. We believe that you should spend at least 12 to 18 minutes analyzing, organizing, and outlining a one-hour question before writing your answer. This will usually provide sufficient time to analyze and organize the question thoroughly **and** enough time to write a relatively complete answer. Remember that each word of the question must be scrutinized to determine if it (1) suggests an issue under the operative rules of law, or (2) can be used in making an argument for the resolution of an issue. Since you can't receive points for an issue you don't spot, it is usually wise to read a question **twice** before starting your outline.

When to Make an Assumption

The instructions for a question may tell you to **assume** facts which are necessary to the answer. Even when these instructions are **not** given, you may be obliged to make certain assumptions about missing facts in order to write a thorough answer. Assumptions should be made only when you are told or when you, as the attorney for one of the parties described in the question, would be obliged to solicit additional information from your client. On the other hand, assumptions should **never be used to change or alter the question**. Don't ever write something like "if the facts in the question were . . . , instead of . . . , then . . . would result." If you do this, you are wasting time on facts which are extraneous to the problem before you. Professors want you to deal with **their** fact patterns, not your own.

Students sometimes try to "write around" information they think is missing. They assume that their professor has failed to include every piece of data necessary for a thorough answer. This is generally **wrong**. The professor may have omitted some facts deliberately to see if the student **can figure out what** *to do* under the circumstances. In some instances, the professor may have omitted them inadvertently (even law professors are sometimes human).

The way to deal with the omission of essential information is to describe (1) what fact (or facts) appear to be missing, and (2) why that information is important. As an example, go back to the "movie shoot" hypothetical we discussed above. In that fact pattern, there was no mention of the relative strength of A and C. This fact could be extremely important. If C weighed 240 pounds and was built like a professional football linebacker, while A tipped the scales at a mere 160 pounds, punching A in the face after he had been pushed to the ground would probably constitute unnecessary force (thereby causing C to forfeit the prevention-of-crime privilege). If the physiques of the parties were reversed, however, C's punch to A's face would probably constitute reasonable behavior. Under the facts, C had to incapacitate A while the opportunity presented itself. The last sentences of the Second Student Answer above show that the student understood these subtleties and correctly supplied the essential missing facts and assumptions.

Assumptions should be made in a manner which keeps the other issues open (i.e., they lead to a discussion of all other possible issues). Don't assume facts which would virtually dispose of the entire hypothetical in a few sentences. For example, suppose that A called B a "convicted felon" (a statement which is inherently defamatory, i.e., a defamatory statement is one which tends to subject the plaintiff to hatred, contempt, or ridicule). If A's statement is true, he has a complete defense to B's action for defamation. If the facts don't tell whether A's statement was true or not, it would *not* be wise to write something like, "We'll assume that A's statement about B is accurate, and therefore B cannot successfully sue A for defamation." So facile an approach would rarely be appreciated by the grader. The proper way to handle this situation would be to state, "If we assume that A's statement about B is not correct, A cannot raise the defense of truth." You've communicated to the grader that you recognize the need to assume an essential fact and that you've assumed it in a way that enables you to proceed to discuss all other issues.

Case Names

A law student is ordinarily *not* expected to recall case names on an exam. The professor knows that you have read several hundred cases for each course, and that you would have to be a memory expert to have all of the names at your fingertips. If you confront a fact pattern which seems similar to a case which you have reviewed (but you cannot recall its name), just write something like, "One case we've read held that . . ." or "It has been held that. . . . " In this manner, you have informed the grader that you are relying on a case which contained a fact pattern similar to the question at issue.

The only exception to this rule is in the case of a landmark decision (e.g., *Roe v. Wade*). Landmark opinions are usually those which change or alter established law.[2] These cases are usually easy to identify, because you will probably have spent an entire class period discussing each of them. *Palsgraf v. Long Island Rail Road* is a prime example of a landmark case in Torts. In these special cases, you may be expected to remember the case by name, as well as the proposition of law which it stands for. However, this represents a very limited exception to the general rule which counsels against wasting precious time trying to memorize and reproduce case names.

How to Handle Time Pressures

What do you do when there are five minutes left in the exam and you have only written down two-thirds of your answer? One thing *not* to do is write something like, "No time left!" or "Not enough time!" This gets you nothing but the satisfaction of knowing you have communicated your personal frustrations to the grader. Another thing *not* to do is insert in the exam booklet the outline you may have made on a piece of scrap paper. Professors will rarely look at these.

First of all, it is not necessarily a bad thing to be pressed for time. The person who finishes five minutes early has very possibly missed some important issues. The more proficient you become in knowing what is expected of you on an exam, the greater the difficulty you may experience in staying within the time limits. Second, remember that (at least to some extent) you're graded against your classmates' answers and they're under exactly the same time pressure as you. In short, don't panic if you can't write the "perfect" answer in the allotted time. Nobody does!

The best hedge against misuse of time is to *review as many old exams as possible*. These exercises will give you a familiarity with the process of organizing and writing an exam answer, which, in turn, should result in an enhanced ability to stay within the time boundaries. If you nevertheless find that you have about 15 minutes of writing to do and five minutes to do

2 In Constitutional Law and Criminal Procedure, many cases will qualify as "landmark" cases. Students studying these subjects should try to associate case names with the corresponding holdings and reproduce both in their exam answers.

it in, write a paragraph which summarizes the remaining issues or arguments you would discuss if time permitted. As long as you've indicated that you're aware of the remaining legal issues, you'll probably receive some credit for them. Your analytical and argumentative skills will already be apparent to the grader by virtue of the issues that you have previously discussed.

Write Legibly

Make sure your answer is legible. Students should *not* assume that their professors will be willing to take their papers to the local pharmacist to have them deciphered. Remember, your professor may have 75 to 150 separate exams to grade. If your answer is difficult to read, you will rarely be given the benefit of the doubt. On the other hand, a legible, well-organized paper creates a very positive mental impact upon the grader.

Many schools allow students to type their exams on a word processor. If you're an adequate typist, you may want seriously to consider this option. Typing has two major advantages. First, it should help assure that your words will be readable (unless, of course, there are numerous typos). Second, it should enable you to put a lot more words onto the paper than if your answer had been handwritten. Most professors prefer a typed answer to a written one.

There are, however, a few disadvantages to using a word processor. For one thing, all the typists are usually in a single room. If the incessant clicking of other keyboards will make it difficult for you to concentrate, typing is probably *not* wise. To offset this problem, some students wear earplugs during the exam. Second, computers sometimes malfunction and word processors can crash. You professor's reaction to a hardware or software failure during an examination might not be as sympathetic as you might hope. Remember always to save answers to both the hard drive and a floppy disk or memory stick, and to save your work frequently.

If you decide against typing, your answer will probably be written in a "bluebook." It is usually a good idea to write only on the odd numbered pages (i.e., 1, 3, 5, etc.). You may also want to leave a blank line between each written line. These things will usually make the answer easier to read. If you discover that you have left out a word or phrase, you can insert it into the proper place by means of a caret sign (^). If you feel that you've omitted an entire issue, you can write it on the facing blank page. A symbol can be used to indicate where the additional portion of the answer should be inserted. While it's not ideal to have your answer take on the appearance of a road map, reference to an adjoining page by means of a symbol is much better than trying to squeeze six lines into one, and the symbol will help to indicate to the grader where the same symbol appears in another part of your answer.

The Importance of Reviewing Prior Exams

As we've mentioned, it is *extremely important to review old exams*. The transition from blackletter law to essay exam can be a difficult experience if the process has not been practiced. Although this book provides a large number of essay and multiple-choice questions, *don't stop here!* Most law schools have recent tests on file in the library, by course. We strongly suggest that you make a copy of every old exam you can obtain (especially those given by your professors) at the beginning of each semester. The demand for these documents usually increases dramatically as "finals time" draws closer.

The exams for each course should be scrutinized *throughout the semester*. They should be reviewed as you complete each chapter in your casebook. Generally, the order of exam questions follows the sequence of the materials in your casebook. Thus, the first question on a law school test may involve the initial three chapters of the casebook; the second question may pertain to the fourth and fifth chapters; etc. In any event, *don't wait* until the semester is nearly over to begin reviewing old exams.

Keep in mind that no one is born with the ability to analyze questions and write superior answers to law school exams. Like any other skill, one can develop and perfect it only through application. If you don't take the time to analyze numerous examinations from prior years, this evolutionary process just won't occur. Don't just *think about* the answers to past exam questions; take the time to *write the answers down*. It's also wise to look back at an answer a day or two after you've written it. You will invariably see (1) ways in which the organization could have been improved, and (2) arguments you missed.

As you practice spotting issues on past exams, you will see how rules of law become the sources of issues on finals. As we've already noted, if you don't *understand* how rules of law translate into issues, you won't be able to achieve superior grades on your exams. Reviewing exams from prior years also should reveal that certain issues tend to be lumped together in the same question. For instance, where a fact pattern involves a false statement made by one person about another, three potential theories of liability are often present—defamation, invasion of privacy (false, public light), and intentional infliction of severe emotional distress. You will need to see if any or all of these legal remedies apply to the facts.

Finally, one of the best means of evaluating if you understand a subject (or a particular area within a subject) is to attempt to create a hypothetical exam for that subject. Your exam should contain as many issues as possible. If you can write an issue-packed exam, you probably know that subject well. If you can't, then you probably haven't yet acquired an adequate understanding of how the principles of law in that subject can spawn issues.

As Always, a Caveat

The suggestions and advice offered in this book represent the product of many years of experience in the field of legal education. We are confident that the techniques and concepts described in these pages will help you prepare for, and succeed, at your exams. Nevertheless, particular professors sometimes have a preference for exam-writing techniques which are not stressed in this book. Some instructors expect at least a nominal reference to the *prima facie* elements of all pertinent legal theories (even though one or more of those principles is *not* placed into issue). Other professors want their students to emphasize public policy considerations in the arguments they make on a particular issue. Because this book is intended for nation-wide consumption, these individualized preferences have *not* been stressed. The best way to find out whether your professor has a penchant for a particular writing approach is to ask her to provide you with a model answer to a previous exam. If a model answer is not available, speak to upper-class students who received a superior grade in that professor's class.

One final point. Although the principles cited in the answers to the questions in this book have been drawn from commonly used sources (i.e., casebooks, hornbooks, etc.), it is conceivable that they may be inconsistent with those taught by your professor. In instances where a conflict exists between our formulation of a legal principle and the one which is taught by your professor, *follow the latter!* Since your grades are determined by your professors, their views should always supplant the views expressed in this book.

Essay Exam Questions

Question 1

On July 1, 1983, Tom properly executed a will, which created a $50,000 trust for Lil, the 65-year-old widow of Tom's brother Bob, who died without issue. The trustee was directed to pay to Lil "as much of the income and, if income be insufficient, as much of the principal, as may be required for her proper support and maintenance, for so long as she lives." After providing for the remainder interest in this trust to go to the American Red Cross on Lil's death, Tom gave "the rest and residue of my estate to the surviving issue of my brothers, per stirpes."

On July 1, 1986, while Tom was confined to the hospital for major surgery, a new will was delivered to Tom in a sealed envelope by two secretaries from his attorney's office. One of them told Tom, "We have a will here that Attorney Smith has asked us to deliver to you for your signature and that we are to witness." Tom opened the envelope, read the document carefully, and then signed it at the end in front of the secretaries. He then handed it to them. The secretaries walked to a small table in the hallway around the corner from Tom's room, signed the paper on the lines provided for their signature, and then immediately returned the paper to Tom. Under the new will, nephew E was made the sole residuary beneficiary; the rest of the will remained the same as the 1983 will. The 1986 will did not expressly revoke the 1983 will.

Tom died in an automobile accident last month. He was never married and left no issue. He is survived by:

1. A and B, grandchildren of his deceased brother Sam and children of Sam's deceased son James;
2. C, son of his deceased brother John;
3. D and E, children of his deceased brother Frank; and
4. Lil, the 65-year-old widow of Tom's brother Bob.

The original of the 1983 will was found in Tom's safe-deposit box. It bears no evidence of acts of revocation. The 1986 will cannot be found but an unsigned copy is in Attorney Smith's possession. The $50,000 trust produces a net annual income of $6,000.

1. Which will, if either, should be admitted to probate? Discuss.
2. Except for the $50,000 trust, what difference, if any, does it make to the family whether they take under the 1983 will or under the laws of intestacy? Discuss.

3. Lil's support needs are approximately $1,000 per month; she has pension and other income of $500 per month and has been making up the difference by withdrawals from savings. If either will is admitted to probate, should the trustee pay Lil $1,000 per month or $500 per month? Discuss.

Question 2

Henry died in the year 2000, leaving an estate consisting entirely of his separate property, valued at $500,000. He is survived by his wife Wanda, his mother Maude, his daughter Sally (by a previous marriage), and his brother Budi. A typewritten will that Henry executed on April 15, 1990, has been filed with the court, and reads as follows:

Will of Henry

1. I give $5,000 to my daughter, Sally.

2. I give the rest of my estate to my mother, Maude.

3. I appoint my friend Wanda as executrix of my will.

The will was published and signed by Henry in the presence of Wanda and Sally who, in Henry's presence and in the presence of each other, signed as subscribing witnesses.

Wanda and Henry were married on January 15, 1991. Shortly thereafter, Henry's lawyer, Lana, prepared a new will for Henry, and that will was properly executed in Lana's office on January 30, 1991. That will left Henry's entire estate to Wanda. The original of that will has not been found, but a photocopy is in Lana's files, and it contains a clause expressly revoking all prior wills.

If called as a witness, Lana will testify that (1) the photocopy in her file is a correct copy of the 1991 will, and (2) in December 1999 she tore up the original of the 1991 will at Henry's direction and in his presence.

If called as a witness, Lana's law clerk, Charles, will testify that (1) he was called into Lana's office one day in December 1999, when Lana and Henry were both present; (2) Lana told him that the scraps of paper on the desk were Henry's 1991 will, which she had destroyed at Henry's request; and (3) Henry then nodded his head affirmatively and said, "Now things are back the way I want them; Wanda won't get a penny of my property."

Assuming Lana and Charles testify as stated above and their testimony is properly admitted, how should Henry's estate be distributed? Discuss.

Question 3

The following events all occurred in State Y.

In 1970, Lear, a widower, executed a valid will that read in part: "I leave my AT&T stock to my sister, Ann, and the residue of my estate to my sons, Ed and Frank, equally." The will was executed in duplicate. Lear kept one executed original and his attorney kept the other duplicate original.

When the will was executed, Lear's son Frank was a reformed alcoholic. Through the years, Lear often threatened, in the presence of various family members, to disinherit Frank if he ever returned to drinking again.

In 1987, Lear was walking with his son Ed, when he saw an obviously inebriated person staggering from a bar. Lear, who had poor eyesight, said, "That looks like Frank." Seizing the opportunity to improve his position, believing (but not being positive) that the person was *not* Frank, Ed said, "It sure looks like Frank."

The next day Lear questioned Frank about the incident at the bar. Frank denied being there and accused Lear of being "a paranoid old fogie." Later that same day, Lear asked his new lawyer to prepare a new will and the new will was properly executed. The will read in part: "I revoke all prior wills. I bequeath my AT&T stock to my sister, Ann, and the residue of my estate to my son, Ed. I leave nothing to my son, Frank." Five days later, Lear tore up his copy of the 1970 will and delivered the new will to Ed for safekeeping.

In 1988, Lear suffered extensive brain damage in an automobile accident. Soon thereafter, he was declared mentally incompetent. Ed was appointed guardian for his father, with power to manage and invest his assets. With court approval, Ed sold the AT&T stock and reinvested the proceeds in a comparable security.

Lear has just died. The executed duplicate original of the 1970 will retained by the first attorney and the 1987 will delivered to Ed are both offered for probate.

Assume the applicable statutory law of State Y is the same as comparable provisions of the Uniform Probate Code.

How should Lear's estate be distributed? Discuss.

Question 4

Three years ago, Alfred Dinsmore executed a will that contained the following provisions:

1. I give my government bonds to Yale College;
2. I give 10 percent of the balance of my estate to my nephew, John, on the condition that he is still married, at the time of my death, to his present wife, Kathleen;
3. I give the residue of my estate to my niece Barbara.

Early last year, Alfred wrote the following letter to his niece Barbara:

> I have established a trust for your children at ABC Bank. This trust is worth approximately $50,000 and is composed of all my U.S. and State X bonds. You can decide how these funds should be used.

This is the only document evidencing Alfred's intention to establish a trust. Barbara's two children, Carol and David, are minors.

When Alfred wrote his will, he owned U.S. bonds worth $20,000, State X bonds worth $30,000, and State Z bonds worth $50,000. Alfred died a few weeks ago. At his death, all of these bonds were still registered in his name and had never been out of his possession.

John and Kathleen were divorced three months before Alfred's death, which was unexpected.

At his death, Alfred was unmarried and was survived by his nephew John (who had no children), his niece Barbara, and Barbara's two children, Carol and David.

1. What are the rights of John and Barbara and of Barbara's children? Discuss.

2. If the court finds a valid trust was created by Alfred's letter to Barbara, what are Yale's rights? Discuss.

Question 5

Bill, a widower, purchased a $100,000 farm (Blackacre), bought a single-payment life insurance policy on his own life (face amount $50,000), and maintained a large balance in his checking account (usually $100,000). Title to the farm and the bank account were always in Bill's name only. Bill's only child, June, was originally named as beneficiary of the insurance policy, but Bill reserved the power to change the beneficiary.

In 1983, Bill signed a formal change of beneficiary form and sent it to his insurance company. The form changed the beneficiary to Joe, Bill's neighbor. After the company informed Bill that the change had been made, Bill wrote to Joe: "I have named you as my life insurance beneficiary. You will collect the proceeds and divide them three ways. You are one; the others I will name later." Joe replied: "Sure, I'll do what you want."

In 1986, Bill executed a deed conveying Blackacre to an old friend, Pete. Later that same day, Bill mailed a signed letter to Pete, directing him to "rent my farm, pay the net income to June yearly, and when she dies, convey the farm to my church." Pete received and read the letter.

A few days later, Bill attempted to deliver the deed to Pete, but learned from Pete's housekeeper that Pete had just left on a three-month sailing trip in the South Pacific. Bill gave the housekeeper the deed and told her to give it to Pete when he returned.

Last month, Bill suffered a heart attack. While he was hospitalized, he executed a valid will that left "all property I own to my daughter, June. I recommend that she look after my 90-year-old Aunt Selma, as long as she lives, making such gifts and provisions for her as she, June, thinks best."

The day after executing this will, Bill wrote the following on a separate piece of paper: "To Joe: the other two beneficiaries are Tom Allen and his wife." Bill did not sign this note.

Bill died the day after he executed the note to Joe. Two days after Bill's death, Pete returned from his trip and his housekeeper handed Pete the deed.

Who is entitled to Bill's assets and why? Discuss.

Question 6

Ten years ago, Daniel, a widower, executed a valid, typed will containing the following dispositive provisions:

1. I give $5,000 to my daughter, Alice.
2. I give $10,000 to my brother, John.
3. I give the residue of my estate to my son, Bill. It is my wish that my son use whatever portion of the residue of my estate he deems appropriate to provide for my sister Karen.

John was one of the two witnesses to Daniel's will.

Shortly before the execution of the will, Daniel and John orally agreed that John would convey any property he would receive under Daniel's will to Daniel's sister, Lois.

One year after executing the will, Daniel drew an ink line through the "$5,000" figure in the bequest to Alice, and then wrote above it in ink the figure "$50,000." Daniel also wrote his initials next to the "$50,000" figure.

For many years prior to his death, Daniel had made regular payments to Karen to help her meet ordinary living expenses.

Daniel recently died and is survived by his children, Alice and Bill; by his brother, John; and by his sisters, Karen and Lois. His net estate is $100,000.

What are the rights of Alice, Bill, John, Karen, and Lois to Daniel's estate? Discuss.

Question 7

Agatha loaned $300,000 to her brother, George. George never repaid any part of the loan. When he died three years later, George left a will that provided that if Agatha forgave the $300,000 debt in writing, a $300,000 trust would be created for her by his executor under his will (Trust #1). Agatha forgave the debt and agreed to look to the trust instrument instead. Under the trust, Agatha is to receive the income for life. Upon her death the corpus is to be distributed to Betty, Agatha's daughter.

After making several other specific bequests, George left his residuary estate in Trust #2, for the benefit of five named beneficiaries. Agatha was not included as a beneficiary of this trust.

Both of the trusts created by George's will contained spendthrift provisions stating that creditors could not reach the income in the trustee's hands.

Nancy, George's accountant, was designated trustee of Trust #1, and Agatha was designated trustee of Trust #2. Each trustee was authorized to sell trust assets.

Before George's death, Agatha borrowed $15,000 from John, a fellow worker. Agatha repaid $5,000 to John and then defaulted. John, who knew about the trust for Agatha, asked her to use her income from the trust to cure the default. She told John that the spendthrift provision prevented her from doing that, but she offered, instead, to sell John 100 shares of TT&A stock from the corpus of Trust #2 for $10,000. The fair market value of the stock was then $21,000. John agreed and purchased the stock from Agatha as trustee of Trust #2 with a check for $10,000.

Six months later, John gave the TT&A stock to his nephew Larry as a wedding present. Larry had no notice of the prior transactions and still has possession of the stock.

What are the rights and liabilities of John, Agatha, and Larry? Discuss.

Question 8

Thirty years ago, Thea executed a trust instrument for "my children," naming State Bank as trustee. At the time of execution, Thea was pregnant with her first child by her husband, Fred.

Thea delivered 80 shares of Disney stock to the Bank under the trust. The trust instrument provided for distribution to Thea's "children" in equal shares upon Thea's death.

Thea died last month. She is survived by her two youngest children. Her oldest child, who was born shortly after the creation of the trust, died two years ago, leaving one son, who also survived Thea.

Eight years ago, Thea executed a valid will in which she gave 100 shares of Disney stock to her husband Fred "out of shares held by me at my death," and "the residue of my estate to my children in equal shares." Six years ago, after she and Fred were divorced, Thea executed a valid codicil. In her codicil, she revoked the gift to Fred and gave 100 shares of Disney stock to her close friend Sal "out of shares held by me at death."

When she executed her will, Thea personally owned 100 shares of Disney stock. After the codicil was executed, a one-for-two stock dividend was declared and issued, and Thea owned 150 shares of Disney stock at her death. After Thea's death, a two-for-three stock dividend was declared, so that her estate held 250 shares at the time of distribution. The trust held 120 shares of Disney stock at Thea's death and, as a result of the two-for-three stock dividend, now holds 200 shares.

Assume that the jurisdiction's applicable statutory provisions are the same as comparable provisions of the Uniform Probate Code.

How should Thea's estate and the trust assets be distributed? Discuss.

Question 9

Alice's husband died more than 20 years ago. Ten years after his death, Alice executed a written instrument transferring $200,000 to Bank in trust for her son Daniel, then 25, and her sister Celia, then 40. Under the terms of the trust, Celia and Daniel were each to receive one-half the income for ten years, at the end of which, each was to receive one-half the principal and any accumulated and undistributed income. If either died during the ten-year period, then, at his or her death, his or her share would be distributed to his or her estate.

Six years ago, Phil, a building contractor, sued Celia for $40,000. While the suit was pending, Alice, Bank, Celia, and Daniel executed a written agreement which amended the trust instrument by adding the following:

> No interest hereunder (i) shall be assigned or alienated by any beneficiary, or (ii) shall be subject to the claims of any creditor of any beneficiary.

After the amendment was executed, Phil obtained a judgment against Celia for $40,000. Celia was insolvent (apart from her interest in the trust) and could not pay the judgment. Phil has tried to attach Celia's interest in the trust to satisfy the judgment.

A year ago, Alice executed a valid will. The will gave $100,000 to Bank as trustee under Alice's trust, $50,000 in cash to Celia, and the remainder of the estate to her old friend Stan. One of the two attesting witnesses to the will was Doris, Celia's daughter. Celia died six months ago. Alice died one month ago.

Alice's only surviving heirs are Doris and Daniel.

In probate proceedings, Daniel asserts the invalidity of Alice's will on the following grounds:

A. Daniel is not mentioned in the will;

B. The $100,000 bequest to Bank as trustee should fail because the trust document was not executed in compliance with the Statute of Wills;

C. The $50,000 bequest to Celia lapsed at her death, and Doris has no claim because she was a witness to the will.

1. How should Alice's estate be distributed? Discuss.

2. Can Phil still reach Celia's interest in the trust? Discuss.

Question 10

Ten years ago, Tina, her husband, Hector, and their two adult children, Charlie and Sally, were residents of the State of Terra. They lived in a house owned by Tina. At that time, Tina wrote, dated and signed her will entirely in her own handwriting. The will provides:

> I want my house to go to my daughter, Sally. All my other property of any kind is to go to my husband, Hector, if he survives me, and otherwise to Sally.

Sally acted as witness to Tina's signing and dating of the will and then added her signature under the word "witness." Terra requires that a handwritten will be witnessed and signed by two witnesses.

Charlie died eight years ago. He was survived by his one-year-old son, George. Five years ago, Tina and Hector moved to the State of Calco. A year later, Hector died intestate. Shortly thereafter, Tina gave Sally $300,000 for the purchase of a home. At the time of the gift, Tina stated in writing that the gift was an advancement.

Recently, Tina died while still a resident of Calco. She never revoked or modified her will. Tina was survived by Sally and by George, who was living with his mother in Terra and whom Tina had never seen. When Tina died, her house in Calco was worth $200,000. Her other assets were worth a total of $50,000.

You may assume that the Probate Code of the State of Calco is the same as the Uniform Probate Code.

1. Is Tina's will effective in Calco? Discuss.
2. How should the assets of Tina's estate be distributed? Discuss.

Question 11

Tippi, a very wealthy woman, decided to endow a public library in her home city. To carry out her plan, Tippi executed the following documents:

1. A declaration stating her intention to create the Tippi Library for the use of the inhabitants of the city. She designated as trustees three persons to serve on the first Tippi Library Board of Governors (the Board), and provided for the selection of successor members of the Board in the event of death or resignation of a member or members;

2. A deed conveying a block of land Tippi owned near the city center to the Board, "in perpetuity," for the purposes stated in her declaration;

3. A check payable to the Board in the sum of $100,000, as an initial contribution for the library; and

4. A document containing an itemized list of a number of Tippi's stocks and bonds having a market value of $2 million, and a statement that these stocks and bonds were to be delivered to the Board in specified installments over a two-year period.

The declaration, check and deed, and the securities list, have all been delivered to the Board. The Board has recorded the deed, cashed the check, and deposited the proceeds in a bank account entitled "Tippi Library Board." No funds have been withdrawn from, or charged to, the account.

Tippi died three months after all these events occurred, but before any of the securities were transferred to the Board under the document for specified installments. Tippi left a valid will naming her only child, Betty, as executrix and sole beneficiary. Tippi's husband predeceased her.

The $100,000 fund held by the Board is not sufficient to construct a library building on the land or to maintain a library. If the specified stocks and bonds are transferred to the Board, a library building can be constructed and the library maintained.

The Board has proposed to use the block of land as a public park if it fails in its efforts to get Tippi's stocks and bonds. The park will be named Tippi Memorial Park. The funds now in the Board's possession are sufficient to maintain the land as a public park for at least ten years.

Betty has brought suit (1) to recover the block of land and all the money in the Tippi Library Board bank account, and (2) for a declaratory judgment that all of the stocks and bonds on Tippi's itemized list are free from any claim by the Board. The Board has responded by asserting all applicable rights and defenses.

To what relief, if any, are Betty and the Board entitled? Discuss.

Question 12

Leonard and Fay Woods had two children, Michael and Linda. Michael was married to Wanda, and they had one adopted child, Roberta. Linda was unmarried and childless. On March 25, 1985, Fay executed a will, with the necessary legal formalities, which contained the following provisions:

> To my daughter, Linda, I give my business property at 1125 Main Street, and such of my jewelry as is enumerated on the list that will be found in my jewel box. To my son, Michael, I give my 1,000 shares of XYZ Class A stock. To my husband, Leonard, I give the rest and residue of my estate.

Leonard and Fay were divorced in November 1986. They had not entered into a property settlement agreement. In January 1987, Michael was killed in a plane crash. In April 1987, Fay sold the business property at 1125 Main Street for $20,000 and deposited one-half the proceeds in her commercial account and the other one-half in a savings account in the name of "Fay Woods, Trustee for Linda Woods." In May 1987, XYZ Corporation declared a stock dividend of one-half share of Class A stock and one-half share of Class B stock for each share of Class A stock held by Fay.

Fay died last month. The following typed note was discovered in her jewel box:

> In accordance with the provisions of my will of March 25, 1985, I want my daughter, Linda, to have the following jewelry found herein: Grandmother Barnes's diamond ring, my wedding rings, and my pearl necklace and earrings.

The note was signed and dated March 25, 1985.

All these events took place, and all of Fay's property was located, in the State of Franklin. Fay's estate, after payment of all taxes, expenses, and debts consists of 1,500 shares of XYZ Class A stock; 500 shares of XYZ Class B stock; the jewelry described in the March 25, 1985, note; $10,000 in the savings account in the name of "Fay Woods, Trustee for Linda Woods"; and $15,000 in her commercial account. All property was Fay's separate property.

Assume that (1) the applicable statutory law of Franklin is the same as comparable provisions of the Uniform Probate Code, and (2) Fay's parents are no longer living.

How should Fay's estate be distributed? Discuss.

Question 13

The following events all occurred in State Y.

On January 5, 1988, Tess executed a valid and attested will naming her mother Martha as her sole beneficiary. In July 1990 Tess married Hubert Jones. Shortly after her marriage, Tess signed a document, entirely in her own handwriting, which reads as follows:

> Codicil to my will of 1/5/88. One-half of my property to my husband Hubert; one-fourth of my property to State University; the rest to my mother.
>
> 8/4/90
>
> Tess Jones

In January 1992 a son, Sonny, was born to Tess and Hubert. Soon thereafter, Tess became upset by the signs of professionalism in college athletics and especially the fact that State University constantly had national championship teams in several sports. After watching State trounce A&M in the Apple Bowl, she signed a document that was entirely in her own handwriting and that read as follows:

> I revoke my codicil of 8/4/90. Nothing to athletic factories like State University. I want to benefit a college that has no athletic program. The one-fourth of my property is to go to Harvale College for academic scholarships.
>
> Tess Jones

Tess died in an auto accident two weeks after making the second codicil. She is survived by Martha, Hubert, and Sonny. Her estate, after payment of all taxes, debts and expenses of administration, consists of cash and securities having a total value of $300,000.

Harvale is a private, nonprofit college. Unbeknownst to Tess, the regents of State University had voted to discontinue all intercollegiate athletic programs prior to Tess's execution of the second codicil. However, their decision was not announced until after Tess's death.

Assume that the applicable statutory law of State Y is the same as the comparable provisions of the Uniform Probate Code.

How should Tess's estate be distributed? Discuss.

Question 14

Nelly died a widow, leaving a two-page handwritten will containing two dispository clauses. Clause 1 provided for bequests of $10,000 "to each of my children, Ann, Brad and Charlie." Clause 2 provided that all of Nelly's stocks and bonds be given to Brad, "to be used as we have agreed." Nelly's home and personal effects, together worth $60,000, were not disposed of by the will.

Nelly signed her name on the bottom of page 1 of the will. Page 2 contained only the date in her handwriting and Brad's signature under the word "Witness." When the will was offered for probate, several lines were drawn through Ann's name in Clause 1.

Brad is prepared to testify that several months after signing the will, Nelly, in his presence, drew lines through Ann's name, and told him she wanted to disinherit Ann. Brad is also prepared to testify that he had agreed with Nelly to use the income from the stocks and bonds for Charlie during his life, but that the stocks and bonds were to be Brad's after Charlie's death. Charlie died several months before Nelly, leaving no spouse or descendants.

The estate includes, in addition to Nelly's home and personal effects, $10,000 in cash, and stocks and bonds worth $70,000.

Assume that the applicable statutory law of the state is the same as the comparable provisions of the Uniform Probate Code.

1. Is the will valid? Discuss.
2. How should the estate be distributed? Discuss.

Question 15

Carol lived for many years as a widow. She had a son, Sam, and a daughter, Dot. At the outset, she told her children that she didn't need a will because "you'll share in everything anyway." Twenty years ago, Carol was notified by the Department of Defense that Sam had been killed in Vietnam. Soon after the notice, Carol overcame her reluctance to execute a will and executed a valid testamentary document. The document provides:

> In view of the death of my son, Sam, I leave one-third of my estate to my brother Tom and my sister Jane, share and share alike; the remaining two-thirds of my estate I give to my daughter Dot. The shares of my brother and sister in the portion of my estate allocated to them should be adjusted to reflect any advancements I may make to each of them, as recorded in a book of account that will be found with my will.

In 1986, Carol made gifts of $5,000 to Jane and $10,000 to Tom. In her ledger, which was later found with her will, under the caption "Advancements," Carol erroneously transposed the amounts, so that the entries read:

4/9/86 - Jane $10,000

Tom $5,000

In 1998, the Department of State wrote Carol that it had received reports that Sam was apparently still being held as a prisoner of war, and that efforts were being made to verify his status and to secure his release. Dot, who lived with Carol, intercepted the letter and concealed it.

When Carol died recently, she left a net estate of $270,000. After Carol's death but before Carol's estate could be distributed, Sam was released and returned home.

1. Under what theories can Sam participate in the distribution of the estate? Discuss.

2. To what other relief, if any, is Sam entitled? Discuss.

3. How should Carol's estate be distributed? Discuss.

Question 16

The following events all occurred in State A.

In November 1997 T. Tate, a widower, instructed his lawyer to prepare the following document:

> I, T. Tate, a widower, dispose of all my estate as follows: I give my sister Sally one-half and my favorite nephew, Sally's son Ron, the other one-half. I have intentionally omitted all of my other heirs.

After reading the document, Tate told the attorney he wanted to think about the matter some more and took the document with him without signing it. A week later, on December 2, 1997, Tate attended a dinner party at Sally's house. After dinner and a few drinks, Tate announced that he wanted to execute his will and took the document from his pocket. Slightly intoxicated, Tate signed and correctly dated the document in the presence of all the dinner guests. Tate then had Sally and two of her guests sign as witnesses.

On January 20, 1998, Tate again consulted his lawyer and told him he wanted a new will prepared, revoking all prior bequests and leaving his entire estate to the Child Care Foundation (CCF), a recognized charitable organization. While Tate was still in the office, the lawyer had his secretary type a memorandum correctly setting forth Tate's requests. Tate signed that memorandum and gave it to the lawyer.

Tate died of a heart attack three weeks after signing the January 20, 1998, memorandum. The document dated December 2, 1997, was found in Tate's desk. Across the document was the following statement, written in Tate's handwriting: "This will is cancelled; I have made a new will. TT"

Tate was survived by his son Art, his sister Sally, and Sally's two sons, Don and Zeke, his only relatives. Tate never had a nephew named Ron.

The applicable statutory law of State A is the same as the Uniform Probate Code.

How should Tate's estate be distributed? Discuss.

Question 17

Tawny, a widow, died a few months ago. In searching through her effects, her children found an undated document in her top desk drawer. The document was in Tawny's handwriting, and was signed by her. It stated:

> My wishes for the distribution of my estate are described on two pieces of paper which are in the bottom drawer of my desk.
>
> (Signed) Tawny

In Tawny's bottom desk drawer, the children found the following papers:

Document #1

On a form of deed that Tawny had purchased at a local stationery store, all the necessary ingredients of a valid conveyance of Tawny's house, designating her daughter Ann as grantee. The deed was properly executed. Attached to the deed with a paper clip was a note stating:

> This is for my beloved daughter. I hope that she enjoys it as much as I have.
>
> (Signed) Tawny
>
> June 1, 1998.

The note was typewritten, except for Tawny's signature and the date.

Document #2

A paper, dated June 1, 1999, stating:

> All my money — brother Bob
>
> ABC stock — sister Shirley
>
> Jewelry — Ann

The note was typewritten, except that the words "brother Bob" had a handwritten line drawn through them. Above them, in Tawny's handwriting, was written: "son Sam".

Document #3

A handwritten, undated piece of paper, stating at the top "Page 2" and continuing:

> I meant to mention in the first page of my will that everything else should be divided equally among Bob, Shirley, and Ann.
>
> (Signed) Tawny

Tawny was survived by her daughter Ann, her son Sam, her brother Bob, and her sister Shirley.

Tawny's estate consists of: her house, valued at $250,000; furniture located in the house worth $10,000; $100,000 in cash; and $50,000 worth of stock in ABC Corp. She owned no jewelry, but did own a $10,000 diamond and ruby-studded jewelry box. ABC stock has split three for one.

How should Tawny's estate be distributed? Discuss.

Question 18

Silver executed a valid will bequeathing his property to Thompson in trust. At his death, Silver's property consisted of a bar and grill, which he owned and operated, and 100 shares of stock of Red Company, a corporation listed on the New York Stock Exchange. Silver's will authorized Thompson to make investments "in his discretion" and, at the end of two years, to distribute the principal and accrued interest to those persons who would be employed at the bar and grill at Silver's death. The members of this group, and the amount to be distributed to each, were to be decided by Thompson.

During the first year after the death of Silver, Thompson operated the bar and grill at a $10,000 profit. At the end of the year, Red Company merged into Blue Company, a new enterprise engaged in experimental electronics. All shareholders of Red Company were given the option of receiving the fair market value of their stock, which was $75 per share, or receiving one-half share of Blue Company stock in exchange for each share of Red Company stock. Thompson elected to take the 50 shares of Blue Company stock.

At the end of the second year, Thompson sold all the Blue Company stock for $3,000, its then fair market value. He also sold the bar and grill, which had lost $15,000 during the preceding year.

Thompson determined that Able, Baker, and Charley were all the eligible employees of the bar and grill, but Thompson died before he could decide what amount to leave to each.

Silver's next of kin now claim the trust property. Assume a lawsuit to settle all rights and liabilities has been initiated by them. Answer and discuss the following:

1. Who is entitled to the trust estate and in what proportions?

2. Has Thompson committed any breaches of trust for which his estate is liable for surcharge and, if so, in what amount?

Question 19

Trisha Tait personally typed this draft of her will:

September 17, 1985

I, Trisha Tait, being of sound mind, hereby publish this as my last will.

First. To my son, Sal I give my 150 shares of Minco stock.

Second. To my daughter, Diane, I give my 500 shares of Oilco stock.

Third. My personal effects located in the wall safe in my living room, I give to my friend Bill.

Fourth. To my husband, Hoby, I give the rest, residue and remainder of my estate.

Tait did not execute this will. The following appears in Tait's handwriting across the bottom of the draft:

June 15, 1986

Being of sound mind, I adopt my draft will, dated September 17, 1985, written above as my last will. TT.

On July 1, 1986, Oilco merged with Zebco. The Oilco shareholders received one share of Zebco stock in exchange for each share of Oilco stock.

Tait died last month.

Tait's son Sal died in August 1990. Sal's sole surviving heirs are his father Hoby, his wife Ann, and his adopted daughter Helen. After payment of all expenses of administration, taxes, and debts, Tait's estate included only the following: 50 shares of Abco stock (worth $5,000) in the living-room wall safe; $100,000 in various bank accounts; personal jewelry in the living-room wall safe; 300 shares of Minco stock (worth $60,000) and 500 shares of Zebco stock (worth $15,000) in a bank safe-deposit box. The personal jewelry was placed in the wall safe on July 1, 1991.

Assume that the applicable statutory law is the same as the comparable provisions of the Uniform Probate Code.

1. Is there a valid will? Discuss.
2. If the will is valid, how should the estate be distributed? Discuss.
3. If the will is not valid, how should the estate be distributed? Discuss.
4. If Hoby predeceased Tait, and Tait had married John one month before her death, how should the estate be distributed? Discuss.

Question 20

The following events all occurred in State Y.

When Timothy Thomas died on July 20, 1998, three documents were found in an envelope in his safe deposit box.

The first read, in its entirety:

> I, Timothy Thomas, make this will, one-half to my sister Bessie and the other one-half to the Boys Club. Sept. 20, 1995.
>
> Witness: William Wordsworth

The second read:

> I'm changing my previous will — Bessie doesn't need all that — all stocks listed in my black book go to Bessie's child — June 30, 1998.
>
> Timothy Thomas

The third was a black notebook containing accurate records of all of Thomas's purchases and sales of securities. All entries were dated prior to June 30, 1998, with the exception of two entries. These showed a sale of 100 shares of ABC stock and the purchase of 100 shares of XYZ stock, both on July 7, 1998.

Each entry in the black notebook was made by Thomas on the actual date of the corresponding transaction.

All writing in the three documents is in Thomas's handwriting, except the words "Witness: William Wordsworth" in the first document. These words are typewritten.

Thomas was never married. His surviving next of kin are his sister Bessie and Bessie's daughter, Dorothy.

Thomas's estate consists of the following: 300 shares of ABC stock purchased prior to June 30, 1998, having a fair market value of $30,000; 100 shares of XYZ stock purchased on July 7, 1998, having a fair market value of $10,000; and $100,000 cash in bank accounts.

Assume that the applicable statutory law of State Y is the same as comparable provisions of the Uniform Probate Code.

As among Bessie, the Boys Club, and Dorothy, how should Timothy Thomas's estate be distributed? Discuss.

Question 21

Ten years ago, Tammy Thor, a widow, validly executed a formal, witnessed will (Will #1) which contained the following dispositive clauses:

> (1) to my friend Robert Rood, $10,000 to be used by him for the education of his daughter Carrie;

> (2) the residue of my estate to my friend Doris Drake, trustee, in trust, to pay the income to my daughter Ethel so long as Ethel may live and upon Ethel's death to distribute the trust corpus to my then living heirs; the trustee may invade the corpus if necessary for the proper care and maintenance of Ethel.

Three years ago, Thor signed a dated, typewritten document purporting to be her last will and testament (Will #2). The document was identical to Will #1, except that the last clause of the residuary bequest, giving the trustee power to invade the corpus, was omitted. This will was attested by only one subscribing witness.

Thor recently died. Will #1 and Will #2 were found in Thor's safe deposit box. Stapled to Will #1 was the following document, in Thor's handwriting:

> This will is hereby cancelled and revoked. I have made a new will.
>
> Tammy Thor

The note was dated, in Thor's handwriting, one day subsequent to the date on Will #2.

Thor was survived by the following heirs and legatees and no others:

A. Ethel, her daughter;

B. Robert Rood, her friend, and Carrie, Robert's 16-year-old daughter;

C. John and Gil, sons of her deceased sister Anne;

D. Warren, grandson of her deceased sister Bessie; and

E. Doris Drake, her friend.

Ethel died before distribution of Thor's estate. By a valid will, Ethel left her entire estate to her friend Sandra.

1. Did Thor die testate or intestate? Discuss.

2. Assuming Thor died testate, what persons are entitled to Thor's estate, and what share or interest will each receive? Discuss.

3. Assuming Thor died intestate, what persons are entitled to Thor's estate, and what share or interest will each receive? Discuss.

Question 22

Ten years ago, Tom, who had never been married, executed a typed will (Will #1) that gave "$50,000 to my niece Mary, $15,000 to my nephew John, $15,000 to my nephew Allen, and the residue of my estate to my niece and nephews, share and share alike." The will was witnessed by Tom's secretary and his niece Mary.

Tom had only one niece, Mary, and three nephews, John, Allen, and David. David had died before the execution of the will, leaving two surviving children.

After Will #1 was executed, John told Tom on numerous occasions that Allen had been unsuccessful in starting a business and had become involved in the sale of stolen automobile parts. In fact, John knew that Allen, who had moved to another city and had not been in contact with Tom for some time, owned a successful business and was not engaged in the sale of stolen goods.

After Tom's recent death, a validly executed second will (Will #2) bearing a date that preceded Tom's death by approximately three years, was found in Tom's safe deposit box. Will #2 gave "$50,000 to my niece Mary, $30,000 to my nephew John, and the residue of my estate to Mary and John, share and share alike."

Will #1, which had lines drawn through each of its provisions, was also found in Tom's safe deposit box.

Tom's only surviving relatives were Mary, John, Allen, and David's two children. Tom's net estate was $200,000.

What are the rights of Mary, John, Allen, and David's two children to Tom's estate? Discuss.

Question 23

Betty and Wilma had been business partners and close friends for many years. Both were widows and each had two children.

In 1990, Betty executed a will in which she bequeathed "$100,000 to my close friend Wilma, if she survives me; otherwise, to the natural persons who are beneficiaries of Wilma's last will and testament, and if she dies intestate, to her next of kin." The residue of Betty's estate was bequeathed "to my children, share and share alike." In 1994, both of Betty's children died, survived by issue. Her son, Charles, left two sons, George and Fred. Her daughter, Jane, left a daughter, Alice.

Wilma had drawn a will in 1985 leaving her entire estate "one-half to my children and one-half to State University." In 1992, thinking that her son Bill had failed to thank her for an expensive present (a new Volvo she had given to him), Wilma drew a codicil, providing "I hereby delete from my will the gift to my son, Bill. Because of his ingratitude, I leave him nothing." In fact, Bill had sent Wilma a "thank you" letter, but it had been lost in the mail.

Last week, Betty and Wilma were killed in an airplane crash while en route to a convention. Betty's next of kin were her three grandchildren. Wilma's next of kin were her two children, Bill and Mary.

Betty and Wilma each left a net estate of $500,000 in cash and marketable securities.

Assume the applicable statutory law is the same as comparable provisions of the Uniform Probate Code.

How should their estates be distributed? Discuss.

Question 24

Ball transferred $100,000 in trust to Trust Company for the benefit of his son Sam. The income was to be distributed to Sam during Sam's life, and the remainder of the trust was to pass to Sam's children living at the time of Sam's death. Ball could, according to the terms of the trust, revoke the trust, provided that the revocation was in writing signed by him and delivered to the trustee. The trust also contained a spendthrift clause.

After the creation of the trust, Sam married Pearl and they had one child, Carol. Two years after the birth of Carol, Pearl divorced Sam. Pearl took this action because Sam had become a chronic alcoholic. When Ball learned of the divorce and that a large alimony award had been given to Pearl, Ball called the trustee and stated, "I revoke the trust and will confirm this revocation by letter." However, Ball died the following day, before he had written the letter. Ball died intestate. Sam was Ball's only child. Sam has no income apart from that paid to him by the trust.

Trust Company has filed a petition for instructions in the appropriate court. The petition alleges the following:

> (A) That Sam has made written demand that the trustee (1) turn over the entire trust estate, free of trust, to the administrator of Ball's estate, or, in the alternative, (2) out of the income and, to the extent necessary, the principal of the trust, pay Pearl the amount now due to her for alimony, and thereafter pay her periodically the amount awarded to her for future alimony.

> (B) That Pearl has made written demand that the trustee, out of the income and, to the extent necessary, the principal of the trust, pay her the amount now due to her for alimony and thereafter pay her periodically the amount awarded to her for future alimony. In her demand, Pearl states that she represents Carol, now age three, and, on Carol's behalf, agrees to an invasion of the trust principal for such purpose.

> (C) That Sam and Pearl, jointly, have made a written election, on their own behalf and on behalf of Carol, to terminate the trust, if the trustee does not agree to the foregoing demands.

The trustee requests instructions with respect to the following:

1. Whether the trust was effectively terminated by Ball in his lifetime;
2. Whether the trustee is obligated to pay Pearl either past or future alimony, or both, out of the income and, to the extent necessary, principal of the trust;
3. Whether Sam and Pearl have the legal power to terminate the trust.

How should the court instruct the trustee? Discuss.

Question 25

The following events all occurred in State Y.

Theresa Taylor died recently. After her death a typewritten document was found in her safe deposit box. It read (in its entirety) as follows:

> To Aunt Marie — my home; to my friend Al — my 200 shares of XYZ stock; to my friend Frank — 20 shares of IBM stock; to my daughter Doris — NOTHING!

Stapled to the typewritten document was another piece of paper on which was written, in Taylor's handwriting: "The attached is the way I want my property to go; all the rest to sister, Sarah. 5-15-90. Theresa Taylor."

Taylor was survived by her daughter Doris, Aunt Marie, friends Al and Frank, and a brother, Ben. Her sister Sarah died in October 1991 without issue but with a will that left everything to Sarah's husband Greg.

Taylor's estate consists of: $50,000 cash on deposit in banks (the proceeds of fire insurance relating to her home, which was destroyed by fire two months ago); 400 shares of XYZ stock (200 shares of which were the result of a stock split in August 1988); and government bonds having a fair market value of $100,000. Taylor did not have, and never had owned, any IBM stock.

Assume that the applicable statutory law of State Y is the same as comparable provisions of the Uniform Probate Code.

How should Taylor's estate be distributed after payment of debts, taxes, and expenses of administration? Discuss.

Essay Exam Answers

Answer to Question 1

1. Which will, if either, should be admitted to probate?

Was the 1986 will valid?

The requirements for will execution vary from state to state. The modern trend, reflected in the Uniform Probate Code, is to liberalize the requirements. Under the UPC, a will is valid if it is witnessed by at least two persons, each of whom signed within a reasonable time after he or she witnessed either the testator's signing of the will or the testator's acknowledgment of: (1) his signature or (2) the will itself. (UPC §2-502). Because (1) Tom (T) executed the will in front of two legal secretaries who knew the document to be his will, and (2) the secretaries signed the document almost immediately thereafter, the 1986 will was valid when executed. There is (at least, under the UPC and in many jurisdictions) no requirement that the witnesses sign in the presence of the testator (or in the presence of each other), so the fact that the witnesses here signed in the hallway outside of T's hospital room does not affect the validity of the will. In some states, the requirements for validity would be more stringent.

If the 1986 will is deemed valid, does it revoke the 1983 will?

A subsequent testamentary instrument need not contain a revocation clause in order to revoke a prior will. A prior will may be revoked either expressly or by inconsistency. (UPC §2-507(a)(1)). Even without a revocation clause, a subsequent will wholly revokes a previous will by inconsistency if the testator intended the subsequent will to replace the old one rather than supplement it. (UPC §2-507(b)). When the later will disposes of the entire estate, that will is presumed to be entirely inconsistent with the earlier will, even if some provisions remain essentially the same in the two wills. (UPC §2-507(c)). Because the 1986 will purports to dispose of T's entire estate, if it is deemed valid it will supersede the 1983 instrument and will be admitted to probate.

Is the 1986 will deemed revoked by being lost?

If a will that was last in the testator's possession (or control) cannot be found upon his or her death, ordinarily a presumption arises that the testator destroyed the will with the intent to revoke it (in many states, it must also be shown that the testator had capacity until death). The presumption does not arise if the will was last known to be in the possession of a third person. If the presumption arises, it is rebuttable. The UPC is silent on the issue of lost wills.

Here, the facts indicate that (1) the 1986 will was last in the testator's (Tom's) possession (after the witnesses signed the will, they "immediately returned" it to Tom); (2) after Tom's death, the will cannot be found; and (3) Tom had capacity until his death. The presumption arises that Tom revoked the will by act. Once the presumption arises, the burden shifts to those who favor probate of the will to offer a more plausible explanation for why the will cannot be found.

T's nephew E can attempt to rebut this presumption by arguing that T knew how to enlist the assistance of Attorney Smith in connection with his will and would have gone back to Smith if he had actually meant to revoke the 1986 will. However, this argument alone would probably *not* be sufficient to rebut the presumption that T had intended to revoke the 1986 will. The fact that T retained the 1983 will in his safe-deposit box supports the presumption that he meant to revoke the 1986 will. If he had meant to substitute the 1986 will for the 1983 will, arguably he would have removed the 1983 will from the deposit box and replaced it with the 1986 will.

Based on these facts, the better and more probable conclusion is that the 1986 will was revoked, and the copy of the 1986 will should ***not*** be admitted to probate.

If, however, the 1986 will is deemed not to have been revoked, the court might probate the 1986 will under the "lost will" doctrine–which in most jurisdictions requires the proponent to prove the terms of the will by clear and convincing evidence. Here, the unsigned copy of the 1986 will in Attorney Smith's possession, coupled with the testimony of Attorney Smith and the two secretaries, would probably constitute clear and convincing evidence of the terms of the 1986 will.

If the 1986 will is deemed revoked, is the 1983 will revived?

What happens to an earlier will when a subsequent will that was intended to revoke the earlier will is itself revoked by destruction or loss? In most states the answer is provided by a specific statute. Some states provide that, once revoked, a prior will may not be revived unless it is properly re-executed with full compliance with requirements for a valid will. In other states and under the UPC, the first will is revived when the second will is destroyed, if that is the testator's intent. The UPC provides that where the later will is revoked by act, "[t]he previous will is revived if it is evident from the circumstances of the revocation of the subsequent will or from the testator's contemporary or subsequent declarations that the testator intended the previous will to take effect as executed." (UPC §2-509(a)).

Here, there is no evidence that T intended or desired the 1983 will to be reinstated. Although the will was preserved in his safe-deposit box, it's possible that T simply neglected to dispose of the 1983 will after the 1986 document was created. However, the aggrieved beneficiaries (*i.e.*, those residuary beneficiaries in the 1983 will who were left out of the 1986 will) might prevail, *if* they could show that T was such a careful and prudent person that he would recognize that his intent would be best expressed by preserving one will and destroying or disposing of the other. On this proof, T's retention of the 1983 will would arguably manifest his desire to have that document constitute his testamentary scheme.

The doctrine of dependent relative revocation is not applicable to these facts. The doctrine comes into play where a testator validly revokes a will based on a mistake, and the testator would not have revoked the will but for the mistake. Where such is the case, it is assumed that the testator would want the revoked will reinstated. The doctrine is not applicable here because there is no evidence that Tom revoked either the 1983 will or the 1986 will based upon a mistake.

Summary:

The probable conclusion is that the 1983 will should not be revived and the testator, Tom, died intestate. If the court were to conclude that the presumption that the 1986 will was revoked is overcome, and the terms of the will are established under the lost will doctrine, Tom's nephew E would take his whole estate. If the court were to conclude that the 1986 will was revoked and the 1983 will was revived, the trust would be established for Lil, and the surviving issue of Tom's brothers would take the residue of his estate per stirpes.

2. What is the difference between the disposition of the residue in the 1983 will and intestacy?

[*Note:* For exam questions such as this one (where there are many potential beneficiaries and you are asked to discuss the difference between testamentary and intestate distribution to those beneficiaries), you should diagram the family tree (on scrap paper, not in your exam bluebook) before attempting to answer.] The family tree for this question would look like this:

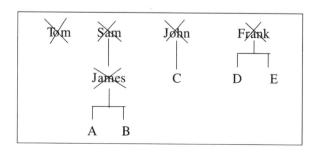

Under the 1983 will, the surviving issue of T's brothers take as directed by T; that is, per stirpes (*i.e.*, through the roots of each brother). Conceptually, the residue is divided into three shares, one for each brother who has issue, and then into subshares for the issue of each brother. Thus, A and B would each receive 1/6 of T's residuary estate (*i.e.*, they get equal shares of the 1/3 that James would have gotten as the sole issue of Sam); C would receive a full 1/3 of T's residuary estate (as the sole issue of John); and D and E would each get 1/6 (sharing equally the 1/3 that would have gone to Frank). As the facts tell us, brother Bob died without issue.

Under intestacy, that part of a decedent's estate not effectively disposed of by will passes to the decedent's heirs as prescribed by statute in each state. Under the Uniform Probate Code, a testator's intestate property would pass to his "descendants by representation." (UPC §2-103(1)). The Uniform Probate Code has adopted the *per capita at each generation* approach. Under this approach the first division of the decedent's estate is made at the highest level where there are living members—one share for each party who is alive at that level, and one share for each party who is dead but survived by issue. (UPC §2-106(b)). Thus, one equal share each would go to C, D, E and one to the issue of deceased James. The final result would be: C, D and E would each get 1/4 of the residuary estate; and A and B would each get 1/8 (splitting James's 1/4 share equally).

3. Should Lil receive $1,000 per month, or $500 per month?

A support trust is a trust that requires the trustee to pay as much income (and, if expressly provided in the trust, principal as well) as necessary for the beneficiary's support. Tom has created a support trust for Lil.

When there are ambiguous provisions in a will or the provisions are capable of different or inconsistent interpretations, the court will attempt to effectuate the testator's intent by inquiring into all the circumstances. Lil could argue that she was intended to be the sole living beneficiary of the trust and that T would naturally prefer her interests to those of a large and well-funded charity. By using the terms "as much of the income, and if income be insufficient, as much of the principal . . . ," T manifested a clear directive to support her from the trust, not to cause her to deplete her savings.

On the other hand, T presumably knew that Lil was receiving funds from other sources. He could have requested Attorney Smith to insert the language, "regardless of Lil's other income" if he had wanted to give a free hand to the trustee. Because (1) the principal would be exhausted in a relatively short period of time if Lil received $12,000 per year from the trust, and (2) the trust was apparently to last for her entire life (the trust language states, "for so long as she lives"), it can be argued that T intended to limit Lil to $500 per month from the trust.

Without additional facts, either interpretation of the will's provision would be reasonable.

Answer to Question 2

We must first decide whether the 1990 will was validly executed, and, if so, whether it was effectively revoked by the 1991 will and, if it was revoked, whether it was revived by the destruction of the 1991 will.

Was the 1990 will executed with the requisite formalities?

The Uniform Probate Code requires that an attested will be in writing, signed by the testator or in the testator's name by some other person in the testator's conscious presence and by the testator's direction, and that it be signed by two persons within a reasonable time after execution. (UPC §2-502)

Historically, persons interested as legatees or beneficiaries under a will could not serve as witnesses. Today, the rule in most states is still either to (1) automatically disqualify interested witnesses, *or* (2) permit them to qualify, but purge them of their gifts. The UPC and a number of states remove this disqualification. (UPC §2-505(b)). Under the UPC, the 1990 will appears to be valid even though Sally was both a beneficiary and a witness. Wanda's appointment as executor would not affect her qualification as a witness, even in a state that does disqualify interested witnesses. The theory is that the executor has a separate interest as recipient of fees for service as a fiduciary. (Note: a lawyer who prepares the will and/or is present at the execution is a valid witness.)

Can the 1991 will be proved as a testamentary instrument although the original is not produced?

In most jurisdictions, a will that cannot be produced in court can nevertheless be proved. However, the burden is on the proponents of the will to prove its valid execution and its terms—and in most jurisdictions the burden of proof under these circumstances is clear and convincing evidence.

In this case, Lana's testimony proves the revocation of the 1991 will and gives the reason why it cannot be produced in court. Lana's testimony that the photocopy is a true and correct copy of the 1991 will may be used to establish its terms. Her testimony is supported by the testimony of Lana's law clerk, who saw the torn scraps of the will and heard Henry confirm that he considered the 1991 will ineffective.

There is probably sufficient evidence that the 1991 will was properly executed. Its execution revoked the 1990 will.

Was the 1991 will revoked?

The UPC allows revocation by "revocatory act." The definition of a revocatory act includes "burning, tearing, canceling, obliterating, or destroying the will or any part of it." The burning, tearing or cancellation of a will are revocatory acts even if the acts do not touch any of the words on the will. The acts must be performed by the testator or another person at (1) the testator's direction, and (2) in his "conscious presence," with the intent of revoking it. (UPC §2-507(a)(2)). Lana's testimony, corroborated by Charles, establishes that the will was destroyed by Lana in Henry's presence and at Henry's direction.

Did the revocation of the 1991 will have the effect of reviving the 1990 will?

In many states, revocation of a later testamentary instrument that by its terms revokes a prior testamentary instrument does ***not*** revive the earlier instrument. The UPC confirms that the previous will "remains revoked, unless it is revived." However, the Code goes on to provide that if the second will was revoked by physical act, the first will is revived if it appears from either (1) the circumstances of the revocation of the second will, or (2) the testator's contemporaneous or subsequent declarations, that the decedent intended the first will to take effect as executed. (UPC §2-509(a)).

Henry's statement that "things are back the way I want them; Wanda won't get a penny of my property," suggests that his intent was to have the 1990 will revived. Wanda will argue, however, that the statement is too ambiguous to prove an intent to revive the 1990 will. Nevertheless, Henry's statement to Lana and Charles would probably be interpreted to mean that he desired reinstatement of the earlier will rather than intestacy.

Assuming the 1990 will is revived, how should the estate be distributed?

Assuming the validity of the first will and its revival, Wanda has two additional arguments she can make to try to gain a share of Henry's estate.

Wanda's first claim would be that she qualifies as an omitted spouse. The UPC provides that if a testator fails to provide for a surviving spouse who married the testator ***after*** the execution of the will, the omitted spouse receives a modified intestate share (see below), unless: (1) it appears from the will or other evidence that the will was made in contemplation of the marriage; (2) the will expresses the intention that it is to be effective notwithstanding any subsequent marriage; or (3) the testator provided for the spouse outside the will with intent that the transfer serve as a substitute for a gift under the will. (UPC §2-301). The difficult issue here is what should be the date of a revived will. The omitted spouse doctrine is based on the assumption that the spouse was "accidentally" omitted from the will. Clearly that was not the case here. The better position is that the date of the revived will should be the date the testator properly revived the will. Here, that is *after* Henry married Wanda. Under this analysis, Wanda would not qualify as an omitted spouse.

On the other hand, the omitted spouse serves a spousal protection purpose of ensuring that surviving spouses are adequately provided for. Wanda will argue that inasmuch as she is not provided for in the 1990 will, and it is the 1990 will that is being probated, the will should be dated as of the date of its original execution, and thus she should qualify as an omitted spouse. If the court were to adopt this analysis, Wanda would receive her omitted spouse share under UPC §2-301, which provides that she receives her intestate share as to that portion of the testator's estate that is devised neither to a child of the testator born before the marriage in question (who is not a child of the surviving spouse) nor to a descendant of such a child. Here, Henry devised $5,000 to his daughter Sally, who is not Wanda's child. Even if Wanda were to qualify as an omitted spouse, she would take her intestate share from the estate passing under the residuary clause only — it would not include the gift to Sally. Under UPC §2-102(4), where one or more of the decedent's surviving descendants are not descendants of the surviving spouse (in this case, his daughter Sally), the surviving spouse's share is $100,000 plus one-half of the balance of the estate ($395,000). Wanda would receive $100,000 plus $197,500, for a total of $297,500. The remaining balance ($197,500) would go to Maude per the terms of the residuary clause. Henry's brother would not share.

Assuming the jurisdiction is a noncommunity property state, Maude could also claim her elective share. The details of the elective share doctrine vary from state to state. Under the current version of the UPC §2-202, the elective share would depend upon how long the parties had been married. They were married in 1991 and Henry died in 2000, so it appears they were married nine years. Under UPC §2-202, Wendy is entitled to 27 percent of Henry's augmented estate (under these facts, the "augmented" estate component is not applicable). Wendy would take $135,000.

Wendy is better off if she can qualify as an omitted spouse, but even if she cannot, she is entitled to her elective share amount.

Assuming the 1990 will is __not__ revived, how should the estate be distributed through intestacy?

If it is determined that the first will was not revived, the estate would be distributed by intestate succession. This would result in Wanda's receiving $300,000 (not $297,500 as calculated above because her intestate share would be determined as against Henry's entire estate as opposed to only that portion of the estate not going to Sally). The balance of the estate would be distributed to Sally as Henry's only surviving descendant. Maude and Budi would not share.

Answer to Question 3

Was the execution of the 1987 will induced by Ed's fraud? If so, what are Frank's remedies?

The burden of proof on the issue of fraud in the inducement is on the contestant. Frank will have to prove that Lear was induced to make the 1987 will by Ed's fraudulent representation that Frank was the person Lear saw outside the bar.

The Uniform Probate Code has no provision that deals specifically with fraud in the inducement. Under the common law, fraud that induces the execution of a will is defined as reliance by the testator upon a false, material statement of fact made with the intention of deceiving him or her into inserting provisions in the will that he or she would not insert in the absence of the deception. In fraud in the inducement, the testator knows the contents of the will. But the contents would be different if he or she were not deceived. Fraud in the inducement is distinguished from fraud in the execution. The following is an example of fraud in the execution: T tells his lawyer to leave the residue of his estate to A and B. The attorney intentionally substitutes C for B. T executes the will believing it names A and B as his residual beneficiaries.

Frank would argue that the facts show all the elements of fraud in the inducement: (1) Ed lied when he stated that the drunkard looked like Frank, when he really believed that the person he saw was *not* Frank; (2) Ed knew that Lear's discovery of Frank's return to alcoholism might lead to his disinheritance by Lear; and (3) Lear relied on Ed's misrepresentation when he changed his will the very next day.

Ed would argue in rebuttal that: (1) Ed could not know the contents of the 1970 will and had no discernible reason to induce Lear to revoke it; and (2) it's possible to conclude that Lear did *not* rely upon Ed's statement in making the new will: (a) Lear asked Frank himself about the incident and Frank had the opportunity to dispel Lear's doubts, and (b) Lear was probably provoked to change his will not by anything Ed said but by Frank's statement that Lear was a "paranoid old fogie."

After reviewing all the facts, the court could reasonably conclude that the execution of the 1987 will was induced by Ed's fraud. The court is likely to rely on Frank's arguments and on the following facts: (1) even if Ed was not aware of the exact disposition of property under Lear's will, he knew how strongly Lear felt about Frank's possible return to drink and had reason to anticipate that Lear would take some action to favor Ed; and (2) the confrontation between Lear and Frank that resulted in Frank's angry response to Lear would not have occurred if Ed had responded to Lear's earlier inquiry truthfully.

In some states, when a new will is determined to be invalid for fraud in the inducement, provisions in the will revoking a prior will fail as well. In those jurisdictions, the 1987 will and its revocatory clause would be void and the 1970 will reinstated (assuming its terms can be proved).

In other states, the remedy for Ed's fraud would be to impose a constructive trust upon one-half of Ed's bequest (*i.e.*, the amount Frank would have received under the 1970 will) for the benefit of Frank.

Can the 1990 will be probated?

If the revocation of the 1970 will in the 1987 will is set aside as having been procured by fraud, the terms of the 1970 will must still be proved. Because the will was executed in duplicate originals, Frank may prove the terms of the 1970 will and its due execution by submission of the duplicate original and the testimony of his attorney. See UPC §3-402(a).

Did the sale of the AT&T stock by Ed result in ademption of the gift to Ann?

At common law, if a testator left a specific bequest and the subject of the bequest was no longer available at his or her death, the bequest was said to fail or be "adeemed." The process was called "ademption." Whichever will is admitted here, the other beneficiaries will argue that Ann takes nothing, because the gift to her was adeemed. Ann will attack this contention on two separate grounds.

First, she will argue that the sale of the AT&T stock was intrinsically fraudulent in nature (*i.e.*, Ed deliberately sold the stock to extinguish the gift to Ann). In light of (1) Ed's earlier lies to Lear about Frank, and (2) the fact that he purchased a comparable security with no real purpose to change the nature of Lear's holdings, her arguments will probably prevail. If so, the court would impose a constructive trust in favor of Ann upon Ed's share, in an amount equal to the value of the AT&T stock when distribution would be due to Ann.

In the alternative, Ann will invoke UPC §2-606(b). Under amendments adopted in 1990, the UPC provides that "if specifically devised property is sold by a conservator, . . . the specific devisee has the right to a general pecuniary devise equal to the net sale price."(UPC §2-606(b)). Thus, Ann would have a right to receive the value of the stock out of the general assets of Lear's estate, *if* she can show that the devise to her was specific (rather than general) in nature.

Whether a testamentary gift is specific or general depends upon the testator's intent, as determined from all of the applicable circumstances. Where a testator utilizes the word "my" before a gift of stock, as happened here, most courts will conclude that a specific gift was intended. Others require that the number of shares be specified (which Lear did not do), or even that the words "All of my . . . ." precede the description of the gift (which Lear also didn't do). Considering all the facts, the court will probably find that the bequest here was specific and that Ann will be entitled to the value of the proceeds from the sale by Ed of the AT&T stock.

Lear's estate would probably be distributed as follows: (1) an amount equal to the sale proceeds of the AT&T stock will be distributed to Ann; and (2) the residue of the estate will be distributed equally between Ed and Frank.

Answer to Question 4

1. What are the rights of John and Barbara and of Barbara's children?

As to John: was the gift to John revoked by failure of the condition?

Barbara will contend that the gift to John was subject to an express condition subsequent that became effective to revoke John's bequest. The condition was that John remain married to Kathleen at Alfred's death.

Unless a condition in a will is deemed against public policy, it will ordinarily be given effect as written. Some conditions are so offensive that they are almost never enforced. Among these are: (1) conditions that restrain a person from marrying, or (2) conditions that encourage divorce. The condition in this case accomplished the very opposite: it encouraged John to preserve his marriage to Kathleen. Because Alfred was childless, he was probably especially concerned to encourage stability in his nephew's life. Also, he may have become fond of Kathleen and wished not to harm her. On these facts, it is likely that the court will enforce the condition as written.

The Uniform Probate Code makes specific provision for devises (other than residuary devises) that fail. The Code provides that a gift that fails for any reason becomes part of the residue of the estate (UPC §2-604(a)). Because the will provides that Barbara take the residue, John's 10 percent interest in the balance of the estate goes to Barbara.

Did Alfred create a valid trust in favor of Barbara's children?

Neither the trust nor Barbara's children are mentioned in the will, and more than two years elapsed between execution of the will and the letter to Barbara. Barbara's children will assert that Alfred had continued to review his affairs and that he intended his letter to Barbara to constitute a valid, *inter vivos*, discretionary trust for their benefit. If a valid living trust existed, then the U.S. and State X bonds would not be part of Alfred's estate when he died, and they would not pass to Yale College.

An *inter vivos* trust requires: (1) manifestation of intent by the settlor to create a trust, (2) funding (that an identifiable property interest be transferred to the trust/trustee), (3) ascertainable beneficiaries, and (4) possibly a writing (if real property is part of the trust res). The children will argue that all these requirements were satisfied by the letter. Alfred's intent to create a trust is clear and emphatic ("I have established a trust ... ."). The beneficiaries are ascertainable. The trust is intended to be for Barbara's "children." Although Alfred does not name them, the description is clear enough that there is an objective means of determining who the beneficiaries are. The trust is an *inter vivos* trust, so it does not have to be in writing unless it holds real property — which here it does not. The problem is the funding requirement. An identifiable property interest must be transferred to the trustee. Alfred stated that the trust property was to be "all of my U.S. and State X bonds," but there is no evidence that he transferred them to the trustee.

The best argument in support of a trust is that he was declaring himself to be the trustee, but where the settlor is also the trustee, most courts require clear evidence of the intent to create a trust and/or proof that the settlor has segregated the assets in question from his or her other assets. Alfred wrote that he was going to segregate the assets by establishing the trust at ABC Bank, but there is no evidence that he put the assets in the bank. In the alternative, Barbara's children can argue that he intended Barbara to be the trustee and gave her full discretion to distribute the income and corpus of the trust as she wished.

Yale will argue that: (1) Alfred may have thought about creating a trust but changed his mind and finally decided not to; (2) his intent was not to be the trustee himself but to make the bank the trustee, and that his failure to execute the necessary documents at the bank clearly proves his change of heart; (3) that no delivery of the trust res ever occurred (*i.e.*, the U.S. and State X bonds were never delivered to anyone but were retained by Alfred, a clear indication that he meant them to go to Yale as originally planned); and (4) that there is no reasonable basis for concluding that he meant Barbara to be the trustee — the language "I have established a trust . . ." instead of the equally simple language "I am establishing a trust," shows that he did not intend Barbara to be the trustee.

Barbara's children will argue in rebuttal that Alfred's unequivocal language in his letter to Barbara ("I *have* established a trust for your children . . . composed of all my U.S. and State X bonds.") should control regardless of the trustee's identity. The retention of the bonds by Alfred simply establishes that he was holding them as both his will and the letter would indicate — the U.S. and State X bonds for the benefit of the children and only the State Z bonds for Yale.

In response, the children will reassert their argument that Alfred intended himself to be the trustee. His statement to Barbara, "You can decide how the funds should be used," meant only that Alfred would consult with Barbara before expending any funds in the children's behalf. Because the trust res (the U.S. bonds and the X bonds only) was clearly identified in Alfred's letter to Barbara, Alfred was not obliged to segregate the bonds from his other assets.

Because the letter to Barbara so clearly designated the components of the trust and so clearly designated the intent to benefit Barbara's children, it is likely that the children will prevail.

If a trust was created with Alfred as trustee, his subsequent death would not cause the trust to fail. A successor trustee (probably Barbara) would simply be appointed.

If, as seems unlikely, no trust at all was created, then the U.S. and State X bonds remained in Alfred's estate and at his death would go to Yale College along with the State Z bonds.

2. Assuming the creation of a valid trust for Barbara's children, what are the rights of Yale College?

If a valid trust *was* created by Alfred, the court will have to decide what effect that will have on the testamentary gift to Yale. Specifically, does Yale get cash equal to the value of the U.S. and State X bonds at Alfred's death? To the extent Yale gets cash, the residuary gift to Alfred's niece Barbara will be reduced accordingly.

Under the common law, a specific devise is adeemed — rendered ineffective — if the property that is devised is not owned by the testator at death. Under the common law, Yale would not get cash in lieu of the value of the U.S. and State X bonds. Instead, it would get only the State Z bonds.

The more modern approach, reflected in the UPC, is to apply ademption only where the facts indicate that the testator intended to extinguish the gift or when ademption is "consistent with the testator's manifested plan of distribution."(UPC §2-606(a)(6)). Yale will argue that ademption is inconsistent with Alfred's overall testamentary scheme. As evidenced in his will, his intent was to give his government bonds, or the value thereof, to Yale. Assuming he created a valid trust of his U.S. and State X bonds, Yale will argue that it is entitled to the monetary equivalent — that all Alfred was doing was shifting his assets around (transferring some of the bonds to benefit Barbara's children, but money should be shifted to Yale to compensate for the shift in the bonds). Alfred made no attempt at revising or revoking the original gift to Yale, arguably indicating that he still wanted the original gift — or its monetary equivalent — to go to Yale. On the other hand, Barbara will argue that even under the modern trend/UPC "intent of the testator" approach, ademption should apply here. The facts indicate that the bonds were a material part of Alfred's assets; it's unlikely he wanted to drain his estate of a matching amount of cash to Yale, especially as that would come at the sole expense of his niece, Barbara. After the failure of the conditional bequest to his nephew John, Barbara was his principal living heir and we may reasonably presume that he would prefer her.

Whether ademption should apply under the UPC approach is a close call. Because Yale bears the burden of proof, and because applying ademption would favor his family over Yale, the more likely result is that a court would apply ademption. Yale would, however, be entitled to the State Z bonds, because these are included in the term "government bonds" and were excluded from the contents of the trust.

Answer to Question 5

The proceeds of the insurance policy:

The issue here is whether Joe gets all the proceeds of the policy or whether Tom Allen and his wife each gets one-third of the proceeds. A subsidiary issue is whether the three share as principal beneficiaries or as beneficiaries of a trust of which Joe is the trustee. One thing is clear — June does not get any part of the insurance proceeds. Although she was originally a beneficiary, the change in beneficiaries was effective to remove her. Nor can she claim any part of the proceeds under the will or in intestacy. The proceeds of an insurance policy are *not* part of the insured's estate.

Bill's letter to Joe following his designation as beneficiary expressed Bill's intent to limit Joe's interest in the policy to one-third of the proceeds. His subsequent note to Joe, although unsigned, confirmed this intent by naming the individuals who would share equally in the other two-thirds. It would be difficult under these facts to argue that Joe should get anything more than Bill intended — that is, one-third and no more than one-third.

Joe will argue that the first letter was ineffective because no specific persons were named to share in the proceeds and that the change of beneficiary form filed with the company controlled the disposition of funds. He will also argue that Bill knew how to accomplish a formal change in beneficiaries and would have done so if he had meant to. He will rely on the fact that the second letter was unsigned and therefore not binding on anyone. Joe is likely to be helped in his arguments by the insurance company, which is unlikely to want to pay the proceeds except as confirmed in the formal designation of beneficiaries. The company will probably deposit the proceeds into court pending the outcome of the litigation.

Tom Allen and his wife will argue that the first letter to Joe, which Joe agreed to respect, constituted a change in beneficiaries that was confirmed and made explicit by the second letter. On this theory, they will claim outright ownership of two-thirds of the insurance proceeds. They will also argue in support of their claim to share in the proceeds outright that they are the third-party beneficiaries of a written agreement between Bill and Joe as expressed in the exchange of letters.

If the claim to receive their share of the proceeds as principal beneficiaries fails, Tom and his wife can then argue that they are the beneficiaries of a trust that arose by reason of Bill's initial letter to Joe, Joe's agreement to be bound by the terms of the letter, and Bill's second letter naming them as beneficiaries. They will argue that Joe became a trustee for the benefit of three designated beneficiaries. Although Bill retained the right to change the beneficiaries until his death, this meant only that the trust was revocable during life and became irrevocable on Bill's death.

If no valid express trust were found to exist, Tom and his wife should also argue in the alternative that the court should impose a *constructive* trust upon two-thirds of the insurance proceeds. The constructive trust doctrine creates an equitable duty to convey property to another when retention of the property would unjustly enrich the holder at the expense of others who are entitled to benefit. Because Joe told Bill that he would do whatever Bill requested (upon which statement Bill presumably relied), Joe would be unjustly enriched if he were to retain more than one-third of the insurance proceeds. Whether the court will impose a constructive trust is a matter of equity and is difficult to predict. If the court is persuaded that Joe acted wrongfully (by inducing Bill to change the beneficiary to him in reliance on his promise he would do whatever Bill requested, or in accepting Bill's second note to him without informing Bill that he would not honor the request), the court should impose a constructive trust on Joe in favor of Tom and his wife with respect to the two-thirds in question.

Blackacre (the Farm):

The circumstances surrounding delivery of the deed to Pete raise several preliminary questions:

Was the deed "delivered"?

Nothing in the facts suggest that there was any defect in the execution of the deed. But before a deed is deemed to transfer title, it must not only be properly executed; it must also be "delivered." The requirement of delivery does not mean that the grantor must hand the deed physically to the grantee. The delivery requirement is satisfied by "words or conduct of the grantor which evidence his intention to make his deed presently operative . . . so as to vest title in the grantee and to surrender his own control over the title."(3 A.L.P. 312). In other words, the requirement revolves around intent to convey rather than any specific physical act.

Here, there is concrete evidence of Bill's intent to convey to Pete. He went to Pete's house for the specific purpose of handing Pete the deed. He left the deed with Pete's housekeeper with instructions to deliver it to Pete. He confirmed the status of Pete as title holder by giving him instructions in his signed letter about the disposition of rental income. The delivery is not qualified by the fact that the deed was handed to the housekeeper instead of

Pete himself. Bill regarded her only as a conduit to Pete, not as a stakeholder or escrowee.

Acceptance by Pete

Some courts hold that a deed does not convey title until there is some manifestation of acceptance by the grantee. It may be argued that Pete could not have accepted the deed because he did not receive it until his return, which followed Bill's death. However, Pete had previously received and read Bill's letter directing him to collect the rents from the farm and to pay the income to June. If he had wished to reject the conveyance, he would presumably have notified Bill of the rejection before he left on his trip.

Was the deed a testamentary transfer that failed to qualify as a will?

June may wish to argue that the transfer of title to Pete was ineffective because the deed was not accepted by Pete until after Bill's death and therefore constituted a testamentary document that did not meet the requirements for a valid will. The consequence would be that title did not pass under the deed but would instead go to June under the will. This argument is not likely to succeed under the facts. When Bill executed the deed, he had no reason to contemplate an imminent death. His execution of the deed and his letter to Pete indicated an immediate intention to convey title to Pete. Pete read the letter and knew its terms. He never rejected the terms. Bill made a deliberate effort to deliver the will. None of these circumstances indicates any intent on Bill's part to consider this a transfer that would take effect only on his death.

Did the deed to Pete create an **inter vivos trust**?

Finally, we ask whether the transfer to Pete created an *inter vivos* trust of income for June during her life, then the fee to Bill's church. Did Bill make the required "manifestation of an intent" to create a trust? Bill executed the deed first, *then* wrote and signed the "trust letter." Pete will argue that he is not bound to observe the trust. He will contend that the deed conveyed unrestricted title to him alone, without any reference to any trust. He will also argue that the letter to him did not meet the formal requirements for creating a trust: it was not executed prior to or at the same time as the deed, and it was not agreed to in writing by Pete as trustee.

June will argue in response that the deed was not "conveyed" until *after* he had properly expressed his intent to Pete that Pete was taking as a trustee.

Bill not only wrote the letter the same day he executed the deed, but Bill did not deliver the deed until "a few days" after he had sent the letter to Pete. Bill's act of writing and mailing the letter to Pete should serve as proof of his intent to create a trust. The letter identifies the beneficiaries. It is in writing. The elements to create a trust are satisfied by the letter, except for funding. The funding requirement is satisfied by the delivery of the deed to Pete. The deed is not effective to transfer title until it is delivered, and Bill did not deliver the deed until *after* he had taken what he thought were the necessary and appropriate steps to set up the trust that was to hold the trust property (the farm). Pete's acceptance of the letter without objection at the time shows Pete's acceptance of Bill's intent to create a trust and Pete's acceptance of the office of trustee — with full responsibility on Pete to fulfill the terms of the trust.

In summary, it is likely that the court will find both that the conveyance to Pete was effective and that Bill created a valid *inter vivos* trust of the income from the farm for the benefit of June.

Did the reference to Aunt Selma in the will create a testamentary trust?

Aunt Selma may contend that the language in Bill's will referring to her created a trust under which June was obliged to supply Selma's needs for life. June can probably overcome this contention by arguing that Bill's language was merely precatory in nature (it was a mere request, not a clear directive). This argument is supported by Bill's use of the word "recommend" and the request to June to do only as she thought best.

There is no indication that Bill had supported Selma during his lifetime and the language in the will is too weak to support a finding that a trust was intended. The court will probably decide that June is *not* obliged to provide any support to Selma, but may do so if she wishes.

Answer to Question 6

Is Daniel's will valid?

Does the fact that John, a beneficiary, acted as witness render Daniel's will ineffective? The answer is "no." The fact that John was an interested witness would not cause the will to fail. Nor would it cause the provision in favor of John to fail. (UPC §2-505(b)). The facts do not suggest any undue influence by John on Daniel, and it is only natural to bestow a testamentary gift upon one's brother.

Bequest to Alice:

As residual beneficiary, Bill might be expected to challenge the specific bequests. He will contend that the $5,000 bequest to Alice was revoked by Daniel's cancellation (*i.e.,* drawing a line through it with the intent to revoke it), and (2) that it was not effectively replaced by the $5,000 bequest, which fails as an attested will because it does not comply with the necessary testamentary formalities (*e.g.* witnesses). See UPC §2-507; §2-502.

Holographic will:

In rebuttal, Alice will argue that the handwritten modification was valid as a holographic will. The statutes controlling holographic wills vary widely from state to state. Some states require that the entire document be in the testator's handwriting, including a full signature. Other states follow the reasoning of the UPC and are much more liberal. In these states writings qualify as holographic wills as long as they contain the handwritten signature of the testator, the "material provisions" are in the testator's handwriting, and the document evidences testamentary intent (the intent that the person intended this document to be his or her last will). (UPC §2-502(b)). Initials will generally suffice as a signature, especially if it is clear that they are in the testator's hand. Bill will argue that the mere insertion of a new number by the testator does not satisfy the "material provisions" requirement. Most courts define the "material provisions" as requiring the testator's handwriting to indicate who takes what. Here, only the amount of the gift is in the testator's handwriting, not who is to take the gift. Most courts would hold that this does not meet the formalities of a holographic will.

Harmless error doctrine:

Even if the court is reluctant to find a holographic will, Alice has a good chance of getting the court to overlook the need for testamentary formalities, under a new provision that was added to the UPC in 1990. Under new UPC §2-503, the lack of formalities will be treated as harmless by the court if there is "clear and convincing evidence" that the document at issue (or an addition or alteration to the document) was intended as the decedent's will. Here, the line through the old amount, the handwritten new amount, and the initials alongside the new amount — taken together — would probably satisfy this standard. Alice should be entitled to the increased amount.

Doctrine of dependent relative revocation:

In the event a court were to rule (1) that Daniel's handwritten provisions do not constitute a holographic codicil, and (2) that Daniel's line through the original gift to Alice constitutes a valid revocation of the original gift of $5,000, Alice's best argument would be to invoke the dependent relative revocation doctrine. This doctrine permits a mistaken revocation to be nullified. Under the doctrine, when a testator revokes a will, or a provision in a will, and substitutes a new will or provision under the mistaken belief that the new will or provision is valid, the revocation is viewed as having been conditional or "dependent" upon the validity of the new will or provision. Applying this principle, if Daniel's changes are not valid, the earlier bequest of $5,000 is restored. Daniel obviously would prefer that Alice get $50,000, but if that change is invalid, the $5,000 gift should certainly be revived. If Alice loses on the "holographic will" and "testamentary intent" arguments, she will almost certainly be permitted to receive the original $5,000 gift under the doctrine of dependent relative revocation.

Pretermitted child:

Alice will *not* be able to claim as a pretermitted child (UPC §2-302) because she was already born when the will was executed. Thus, she is not entitled to an intestate share.

Possible trust in favor of Karen:

Karen will contend that the bequest to Bill was subject to a trust for her benefit; that Bill was obligated to provide for her needs. This contention is supported by the fact that Daniel had helped Karen to meet her living expenses during his life and presumably would want Karen to be cared for in a similar manner after his death. Bill will argue that the phrasing in the will with respect to Karen is only precatory. Precatory phrasing imposes only a moral obligation on the donee (here Bill) to use the gift for the benefit of the third party (here Karen), not a legal obligation. It is a close call here. The phrasing in the will ("it is my *wish* ...") is not enough, standing alone, to impose a legal obligation on Bill. But when coupled with Daniel's history of helping to care for Karen, it is a close call. Ultimately it is a question of the testator's (Daniel's) intent. A court could go either way on this issue.

Is Lois entitled to John's $10,000?

The law distinguishes between a beneficiary who receives property under a promise to convey to another but who changes his or her mind *after* the testator's death and one who receives property under a similar promise but who never intended to keep the promise in the first place, or who did intend to keep the promise but changed his or her mind *before* the testator's death. In the former case, the beneficiary is generally allowed to keep the property free of the promise. In the latter case, a constructive trust is generally applied in favor of the person who will benefit from the promise.

Lois will contend that she is entitled to the $10,000 that Daniel left to John, on the theory that a constructive trust arose because Daniel relied on John's promise to convey the money to Lois, even though the promise was oral. Where there is adequate extrinsic evidence of the testator's reliance upon the beneficiary's promise, most courts will impose a *constructive trust* in favor of the intended beneficiary. As we have pointed out, the court is more likely to do this if it believes that John never intended to keep the promise — or that he did intend to keep the promise but changed his mind before the testator's death — than if it believes he originally intended to comply and changed his mind after the testator's death. We don't know from these facts what John's state of mind was, nor are we told that John has manifested an intent not to convey to Lois. If there is a dispute between them, Lois is likely to prevail.

Summary:

Probably, Alice will receive $50,000; either Lois or John will receive $10,000; and Bill will receive $40,000 — which may be subject to an obligation to care for Karen.

Answer to Question 7

Beneficiaries of Trust #2 (Beneficiaries) v. Agatha

A testamentary trustee derives authority from both his or her designation under the will and his or her appointment by the court. Once appointed, the trustee owes a duty of loyalty to the beneficiaries of the trust. She or he may not, for example, sell any trust property to herself or himself, regardless of the fairness or good faith of the transaction, without (1) authorization from the trust, (2) court approval, or (3) approval of the beneficiaries after full disclosure. (Uniform Trust Code [UTC] §802(b)). The duty of loyalty precludes the trustee from making any personal profit from trust transactions. When the duty of loyalty is breached, beneficiaries can recover from the trustee: (a) any loss resulting from the breach, (b) any profit resulting from the breach, and (c) any profit the trust would have made if the breach had not occurred. The beneficiaries have several equitable remedies as well (*e.g.*, an injunction to prevent the trustee's breach, an action to appoint a receiver, an action to compel a waiver of the trustee's compensation). In addition, when trust property is wrongfully transferred to a third party, the beneficiaries may trace the property and/or its product into the hands of the third party and secure its return to the trust.

There is little doubt on these facts that Agatha breached her duty of loyalty by utilizing trust property to satisfy a personal obligation. Her actions resulted in a substantial loss to the Beneficiaries. She is therefore liable to the Beneficiaries for at least the loss in the TT&A stock's value to Trust #2 at the time of transfer ($11,000). In many states, she would also be liable for any increase in the stock's value **to the time of trial** (plus any lost dividends).

Beneficiaries of Trust #2 (Beneficiaries) v. Larry

If the Beneficiaries believe that TT&A stock will continue to increase in value, they can seek to trace the stock and recover the shares directly from Larry.

Under the constructive trust doctrine, when the retention of identifiable property would result in unjust enrichment to the recipient at the expense of the intended beneficiary, the court may deem the item to be held in trust for the benefit of the intended beneficiary. The Beneficiaries will contend that, because Larry received the stock as a gift, the constructive trust doctrine should be applied to require him to return the stock to them.

Larry will respond that he received the stock from his uncle John, a *bona fide* purchaser for value and that he stands in John's shoes. But this argument will probably fail because John did not act in good faith. He knew or should have known that: (1) Agatha was transferring trust assets, and (2) the assets were worth much more than he paid for them — that is, enough to enable Agatha to pay off her entire loan balance, plus 10 percent interest. Equity requires that the Beneficiaries prevail against Larry.

If the TT&A stock is recovered by the Beneficiaries, can John invade Trust #1 to satisfy Agatha's obligation to him? If the Beneficiaries obtain a judgment against Agatha, can they invade Trust #1?

If Larry is forced to return the stock to the trust, John will probably stop at nothing in a renewed effort to recover Agatha's $10,000 from the assets of Trust #1. He will argue that there has been a material failure of consideration and that he released Agatha from her obligation without receiving anything in return. The question is whether John can invade Trust #1 to satisfy his $10,000 debt.

Ordinarily, a trust beneficiary may assign or transfer his or her interest in the same way as a fee owner. When the testator wishes to prevent unlimited transfer by the beneficiary, he or she may use one of several restraints. One of these is a spendthrift trust. A spendthrift trust is one that includes an express provision prohibiting alienation of a beneficiary's right to receive a benefit, whether principal or interest or both. The provision may be limited to voluntary transfers, but it may also be written to apply to involuntary transfers. A majority of states enforce spendthrift provisions; a minority do not.

Most spendthrift clauses express two restraints: (1) one that prevents the beneficiary from voluntarily alienating his or her interest in the trust income or corpus, and (2) one that prevents creditors of the beneficiary from reaching the interest of the beneficiary. Most courts that enforce spendthrift clauses will construe a will that contains either restraint as intending both. These courts hold that it is against public policy to permit a settlor to restrain involuntary alienation without also restraining voluntary alienation. Some courts will not enforce a restraint against involuntary transfer unless there is also a restraint against voluntary transfer. These courts permit creditors to reach the beneficiary's interest if the beneficiary is not also restrained.

Both of George's trusts stated that creditors could not reach the income in the trustee's hands. We may reasonably conclude that there was no corresponding provision specifically enjoining voluntary alienation by the beneficiaries. In those states in which a spendthrift provision will not be enforced without such a clause, Agatha's creditors may invade the trust (at least to the extent of her income interest).

In the majority of states, however, the restraint against creditors will be construed as including a restraint against voluntary alienation as well. In those states, John will be prevented from reaching Agatha's interest.

John may have one final ace up his sleeve. The general rule is that a settlor may not create a spendthrift trust for himself or herself. John will argue that the agreement between George and Agatha was a skillful effort to avoid this rule.

John will argue that Agatha really acted as settlor of her own trust by forgiving the $300,000 debt to George's estate and agreeing to substitute the trust instead. He may be able to prove that the arrangement between Agatha and George was a ruse to limit access to Agatha's assets by her creditors.

The same arguments made by John will be made by Agatha's other creditors, including the beneficiaries of Trust #2.

Answer to Question 8

Was a valid trust created thirty years ago?

An *inter vivos* trust requires: (1) manifestation of intent by the settlor to create a trust, (2) funding (that an identifiable property interest be delivered to the trust/trustee), (3) ascertainable beneficiaries (either immediately or within the period of the Rule Against Perpetuities), and (4) possibly a writing (if real property is part of the trust res). The facts here state that a trust instrument was executed, that State Bank was named trustee, and that 80 shares of Disney stock were delivered to the trustee. Thus, three of the four elements are clearly satisfied. The only issue is whether the ascertainable beneficiaries element is satisfied.

Because Thea had no children "in being" at the time the trust was created, it may be argued that the fourth requirement is not satisfied because there is no living person who may be identified as the beneficiary and therefore no person to ensure the enforceability of the trust. A trust for unborn children, however, is a widely accepted exception to the requirement that there must be ascertainable beneficiaries. Most courts and the Uniform Trust Code permit trusts for unborn children as long as the beneficiaries may become ascertainable within the period of the Rule Against Perpetuities. (UTC §402 Comment). Moreover, for probate purposes, the traditional rule has been that a child born alive is treated as alive from the moment of conception. Inasmuch as Thea was pregnant when she created the trust, and the child was born alive, there is also the traditional argument that there was an ascertainable beneficiary from the moment the trust was created.

Therefore Thea's trust was validly created thirty years ago.

Did the bequest to Fred in Thea's will revoke the trust?

Sal might contend that the gift of 100 shares to Fred revoked the *inter vivos* trust, on the theory that the "out of shares held by me" language implied that Thea owned more than 100 shares and that only some of her shares would be taken "out of" the total to satisfy the gift to Fred. Because this would be true only if we included the shares in the trust, Thea arguably meant to revoke the trust. But the children are likely to prevail against this argument. They will contend: (1) in most states, an *inter vivos* trust cannot be revoked unless the power to revoke is expressly retained by the settlor, and (2) even if the power to revoke was specifically reserved in the trust document (the facts are silent on this point), revocation of a trust must be clear and unequivocal. The will stated that Fred was to receive the stock "out of shares held by me at my death." Technically, Thea did not own the shares in the trust; the trust/trustee held legal title to the shares in the trust at the time of her death. Most likely, Thea anticipated the acquisition of more shares of Disney stock prior to her death, but intended nothing more by this language. Furthermore, the will contained no reference to the trust agreement, and we are not told that Thea made any effort to reclaim the Disney stock from State Bank. It's unlikely that the court will decide that the trust agreement was revoked.

To whom should the trust assets be distributed?

[This issue is complicated because the fact pattern does not give us all of the facts — in particular, who has what interest, if any, in the trust while the settlor is alive; and do Thea's children hold any interest while Thea is alive, or only upon her death?]

When Thea created the trust for the benefit of her "children," she created a class gift. When the term "children" is used in a trust document, it is generally construed as including only the generation immediately following the settlor (*i.e.*, it does not include grandchildren). Her two youngest children will be entitled to shares. The issue is what should happen to the share for her oldest child, who died two years before Thea, leaving a son who survived Thea.

The son will argue that once his parent was born, the interest in Thea's trust vested. As a vested interest, it is inheritable and devisable. If Thea's oldest child died intestate, the interest would pass through intestacy to the child's heirs (including the son — again the facts are incomplete). If Thea's oldest child died testate, the interest would pass under the terms of his or her will (most likely to the residual donee).

The Uniform Probate Code adopts a different approach. Section 2-707 requires holders of future interests to survive to the time of distribution (assuming the right to distribution can be characterized as a future interest — an issue that turns on the precise terms of the trust, which the facts do not provide). If a remainderman does not survive to the time for distribution, the UPC provides for a gift over to the remainderman's issue; and if there are none, the gift fails and is returned to the settlor's estate — unless there is an express default taker who is to take in the event the gift fails. Under the UPC approach, one-third of the trust assets would be distributed to the son of Thea's child who predeceased her. The other two-thirds would be divided equally between her surviving children.

What is the effect of Thea's divorce from Fred?

The UPC provides that the dissolution of a marriage has the effect of revoking a testamentary gift to the former spouse (UPC §2-804(b)), unless the will or a court order or a marital agreement expressly provides to the contrary. Therefore, Fred gets nothing. (This would be so even if there were no codicil or the codicil were, for some reason, invalidated.)

What does Sal receive?

The UPC provides that where a testator devises stock, and at the time the testator executed the will, the testator owned matching shares of stock, if thereafter the stock changes due to action initiated by the corporate entity, the beneficiary receives the benefit of the change — regardless of whether the language of the gift makes it look like a general or specific gift. (UPC §2-605(a)(1)). At the time Thea executed her codicil, she owned matching shares of Disney stock. Therefore, Sal is entitled to the 50-share increase that occurred between the time the codicil was executed and the testator's death. His gift includes the 100 shares allocated to him in the will, plus the additional 50 shares issued as a stock dividend before Thea's death.

What is the effect of the stock dividend that occurred after Thea's death?

Because all interests in the estate became vested at Thea's death, the stock dividend during the period of administration is allocated 100 percent to the party who holds the underlying stock interest. Here, the stock dividend on the shares held in trust will go to the trust beneficiaries; the stock dividend on the shares held by the probate estate will go to the devisee under the will — Sal.

Answer to Question 9

1. How should Alice's estate be distributed?

Does it matter that Daniel was not mentioned in the will?

In general, a testator is free to disinherit a child in his or her will. Some states have attempted to mitigate the effect of this general principle. Thus, in some states a child is barred from taking only if the intent to disinherit is expressed in the will. In some states, only children who are born after the will is executed are protected. The UPC now protects after-born children only, in circumstances that are not relevant under these facts. (UPC §2-302). But the UPC makes no provision for a child who is alive when the will is executed unless the testator erroneously believes that the child is dead (in which case the child is treated as an omitted after-born child). Daniel's arguments will fall on deaf ears. Alice made adequate provision for Daniel both in the original trust and also through her additional bequest to the trust in her will. There is no reason to conclude that she meant to do anything more for Daniel.

Should the $100,000 bequest to the trustee fail?

According to the facts, Daniel has asserted that the $100,000 bequest to Bank as trustee should fail because the trust document was not executed in compliance with the Statute of Wills. This argument will also fail.

There is nothing in the facts to suggest that the original trust instrument was defective in any way or that it was invalid. The bequest to Bank will simply operate as a gift to an existing valid legal entity. An existing trust is an eligible devisee, and the gift to the trust will be held and distributed pursuant to the terms of the trust. (UPC §1-201(11)). Daniel's challenge of the $100,000 bequest to Alice's trust is without merit.

[In the alternative, the beneficiaries under the trust can argue incorporation by reference. The doctrine of incorporation by reference permits a separate writing that is in existence when a will is made to be incorporated within the will, if the language of the will (1) manifests an intent to incorporate the document, and (2) describes the document sufficiently to permit its identification. Although the doctrine is generally applied to informal documents of the testator that he or she wants to include within his or her will, it can be applied to the trust here. The trust agreement (including the amendment signed by Daniel himself) was already in existence when the will was executed, and it was specifically mentioned in the will.]

Did the bequest to Celia lapse at her death?

A will is deemed effective as of the date of the testator's death. A gift to a named beneficiary who has died before the testator is therefore deemed invalid. It is said to lapse. Most states have statutes that control the disposition of a lapsed bequest. Under the UPC's antilapse provision, when a beneficiary who is a lineal descendant of the testator's grandparent predeceases the decedent, the gift passes to his or her surviving descendants. (UPC §2-603(b)(1)). As Alice's sister, Celia was protected by this provision. Doris is entitled to receive the $50,000 devise to Celia as Celia's sole surviving descendant.

Is Doris's claim affected by her witnessing of the will?

At common law, any person having a pecuniary interest in the testator's estate was incompetent to act as witness to the testator's will. This impediment has been changed by statute in most states. Under the UPC, "[i]nterest no longer disqualifies a person as a witness, nor does it invalidate or forfeit a gift under the will."(UPC §2-505, Official Comment). Furthermore, Doris did not have a pecuniary interest at the time she signed the will. Celia was still alive to take the gift and Doris was not an "interested person" as that term is defined in the UPC. (UPC §1-201(24)).

Conclusion:

Based upon the foregoing, (1) Bank, in its capacity as trustee of the trust established by Alice, would receive $100,000 from her estate; (2) Doris would receive $50,000; and (3) the balance would pass to Stan.

2. Can Phil reach Celia's interest in the trust?

In his attempts to reach Celia's assets in the trust, Phil has probably asserted that the spendthrift provisions added to the trust were invalid against him as a pre-existing creditor of Celia.

Phil might have initially argued that an *inter vivos* trust cannot ordinarily be terminated or modified by the settlor, unless this power has been specifically retained by him or her. However, most jurisdictions permit a settlor to terminate or modify an *inter vivos* trust provided the trustee and ***all*** of the outstanding beneficiaries agree. See Restatement 2d of Trusts, §338(1). Because Bank, Alice, Celia, and Daniel were the trustee, the settlor, and all the beneficiaries, they had the power to modify the trust by adding the spendthrift provision.

Phil might make a second, more powerful, argument: that Celia's conduct in securing and participating in the execution of the amendment constituted a *fraud upon Phil as Celia's creditor*. Fraud on creditors occurs when a debtor attempts to place his or her assets beyond the reach of creditors without giving fair value for the assets or while retaining a concealed interest in the assets. Celia was arguably guilty of such conduct because she entered into a modification of the trust only to insulate her interest from Phil, while preserving her ability to receive income from the trust. When a fraud upon a creditor has occurred, the creditor may invade the trust to the extent of his debtor's interest.

The facts don't tell us whether Celia's consent was in fact necessary to effectuate a modification of the trust, or whether her consent was superfluous because Alice reserved the power to amend in the original instrument. If Celia's consent was crucial to the modification, Phil's "fraud upon creditors" argument should prevail. However, if Alice had reserved the power to amend the trust without Celia's consent, Phil's contention would be weaker. Even then, however, if it were shown that Celia induced Alice to make the change for the purpose of defeating Phil's rights as a creditor, a court might find that Phil had been defrauded.

[Note that the modern trend is to allow certain classes of creditors to reach a beneficiary's interest in a spendthrift trust. In some states a creditor who has rendered basic necessities to the beneficiary may reach the beneficiary's interest. Phil might be able to persuade the court that his services as building contractor should be included in the definition of basic necessities. Other creditors who may reach spendthrift trust interests, depending on the jurisdiction and the approach, are: (1) ex-spouses entitled to alimony; (2) children entitled to child support; and/or (3) federal and state governments entitled to taxes.]

Answer to Question 10

1. Is Tina's will valid in Calco?

Under UPC §2-506, a will is valid if it was executed in compliance with the law of the place where the will was executed, or with the law of the place where the testator was domiciled or had "an abode" at either the time of the execution or at the time of his or her death. Thus, while we are told that Tina's will was not valid under the law of Terra, it is valid in Calco — the place of Tina's domicile at death. The facts tell us that Calco's probate code is the same as the UPC. Tina's will qualifies as a holographic will (*i.e.,* a will that is signed by the testator and the material terms of which are in the testator's handwriting). See UPC §2-502(b). In the alternative, there is also a good chance that the document could be validated as an attested will under the harmless error doctrine. (UPC §2-503).

Although Sally is an interested person as defined in UPC §1-201(23), her signature does not invalidate the will. First, a holographic will does not need to be witnessed at all, so Sally's signature was irrelevant to the validity of the will. Second, under the UPC, the signing of a will by an interested witness does not invalidate the will or any provision of it. (UPC §2-505(b)). Of course, a person opposing the will may be able to show that the witness — especially one who receives a substantial benefit under the will — exerted undue influence on the testator. See Comment, UPC §2-505.

2. How should Tina's estate be distributed?

Claims on behalf of George:

Can George's guardian claim an interest by George under the pretermitted child doctrine? UPC §2-302 deals with "omitted children." Was George's father Charlie an omitted child of Tina? The answer is "no." The UPC protects an omitted child only if (1) the testator erroneously believed the child, though alive, was deceased, or (2) the child was born or adopted *after* the execution of the will. Charlie was not an omitted child as that term is defined and George cannot claim through him. Further, the protection accorded to omitted children under UPC §2-302 does not extend to omitted grandchildren. The term "child" specifically excludes grandchildren of a testator. See General Definitions, UPC §1-201(5). A grandchild — even one born or adopted after the will is executed — cannot take advantage of the omitted child provisions of the UPC. George will receive nothing, even though he is an after-born issue of a child of the testator.

Gifts to Sally:

We have determined that Tina's will is valid in Calco. Does Sally's status as witness affect her status as beneficiary under the will? Under UPC §2-505, the signing of a will by an interested witness does not invalidate either the will or any of its provisions. The provisions for Sally's benefit remain intact. Sally was Tina's daughter and the natural object of Tina's affection and her largesse. Nothing in the facts indicates that Sally exercised any undue influence on her mother. On the contrary, we know that Tina later gave Sally enough money to buy a house.

Which house is "the house" referred to in the will?

George's guardian may contend that Tina meant to give Sally only the house in Terra, and that when the Terra house was sold, the doctrine of ademption by extinction applied and made the gift ineffective. At common law, ademption was applied mechanically; if the property referred to in the will was not in the estate at death, the gift failed. The modern trend is to soften the impact of ademption. One device is to construe the will as though it read at the death of the testator, not at the date of execution. Under this device, the original gift is deemed replaced by any substitute that may exist at death. Another device is to read the disposition in its most general sense instead of as referring to specific property. Thus, "my" house becomes not a specific house, but any building in which the testator resides.

The Uniform Probate Code offers relief in the case of substituted real or tangible personal property. UPC §2-606(a) provides: "A specific devisee has a right to the specifically devised property in the testator's estate at death and: . . . (5) real or tangible personal property owned by the testator at death which the testator acquired as a replacement for specifically devised real or tangible personal property; . . ." Under this provision, the Calco house would be substituted for the Terra house under the will.

Even if the specific bequest fails, the Calco house will still go to Sally under the residuary clause.

The significance of the $300,000 "advancement":

Tina did not use the term "advancement" correctly. The term is applied only in the case of total or partial intestacy. An advancement is an *inter vivos* transfer made by a deceased before his or her death to a person who is entitled to take in intestacy, which the testator intended as an advance against the person's final disposition from the intestate estate. Example:

A has two sons, B and C. A dies intestate, leaving $100,000 in cash. Two years before his death, A gave son B $50,000 with the admonition, "This is an advance against your money when I die." Under the advancement doctrine, A's "hotchpot" estate would be $150,000. Inasmuch as B has already received $50,000, his share of the hotchpot is only $25,000. C would take the remaining $75,000 (remember the "real" probate estate is only $100,000, so the math works out fine). Under the UPC, an *inter vivos* gift to an heir of an individual who dies intestate is treated as an advancement only if: (1) the testator declares in a contemporaneous writing that the gift is an advancement, or the donee acknowledges it in writing; or (2) a writing of the decedent, or a written acknowledgment of the donee, indicates that the gift is to be taken into account in computing the division and distribution of the intestate estate.

Here, it's clear that by using the word "advancement" Tina meant only that she was giving Sally some money she needed then instead of keeping it for Sally as part of the residue of Tina's estate under her will.

Was the devise of the house to Sally satisfied by the inter vivos gift of $300,000?

When Tina gave Sally $300,000 to purchase the house, did Tina intend for the gift of cash to be in satisfaction of the bequest of the house? The effect of construing the gift as a satisfaction would be to revoke the bequest of the house. At common law, there was authority for the proposition that a substantial *inter vivos* gift to a child who was also a legatee presumably satisfied the legacy if the other beneficiaries of the will were other children of the testator. The presumption was rebuttable by evidence of a contrary intent by the testator.

Under UPC §2-609, an *inter vivos* gift is treated as a satisfaction only if the will provides for deduction, or if the testator declares in writing that the gift is in satisfaction of the devise, or if the devisee acknowledges in writing that the gift is in satisfaction. Although Tina did not use the word "advancement" correctly (as she died testate), one could argue that she was expressing the intent that her *inter vivos* gift to Sally should count against Sally's share of Tina's estate and that satisfaction should apply. The problem with this argument under these facts is that because Hector died before Tina, Sally stands to take all of Tina's estate. Application of the satisfaction doctrine is moot. Sally takes all of Tina's estate as the alternative taker under the residuary clause whether satisfaction applies or not. (Had Hector not predeceased Tina, he would have had a strong argument that satisfaction should apply under these facts and it would have affected Sally's gift under the will.)

Summary:

Sally receives Tina's entire estate.

Answer to Question 11

Has Tippi created a valid charitable trust?

An *inter vivos* charitable trust requires: (1) the settlor's intent to create a charitable trust; (2) funding (delivery of an identifiable property interest to the trust/trustee); and (3) possibly a writing (if the trust is to hold real property). A charitable trust does not require ascertainable beneficiaries because it is deemed to be for the benefit of the public at large or a large subset of the public. (The state attorney general typically has standing to enforce the trust on behalf of the public).

The intent to create a trust arises anytime one person transfers property to a second for the benefit of a third (or if the person uses traditional trust terminology). Here, although the facts do not indicate that Tippi used the term "trust" in her documents, she used the term "trustees," and she transferred the land and $100,000 to the trustees for the benefit of the public at large. Tippi intended to create a trust. She expressed her intent in writing, as required by the Statute of Frauds, because the trust holds real property. And she validly transferred an identifiable property interest (the land and $100,000 to the trust/trustees). If the trust purpose qualifies as a valid charitable purpose, Tippi has created a valid charitable trust.

Any function of a governmental or municipal nature, or any activity that is beneficial to the general community, is usually accepted as a "charitable" purpose. Because one of the traditional functions of government or of any organized society is to provide libraries for its citizens, Tippi's purpose is clearly charitable. The trust res consists of the land and the proceeds of Tippi's $100,000 check.

Who gets Tippi's stocks and bonds?

Who gets Tippi's stocks and bonds depends on whether they were "delivered" to the trust/trustee before she died. A trust instrument applies only to those assets that are transferred to the trust. Tippi's will leaves all of her assets to her daughter. The only claim the trust has to the stocks and bonds is that she transferred them to the trust *inter vivos* — before she died.

The trustees will claim that she transferred the assets to the trust when she created the trust. The facts state that the declaration of trust contained an "itemized list" of her stocks and bonds with a market value of $2 million. The trustees will argue that by itemizing the stocks and bonds in the document that declared her intent to create the trust, she was also declaring her intent to transfer the stocks and bonds to the trust. Because the stocks and bonds are intangible personal property, symbolic delivery is all that is necessary. The trustees will argue that by listing the property in the document creating the trust, the list constituted a symbolic delivery of the assets to the trust.

Absent other facts, listing personal property in the documents creating the trust is often sufficient to constitute delivery of the assets to the trust. The problem here is that the document expressing the intent to create the trust and listing the stocks and bonds goes on to expressly state that these "stocks and bonds *will be delivered*" to the trustees in installments in the future. Valid transfer of a property interest requires the intent to make a **present** transfer of the property interest and delivery. Betty, Tippi's only child and the beneficiary under her will, will argue that Tippi's statement that the stocks and bonds "*will be delivered*" constitutes merely a gratuitous promise to make a gift in the future — not a present transfer of the property interest. If the language is construed as constituting nothing more than a gratuitous promise to make a gift in the future, under traditional property principles, there is no transfer, and Betty is entitled to the stocks and bonds under the terms of the will.

The trustees have one final argument, however. The modern trend is to loosen the delivery requirements where there is clear and convincing evidence of the intent to make an *inter vivos* gift but the gift fails for want of delivery under traditional delivery standards. The modern trend is to uphold the gift despite the absence of traditional delivery.

In the end, who gets Tippi's stocks and bonds will probably turn on whether the court follows the traditional approach to delivery of gifts or adopts the modern trend. Most courts still follow the traditional approach.

Can the Board use the block of land as a public park and maintain it with the trust funds?

When a charitable trust is created for a particular purpose and the purpose cannot be accomplished, the trust is said to fail. A resulting trust in favor of the settlor is then imposed. Betty will contend that the trust purpose here (the construction and maintenance of a public library) has failed, and that a resulting trust should be imposed for the benefit of Tippi and her estate. On this theory, the Board should be ordered to transfer title to the trust res back to Tippi's estate.

However, the Board will argue that the *cy pres* doctrine should be applied to permit the use of the trust res for a public park. Under this doctrine, when the specific purpose for which a charitable trust has been created cannot be carried out, the court may permit the trust to continue for a *similar* purpose, provided this similar purpose fits within the testator's "general charitable intent." The court attempts to put itself into the testator's mind and decide whether the testator would prefer to support some reasonably comparable charitable purpose or to cause the assets to revert to his or her heirs.

Betty will contend that Tippi wanted to build only a library and would not have made any gift to the Board if she had known that it would not be used for this purpose. The Board will argue in rebuttal that the deed to the property was "in perpetuity," proving that Tippi intended the Board to keep the land even if some other good purpose had to be substituted.

Because courts ordinarily prefer to validate a charitable trust rather than destroy it, it is likely that the *cy pres* doctrine will be applied. Thus, the Board will likely be allowed to create and maintain the park with the land and funds given to the trust by Tippi, even if the Board doesn't get to use the proceeds of the stocks and bonds. (But the fact that the funds in the Board's possession are sufficient to maintain the land as a public park for only a little over ten years argues against bothering to create the park at all).

Answer to Question 12

What is the effect of the divorce upon the gift to Leonard?

Except as may otherwise be provided in a court order, another "governing instrument," or a contract providing for the division of the marital estate, a divorce has the effect of revoking a testamentary gift to the former spouse. Here, there is no property settlement agreement and no evidence of any court order, so Leonard would *not* be entitled to take anything from the estate. (UPC §2-804(b)). If Fay's estate is not disposed of by the other bequests, the residuary will be disposed of as if Fay had died intestate. If the other bequests exhaust all of Fay's assets, there will be no residue.

The UPC provides that, if the testator dies leaving descendants (but no spouse), the residuary estate passes to the descendants by representation. The estate is divided at the earliest level at which there are living descendants. (UPC §2-103(1); UPC §2-106(b)). This means that, assuming both were alive, Linda and Michael would each receive one-half of the residuary estate. But because Michael is deceased, Roberta, his adopted daughter, would take his half of the residuary estate by representation.

How will the proceeds of the sale of the "business property" be disposed of?

Ademption:

At common law, a *specific* devise of property that was no longer in the testator's estate at his or her death was usually treated as "adeemed" — that is, cancelled. A specific devise is a gift that is clearly identifiable as against all other assets of the estate. Because the Main Street property was disposed of by Fay many years before her death, ademption would appear to apply, wiping out the gift of this property to Linda.

However, the modern trend is to discourage ademption. Some states have statutes that create the presumption that the testator does not intend ademption if the proceeds of the specific bequest can be followed into other assets of the testator at his or her death. Some courts interpret the bequest as one of form only; a change in the form of a gift is not relevant if the testator intends one form to replace another.

The current version of UPC §2-606 adopts the presumption against ademption. It provides that even if the substituted assets are not clearly a replacement for the original bequest (in this case, one business property for another), a specific beneficiary is entitled to the value of any specific bequest, real or personal, to the extent that such property is not in the testator's estate at death, and to the extent that it is established that ademption would be inconsistent with the testator's manifested plan of disposition.

Here, however, there is strong evidence that ademption is *consistent* with the testator's plan of disposition. Following the sale of the business property, Fay put half of it in her commercial account and the other half in a savings account in the name of "Fay Woods, Trustee for Linda Woods." Based on Fay's actions, a strong argument can be made that Fay *did* intend for ademption to apply. Fay did not intend for Linda to get a pecuniary devise equal to the value of the business property as of its date of disposition ($20,000). Fay intended for Linda to get only $10,000 of the proceeds as evidenced by Fay putting only half of the sale proceeds in the savings account for Linda. Applying ademption therefore is more consistent with Fay's apparent manifested plan of disposition than not applying it. Ademption should apply to the business property (however, Linda should get the $10,000, but under a different doctrine — see below).

Is Linda entitled to the $10,000 in the savings account?

One of Fay's cash assets was the $10,000 deposited into a bank account designated "Fay Woods, Trustee for Linda Woods." Under traditional trust principles, this will probably be construed as a Totten trust (*i.e.*, the trust relationship is created by the designation upon the savings account). A Totten trust is in the nature of a revocable trust. The trust res is owned by the trustee during his or her lifetime and may be used or withdrawn by him or her, but passes to the beneficiary upon the death of the trustee. Thus, Linda should be entitled to the $10,000.

Under the modern trend, the money in the savings account can also be characterized as a payment-on-death account. While such accounts were invalid under common law, they are permitted under the UPC. (UPC §6-101). Such payment-on-death designations are valid nonprobate transfers, and Linda would be entitled to it as such.

As for the half of the proceeds from the sale of the business property that Fay deposited in her commercial account, that money (along with the other $5,000 in the commercial account) would ordinarily fall to the residuary clause of her will. Because Fay and Leonard divorced, the residuary clause in favor of Leonard fails, and the property that otherwise would have passed under it falls to intestacy. Under intestacy Linda will receive one-half (or $7,500), and the other half that would have passed to Michael will pass to his adopted child, Roberta.

What disposition should be made of the jewelry described in the typed note?

The note designating the specific jewelry that would pass to Linda was not executed with the requisite testamentary formalities. The execution was not witnessed and therefore, the note does not qualify as a codicil. No part of the note except the signature and date was in the testator's handwriting, so it was not a valid holographic will. But Linda should still be able to convince the court to admit the list as part of the will.

First, under the doctrine of incorporation by reference, material extraneous to the will that was (1) in existence when the will was created; (2) referred to in the will in a way that shows the testator's intent to incorporate it; and (3) described sufficiently to permit its identification, will become part of the will. (UPC §2-510). Of course, the UPC does require that the extraneous writing be in existence when the will was executed, and it is not clear from these facts which document came first. However, because they are both dated on the same day and the will refers to jewelry "as is enumerated" on the list, the court will probably presume that the list preceded the will and should be incorporated.

Second, even if the list was not in existence at the time the will was created, it will probably still be incorporated under UPC §2-513. This provision states that a will may refer to an extraneous written list to dispose of specific items of tangible personal property provided that: (1) the writing is signed by the testator; (2) the items and the devisee of the items are clearly identified; and (3) the items are "tangible personal property not otherwise specifically disposed of by the will, other than money." In addition, UPC §2-513 provides that "[t]he writing may be referred to as one to be in existence at the time of the testator's death; it may be prepared before or after the execution of the will; it may be altered by the testator after its preparation; and it may be a writing that has no significance apart from its effect on the dispositions made by the will."Because the note in question satisfies all of the requirements, it will be effective to constitute a gift to Linda of the jewelry mentioned in it.

How does Michael's death affect the gift of stock in the will?

Because Michael was a lineal descendant of Fay, the gift of stock to him (which would otherwise lapse because of his failure to survive Fay) will pass to Roberta, his descendant. (UPC §2-603(b)). Although adopted, Roberta is considered to be a child of both Wanda and Michael. (UPC §2-114(b)).

How does the stock dividend affect the testamentary gift to Michael?

Under the UPC, where the testator makes a gift of stock in the will, and the testator owns matching shares at the time the will is executed, the beneficiary gets all the additional shares of securities in the testator's estate as long as the additional shares were acquired as the result of action initiated by the corporate entity. (UPC §2-605). This would include stock dividends. It doesn't matter that some of the securities included in the dividend are of a different class (*e.g.*, Class B) from those that were the direct subject of the bequest — so long as the issuing organization is the same, UPC §2-605 applies. Thus, both the original stock and the stock dividends would pass to Roberta by reason of the antilapse provision.

In summary, Linda gets the $10,000 in the savings account and the jewelry listed in the note. Roberta gets all the XYZ stock. Linda and Roberta share equally the $15,000 in the commercial account.

Answer to Question 13

The impact of Tess's marriage on her 1988 will:

If Tess had not executed any other testamentary documents after she executed the will, her marriage to Hubert would have had a significant impact on her testamentary plans. Under the UPC, a surviving spouse who marries the testator *after* his or her will is executed is entitled under most circumstances to receive the value of his or her intestate share of all assets left by the testator, at least to the extent that the assets are not left to a child of the testator who was born before the marriage. (UPC §2-301). Because it does not appear that Tess had a child before the marriage, Hubert would have been entitled to take his intestate share.

Effect of the 1990 "codicil":

When a testator labels a testamentary document a "codicil" rather than a "will," the normal assumption is that he or she intends only to alter, amend, or clarify a prior will. But when the document — although labelled a "codicil" — completely disposes of the testator's property, it will be strongly presumed that the testator intended a new will revoking all prior wills, not an amendment. See UPC §2-507(c). Under this rule of interpretation, the August 4, 1990, document will be presumed to represent a new and complete will, because it completely disposes of Tess's estate. The document satisfies the UPC's holographic will requirements (*i.e.*, a writing, with the material provisions in the testator's handwriting, signed by the testator, and which has testamentary intent). (UPC §2-502(b).) The so-called codicil became Tess's new will.

Effect of Sonny's birth:

If the 1990 document continued to control Tess's estate, Sonny would have the right to take his intestate share of her estate. Under UPC §2-302, if a testator has no child living at the time he or she executes the will, an omitted after-born child takes an intestate share, unless (1) it appears from the will that the omission was intentional; (2) the testator provided for the child outside of the will and intended for that gift to be in lieu of the child taking under the will; or (3) the will devises all or substantially all the estate to the omitted child's other parent. Sonny qualifies as an omitted child relative to the 1990 will, and none of the exceptions apply (Hubert does not take "substantially" all of the estate). Sonny would have been entitled to an intestate share. However, as we shall see, Tess's second codicil may have the effect of preventing Sonny from receiving his intestate share.

Did the second codicil revoke the first one?

On first reading, the second "codicil" appears to have revoked the August 4, 1990, document. The first sentence of the second codicil states, "I revoke my codicil of August 4, 1990."

If the codicil is construed as revoking the 1990 document, we are left with two options: either (1) one-fourth of the estate goes to Harvale College, the rest to intestacy; or (2) the 1988 will is revived. There is no evidence to support the latter. As for the former, despite the clear statement in the codicil revoking the first codicil, one can argue that Tess merely wanted to abort the gift to State University. This is a tough call, but there is a good chance that the court will read both "codicils" in their entirety and conclude that Tess intended the second codicil to be merely an amendatory document (remember both "codicils" are *holographic* documents, a fact that should not be lost on the court). Extrinsic evidence is generally admissible to explain ambiguities in a will or codicil, and the fact that the second codicil resulted from Tess's dissatisfaction with professionalism in college athletics presumably can be proven. As a consequence of the strong desire by most courts to attempt to effectuate a testator's intent and to avoid intestacy, the second codicil will probably be deemed to have merely modified, *not* revoked, the August 4, 1990, document.

We have assumed in our discussion that the second codicil meets the formal requirements for a testamentary document under the UPC — even though it was unwitnessed, it is in the testator's handwriting and signed by her, so it is valid as a holographic testament. (UPC §2-502(b)).

Effect of the second codicil:

If we proceed under the assumption that the second codicil merely modified the first, it will have affected Tess's previous testamentary scheme in two ways.

First, a codicil is usually deemed to republish and reconfirm a prior will to the extent it does not change or modify the prior will. When Tess executed the second codicil, Sonny was already born. As a child in being, he would no longer qualify as a pretermitted child. Presumably, if Tess had intended otherwise, she would have made provision for Sonny in the second codicil. Because she chose not to, and because the second codicil is valid, Sonny will receive nothing from Tess's estate.

Second, the codicil probably effectively revoked the devise to State University. While Tess's statement, "Nothing to athletic factories like State

University," does not specify that the gift is revoked, this conclusion is virtually inescapable, especially as Tess clearly expressed the terms of the alternative gift to Harvale. As we've discussed, extrinsic evidence is ordinarily admissible to explain ambiguities in a will or codicil, and proof that Tess was upset with professionalism in college athletics at the time the second codicil was made would be admissible. The second codicil revoked the devise to State University and substituted the Harvale academic scholarship fund for the earlier gift.

What is the effect of Tess's mistake?

State University will contend that under dependent relative revocation, in which there is a valid revocation based upon a mistake, and the testator would not have revoked but for the mistake, the revocation is not given effect — and the original gift is reinstated. State University will argue that although Tess validly revoked the gift to it in her second codicil, she acted under a mistaken fact (that the college was an athletic factory) and that had she known that the University had voted to discontinue all intercollegiate athletic programs, she would not have revoked the gift. (Where the revocation is by writing, invariably courts also require the mistake to be set forth in the revoking instrument — which is the case here).

The problem with application of dependent relative revocation under these facts is that Tess made an express gift of the property in question to Harvale College. Dependent relative revocation typically applies where the requirements are otherwise satisfied and there is no valid express new gift. Here, the valid express new gift to a completely different university would make it extremely difficult, if not impossible, for the court to apply dependent relative revocation.

The general rule is that courts do not correct mistakes. Dependent relative revocation is a narrow exception to that general rule, which probably does not apply to these facts. The gift to State University is revoked.

Is the gift to Harvale College valid?

At common law, a gift to charity within the period — usually six months — immediately before the testator's death was invalid under statutes called mortmain statutes. Under such a statute, the gift to Harvale would be invalid. But very few states still have mortmain statutes, and the Uniform Probate Code does not recognize the mortmain concept. The gift to Harvale is valid.

How should Tess's estate be distributed?

If we assume that the second codicil controls the disposition of Tess's estate, then Harvale College would receive one-fourth of Tess's estate, Hubert would receive one-half, and Martha one-fourth. This is the most likely result.

Answer to Question 14

1. Is the will valid?

Nelly's will should qualify as a holographic will. A holographic will is valid if it is signed by the testator and the material provisions are in her handwriting. Because Nelly's will is written in her own hand and signed by her, it should be probated. The fact that she signed at the bottom of page 1, instead of at the end of the document, should not invalidate the will; there is no requirement in most states, or under the UPC, that the signature be at the end of the document. See UPC §2-502, Official Comment. In any event, the two items that were written on page 2 (the date and Brad's signature) were not vital to the integrity of the document. The first page was sufficient to constitute a valid holographic will.

2. How should Nelly's estate be distributed?

Brad as interested witness:

Brad's signature as witness on the will will probably not invoke the common law interested witness doctrine to invalidate the will. True, he received a bequest under Nelly's will, but his signature was superfluous. No witness is required to support a holographic will. Brad's signature would ordinarily be ignored on the issue of the will's validity. In any case, under the UPC, the "signing of a will by an interested witness does not invalidate the will or any provision of it." (UPC §2-505(b)).

Was Ann's gift revoked by striking through her name?

Although not all states recognize partial revocation by act, the UPC permits revocation of any part or all of a will if the testator, or another in the testator's presence and at the testator's direction, performs the revocatory act on the will itself with the intent and purpose of revoking the will. (UPC §2-507). The rule applies equally to a holographic will and a will that has been executed before witnesses. The revocatory act may consist of "burning, tearing, canceling, obliterating, or destroying" the will or any part of it. See UPC §2-507(a)(2).

There is no doubt that the lines through Ann's name constitute a revocatory act *if* performed by the testator with the intent to revoke or by another in the testator's presence and at her direction. The problem here is that it is impossible to tell who drew the lines through the gift to Ann. Brad is prepared to testify that, in his presence, he saw the testator draw the lines with the intent to revoke. The problem is that Brad is an interested witness with respect to this claimed act (he stands to take a share of the money in question if it falls to intestacy — see below). Moreover, the potential for fraud (maybe Brad drew the lines because he did not like Ann or just to increase the size of his share of the estate) is one of the primary reasons some states do not recognize partial revocation by act at all.

Brad could also invoke revocation by presumption. Where a will is last in the testator's possession and cannot be found following the testator's death, a presumption arises that the testator destroyed the will by act with the intent to revoke (at least where the testator had capacity until death). A variation on the presumption doctrine is where the will is found with revocatory marks on it. In this case the presumption arises that the testator made the marks with the intent to revoke. The presumption, however, is rebuttable if there is a more plausible explanation for why the will cannot be found (or why it has revocatory marks on it). Here, if there is evidence that Brad had access to the will either immediately before or immediately after Nelly died, Ann could argue that the more plausible explanation is that Brad drew the lines through the gift.

This is a close call and will depend on the credibility of the witnesses. Brad's credibility will be critical to this issue, but the facts look rather suspicious, particularly when coupled with his behavior and comments with respect to the gift of Nelly's stocks and bonds. Although it is a close call, it is more likely that the court will conclude that there is not enough evidence to establish that the gift to Ann was validly revoked.

Lapse of Charlie's share:

A devise is said to lapse when the beneficiary dies before the testator and the will fails to provide an alternative disposition of the property. Because Charlie predeceased Nelly, his $10,000 gift will lapse. Most states and the UPC have adopted antilapse provisions to protect certain devisees. If the devise is to a child of the testator who predeceases the testator, his or her surviving issue will take the devise in his or her place. (UPC §2-603). Because Charlie had no descendants, there is no one to take his share under the antilapse provision. The failed gift will fall to the residuary clause, if there is one, otherwise to intestacy.

(The class gift doctrine does not apply here because the gift is not a single gift to a class — it is three separate bequests of $10,000 to three individuals. The will made bequests of $10,000 to "*each* of my children." Any attempt to characterize the gift as a class gift would fail.)

The stocks and bonds:

A secret trust arises when a bequest in a will appears unconditional and unequivocal but was made upon the oral promise of the devisee to hold the devise in trust for someone else. No reference to the trust is made in the will. In a semisecret trust, the will makes reference to the existence of a trust but no beneficiary of the trust is specified. Presumably, the testator and the devisee have agreed orally who is to benefit from the trust. Here, because the language in Nelly's will directed Brad to use the stocks and bonds "as we have agreed," the arrangement would be viewed as a semisecret trust. The majority view under these facts is that the trust fails for lack of a designated beneficiary. Under these circumstances, the named trustee (*i.e.,* Brad) holds the stocks and bonds in a resulting trust for the benefit of the residuary beneficiaries. See Restatement 3d of Trusts, §8. If there is no residuary clause, they go to the testator's heirs as in intestacy. In a few jurisdictions, a constructive trust is imposed in favor of the intended beneficiary. See Restatement 2d of Trusts, §55, Comment h, applying the minority approach.

If the majority view is followed, the stocks and bonds here will pass by intestacy because there is no residuary clause. If the minority view is followed, the trust will be enforced according to its (secret) terms. Thus under the minority view, if Brad's testimony is believed, he will take outright (he is the remainderman after the life estate to Charlie), and if his testimony is *not* believed, the gift will fail and pass by intestacy. (Inasmuch as Brad is an interested witness who stands to benefit more if a constructive trust is imposed, the court may be suspicious of his self-serving testimony as to the terms of the semisecret trust and may favor a resulting trust so that Ann can share in the property.)

The house and Nelly's other personal effects:

When a testator fails to dispose of some of his or her property by an existing valid will, the property passes by intestacy. On these facts, the house and other personal effects would be shared equally by Brad and Ann. If the semisecret trust of Nelly's stock and bonds is deemed to fail (see above), then the stock and bonds will also pass to both by intestacy.

If we assume for the purpose of argument that Nelly herself struck through Ann's name and that the specific bequest to Ann was therefore invalid, does this also mean that Ann will be completely disinherited — that is, that she will not even receive her intestate share? Under the UPC, the testator may disinherit anyone, including a child, but he or she must do so "expressly."

See UPC §2-101(b). It is unlikely that a court would find that by striking through Ann's name in a clause providing for a specific bequest of a limited amount, Nelly intended to disinherit Ann entirely. It's likely that Ann will be permitted to take her one-half intestate share along with Brad, whose testimony is likely to be discounted.

Answer to Question 15

1. Theories upon which Sam may participate in the distribution of Carol's estate.

As mistakenly omitted child: Under the UPC, when a testator fails to provide for a child because he or she mistakenly believes that the child is dead, the child is entitled to a share of the estate as a mistakenly omitted child. (UPC §2-302(c)). Carol had no reason to doubt that Sam was dead. She had the army's letter and she confirmed her belief in his death by stating in the will, "In view of the death of my son, Sam . . . ." If a testator had one or more children living when he or she executed a will and the will devised property to one or more of those children, then a pretermitted or mistakenly omitted child is entitled to a pro-rata share of the gifts to such child or children. (UPC §2-302(a)(2)). Therefore, Sam takes one-half of the portion of the estate given to his sister, Dot (*i.e.*, one-half of two-thirds of the estate, or one-third of the total).

Fraud — constructive trust: The general rule is that anyone deprived of a benefit under a will because of fraud or duress is entitled to relief. This general principle is incorporated in UPC §1-106. The default relief is to invalidate as much of the will as was affected by the wrongful conduct, but where that relief is not sufficient, the court may impose a constructive trust. Section 1-106 of the UPC specifically provides that any person injured by fraud in connection with a will may obtain "appropriate relief against the perpetrator of the fraud or restitution from any person (other than a bona fide purchaser) benefiting from the fraud, *whether innocent or not.*" (Emphasis added.)

There is little doubt that Dot has committed fraud. Dot fraudulently concealed the army's letter raising doubts about Sam's death (and because of the concealment Carol did not have an opportunity to make provision for Sam). Dot will argue that the letter did not confirm that Sam was alive, and that even if Carol had seen the letter, she might not have changed her will until it was confirmed that he was alive. But these arguments will probably fail. On these facts, the court is not likely to be sympathetic to Dot and will probably find that she engaged in fraud. (Technically this form of fraud is called fraud in the inducement as opposed to fraud in the execution.)

The more difficult issue is the question of the appropriate relief. The presumed relief is to strike as much of the will as was affected by the wrongful conduct (or the whole will if necessary). Where striking a provision of the will, or the whole will, is not sufficient relief, however, the court may impose a constructive trust in favor of the aggrieved party. Here, Sam will argue for striking the whole will. When Carol thought that both

Sam and Dot were alive, she told both children that she did not need a will because "you'll share in everything anyway." Carol executed the will only because she thought Sam was dead. Striking the whole will would return Carol to the position she was in before she mistakenly was told that Sam was dead — it would cause her estate to be distributed to her children equally, which was her original intent.

It can be assumed that Tom and Jane, Carol's brother and sister, would oppose such relief. They did not engage in the fraud and therefore would argue that the gift of one-third of Carol's estate to them under her will should not be affected. Section 1-106 of the UPC, however, expressly authorizes appropriate relief from any person benefiting from the fraud, "whether innocent or not." The gift to Tom and Jane is introduced by the clause "In view of the death of my son, Sam, ..." A strong argument can be made that Tom and Jane, though innocent of any wrongdoing, would also benefit from Dot's wrongdoing if the whole will were not stricken. The court could either strike the whole will, or impose a constructive trust on the gift going to Tom and Jane in favor of Sam.

At a minimum Sam should share equally in the gift to Dot (by imposing a constructive trust on the gift to Dot). In addition, a strong case can be made that the gift to Tom and Jane should be included in the relief (either by striking the whole will or by imposing a constructive trust on the gift to Tom and Jane in favor of Sam.)

Mistake: If a testator includes or omits a particular bequest because of a mistake in a material fact, the courts are loath to invalidate the will, even though the will may not represent the testator's true intent. (Example: the testator intentionally omits a bequest to his nephew because he believes the nephew has dropped out of law school; in fact, the nephew has graduated with honors.) A mistake of this kind is called a mistake in the inducement. Generally, it will not impede probate of the will. The reason the courts are reluctant to refuse probate: if the will is refused, the estate will be distributed as in intestacy. This is not likely to be the testator's wish. In the limited case in which the testator fails to include a child in the will believing the child is dead, the UPC ignores the usual rule regarding mistakes in the inducement and allows the pretermitted or omitted child to share pro rata in any gift made to his or her siblings. See discussion of UPC §2-302(a)(2), above.

2. Other relief to which Sam may be entitled:

Sam may be able to assert claims against Dot individually, for (1) fraud, (2) tortious interference with an expectancy, (3) interference with a prospective economic advantage, and (4) intentional infliction of severe emotional distress.

Sam can contend that Dot's deceit in withholding the letter was deliberately intended to deprive him of his inheritance. Dot knew that it would cause Sam emotional distress to learn he had been disinherited by his mother, especially when he realized that his mother had continued to suffer under the illusion that he was dead. If Sam is successful on any of these theories, he may be able to recover punitive damages from Dot, in addition to his actual losses.

3. How should Carol's estate be distributed?

[The issue raised by this question is how the "advancements" to Tom and Jane should be treated. This issue assumes, however, that Tom and Jane are still entitled to take under Carol's will. As discussed above, Sam can make a strong argument that even though they are innocent of any wrongdoing, they should not take at all under the will. If the court were to adopt that remedy, the only issue is whether Tom and Jane should have to repay the *inter vivos* gifts that were to count against their gift under the will. The answer to that issue is "no" — they are entitled to keep whatever gifts they received *inter vivos*. The rest of this discussion assumes that Tom and Jane are still entitled to take their one-third of the estate under the terms of the will.]

Although Carol characterized the *inter vivos* gifts to Tom and Jane as "advancements," she probably intended such gifts to constitute partial "satisfaction" of their testamentary gifts. ("Advancements" pertain to *inter vivos* satisfactions of a beneficiary's *intestate* share of the decedent's estate.)

Jane and Tom could contend that, because the statements made in the ledger were *not* accompanied by the requisite testamentary formalities (*i.e.*, they were not embodied in a formal or holographic will), they are not admissible.

Sam and Dot could argue in rebuttal, however, that UPC §2-609 provides that a satisfaction occurs where either: (1) the will provides for deduction of an *inter vivos* gift, (2) the testator declares in a contemporaneous writing that the *inter vivos* gift is to be deducted from a testamentary gift, or (3) the devisee acknowledges in writing that the gift is in satisfaction of the devise or that its value is to be deducted from the value of the devise. Because Carol's will referred to the possibility of *inter vivos* satisfactions (the first test above), the court will almost certainly treat the gifts to Jane and Tom as partial satisfactions. (The ledger, although it reverses the numbers, would probably satisfy test (2) above, making it even more likely that the court would find the gifts to have been partial satisfactions.)

Tom might contend that extrinsic evidence generally is not permissible to vary the plain meaning of a will, and therefore that proof of the erroneous transposition in the ledger should not be admissible. This argument, however, should fail for several reasons. First, the ledger is not a part of the will and therefore should not be subject to the rules that ordinarily apply to wills. The will simply indicates that Carol wanted the doctrine of satisfaction (or partial satisfaction as the case may be) to apply to the gifts in her will to Tom and Jane. The amount of partial satisfaction to apply is beyond the express terms of the will. To the extent there is a dispute as to the amount, extrinsic evidence should be admissible to resolve the issue. Second, even if the wills rules were to apply to the issue, increasingly the modern trend is to permit extrinsic evidence to prove a mistake in transcription and to establish and correct the scrivener's error. It is likely that Jane will prevail and be permitted to prove Carol's mistake. In that event, the court will deduct $5,000 from Jane's share and $10,000 from Tom's, as partial satisfaction.

Summary:

At a minimum, Sam is entitled to a share of Carol's estate as a mistakenly omitted child. He is entitled to one-half of two-thirds of Carol's estate, or $95,000. (The total estate, $285,000, consists of the present estate of $270,000 plus the $15,000 *inter vivos* partial satisfactions.) Dot would be entitled to the other half, $95,000. Jane and Tom would divide the remaining cash, $80,000, in a manner resulting in Jane's receiving $5,000 more than Tom — that is, $42,500 for Jane and $37,500 for Tom.

If the constructive trust doctrine were applied, but only to Dot's share, Dot would receive two-thirds of $285,000 ($190,000), but a constructive trust would be imposed on the devise in favor of Sam in the amount of one-half of the gift ($95,000). Jane and Tom would divide the remainder, $80,000, as follows: $42,500 for Jane and $37,500 for Tom.

If the constructive trust doctrine were applied to the gifts to Dot and to Tom and Jane, Dot would receive two-thirds of $285,000 ($190,000), and Tom and Jane would receive one-third ($80,000 — that is, $42,500 to Jane and $37,500 to Tom), but a constructive trust would be imposed on the devises in favor of Sam so that Sam would take 100 percent of the gift to Tom and Jane ($80,000), and a constructive trust would be imposed on 30.5 percent ($55,000) of the gift to Dot. Under that approach, Sam and Dot would end up splitting the estate equally, and Tom and Jane would end up with nothing.

Answer to Question 16

Was the document that Tate signed on December 2, 1997, a valid will?

Although the document prepared by Tate's lawyer in 1997 did not use or mention the word "will," it would appear to have been intended as Tate's will. This is evidenced by the following facts: (1) the document used the words, "I . . . dispose of all my estate as follows . . . ," and the words, ". . . I have intentionally omitted all my other heirs"; (2) it disposed of Tate's entire estate; (3) it was prepared at Tate's request by an attorney; and (4) Tate declared it to be his "will" when he withdrew it from his pocket during the party.

Tate's son, Art, will contend that Tate did not have the requisite testamentary capacity when he signed the document at the party. To be a valid will, the testator must be at least 18 years old and of sound mind at the time he or she executes the will. Sound mind generally requires that the testator have the ability to know (1) the natural objects of his or her bounty; (2) the nature and extent of his or her property; (3) the nature of the testamentary act he or she is performing; and (4) how all of these factors relate together to form an orderly disposition of the testator's property.

Here the facts indicate that Tate was "slightly intoxicated" when the will was executed. Sally will argue that Tate displayed the requisite testamentary capacity because (1) he characterized the document as his "will"; (2) he had the presence of mind to have the document witnessed; and (3) he later referred to the document as his will when he tried to cancel it. Art will emphasize (1) that Tate had had "several drinks"; (2) that Tate was "intoxicated" at the time he signed the document and asked the others to witness it; and (3) that as a matter of public policy individuals should be discouraged from executing wills while under the influence of alcohol. The mere fact that a testator has a drink before signing a will should not be enough to cause him or her to lose his or her testamentary capacity; but if a testator is drunk, it is unlikely that he or she has the requisite testamentary capacity. This is a close call under these facts and depends on how intoxicated Tate was (the facts are ambiguous on this issue — saying he was "intoxicated" but only "slightly.") This issue could go either way.

The fact that Sally was one of the witnesses to the will is not significant. Interested persons (*i.e.*, those receiving a bequest under the will) qualify as witnesses. (UPC §2-505(b)). Besides, because only two witnesses are needed under the UPC (UPC §2-502(a)(3)), Sally's signature as a third witness would be superfluous.

In summary, it is unclear whether the document Tate executed on December 2, 1997, is a valid will.

Was the typed document that Tate signed on January 20, 1998, a valid will?

Art and Sally will both contend that the document that Tate signed in his lawyer's office on January 20, 1998, was not intended to serve as a codicil to Tate's will, but only as a nonbinding memorandum that the lawyer would reduce to a more formal document that Tate would execute at a later date. There is no indication that the January 20, 1998, document was properly witnessed. Tate was in his lawyer's office when the memo was prepared and signed. If he had intended the memo to constitute his will, witnesses were available (the lawyer and his secretary were there). The memo did not satisfy the requirement of UPC §2-502 that two witnesses sign the will.

Nor could the January 20, 1998, memorandum be probated as a holographic will. The "material provisions" were not in Tate's handwriting. (UPC §2-502(b)).

An argument can be made that the January 20, 1998, memorandum should be treated as a valid will under UPC §2-503. This section allows a document not satisfying the formalities for a will to be treated as one, "if the proponent . . . establishes by clear and convincing evidence that the decedent intended the document . . . to constitute . . . the decedent's will . . . ." On these facts, CCF could argue that the handwritten statement written by Tate across the December 1997 will ("I have made a new will") shows that he intended the January 20, 1998, document to be his will. It is debatable whether this argument will be enough to meet the "clear and convincing evidence" standard of UPC §2-503.

It is unclear whether the January 20, 1998, document will qualify as a will. If it does, and if the December 2, 1997, will also qualified as a will, the latter will completely revokes the prior will by inconsistency. (UPC §2-507(a)(1)). If the January 20, 1998, document does not qualify as a will, whether Tate has a will depends on whether the December 2, 1997, document qualifies as a will.

Did Tate revoke the December 1997 will by the statement he wrote across it?

Assuming, *arguendo*, that the December 1997 document was validly executed, Art will contend that it was validly revoked by two independent means. First, he will argue that the words Tate wrote across the will constituted a valid holographic revocation that incorporated the will by reference. An express revocation can be accomplished by utilizing the steps necessary to make a valid holographic will: that is, the material terms must be in the testator's handwriting, and the document must be signed by the testator. Because the revocation was in Tate's handwriting and was initialed by him (the initials "TT" are sufficient to count as a "signature" — see UPC §2-502, Comment), these requirements were satisfied.

Art will also argue that the statement written on the will was a valid "revocatory act." UPC §2-507(a)(2) defines "revocatory act" to include a "canceling" of the will. Cancellation is effective "whether or not the . . . cancellation touched any of the words on the will." The statement here qualifies under this section, and it serves to revoke the will.

Art's argument that the December 1997 will was validly revoked by the handwritten statements across it will probably succeed.

Should the December 1997 will still be probated under the doctrine of dependent relative revocation (DRR)?

Under the doctrine of dependent relative revocation (DRR), where the testator validly revokes his or her will because of a mistake, and the testator would not have revoked the will but for the mistake, the doctrine of DRR authorizes the court to ignore the valid revocation and probate the will. Where the valid revocation is by act, invariably the courts also require proof of an alternative plan of disposition that fails. Where the valid revocation is by writing, invariably the courts require the writing to set forth the mistake and the mistake must be beyond the testator's knowledge. Sally will argue that if the court concludes that the December 1997 will was validly revoked but the January 1998 document is *not* a valid will, then the court should apply DRR to give effect to the December 1997 will.

Here, the December 1997 will was validly revoked. It appears that it was revoked because Tate assumed his January 20, 1998, document was a valid will. If that is not the case, Sally can successfully argue that the revocation was based upon a mistake. If the revocation is deemed to have been by act (see above discussion), the failed alternative testamentary scheme is the January 20, 1998, document. If the revocation is deemed to have been by writing (see above discussion), the writing sets forth the mistake ("I have made a new will.") and the mistake is beyond the testator's knowledge. (Tate did not know that the January 20, 1998, document would not qualify as a valid will.) The only issue is whether Tate would prefer that the revocation be ignored if he had known of the mistake; that is., if he had known that the January 20, 1998, document was not a valid will.

Because Art would be the sole recipient of Tate's estate if Tate were deemed to have died intestate, Art would contend that DRR should *not* be applied.

There is no reason to believe that Tate would have wanted the initial will revived — the January 20, 1998, memorandum contained a completely different dispository scheme, and the facts do not show that Tate would have preferred his original scheme over intestacy.

Sally would argue in rebuttal that Tate would have preferred that his estate be distributed in accordance with the December 1997 will rather than according to an arbitrary state-drafted intestacy scheme. Sally will emphasize that as evidenced by both documents, the December 1997 document and the January 1998 document, Tate did not want his son to take a dime of his estate, and if the court were *not* to apply DRR, Tate's son would take *all* of his estate.

This is a close call. Although there is no affirmative evidence that Tate would have preferred the December 1997 will over intestacy, there is the argument that both documents evidence the intent that Tate's son not take any of Tate's estate. The court could go either way on this issue — but courts tend to favor decedents' family members, which would mean here that it is unlikely that the court would apply DRR.

The more probable result is that Tate will be deemed to have died intestate. His son Art will inherit Tate's entire estate. Section 2-103(1) of the UPC gives the entire estate of one who dies without a spouse to the testator's "descendants" — and Art is Tate's only descendant.

Assume Tate's December 1997 will was probated under DRR. How would his estate be distributed?

For purposes of discussion, two questions arise if the December 1997 will is deemed revived. First question: Was Art alive when the will was made? If he was, then he would receive nothing. But if he was born after Tate made the December 1997 will, he would be considered a pretermitted child and he would receive his intestate share (the entire estate). (UPC §2-302).

Second question: What was the consequence of Tate's mistake in describing his nephew as "Ron" instead of "Don"? Because (1) Tate has no nephew named "Ron," and (2) the description of the recipient in the will is otherwise ambiguous ("my favorite nephew"), we don't know on the face of the will which of his two nephews Tate preferred. In this instance, virtually all courts permit extrinsic evidence to prove the identity of the intended beneficiary. Under common law terminology, this is known as a latent ambiguity. Under the misdescription doctrine, extrinsic evidence would be admissible to establish the latent ambiguity. The court would strike the first letter of the nephew's name (the "R") and then decide whether the testator's intent is clear enough that it would feel comfortable giving the gift to Don (assuming that is what Tate intended — if he intended Zeke, the court probably would not be able to construe the will in favor of Zeke and the gift would be deemed to fail). Under the modern trend, courts are much more likely to admit extrinsic evidence to reform the will. In particular, under the scrivener's error doctrine, as long as there is clear and convincing evidence of the error and clear and convincing evidence of its effect upon testator's intent, the evidence is admitted to prove and correct the mistake (whether the favorite nephew is Don or Zeke).

If the gift to the "favorite nephew" cannot be saved, it will fail. Under the modern trend, the UPC approach, where part of a residuary gift fails, it goes to the other residuary takers. Here, particularly if the court applies the traditional common law approach, there is a good chance the gift may fail, in which event Sally would take all of Tate's estate. On the other hand, if the court applies the modern trend approach, it is likely that the court will reform the will and give half of the residuary estate to Tate's favorite nephew (whomever that may be) and the other half to Sally.

Answer to Question 17

Do any of the documents, either alone or together, constitute a valid will?

These facts require that we scrutinize all of the documents both separately and together. We will call the document found in Tawny's top desk drawer the "primary document."

Is the primary document, standing alone, a valid will?

For a holographic will to be valid, there must be a writing, with the material provisions in the testator's handwriting, signed by the testator, and the document must have testamentary intent. (UPC §2-502). The primary document is in writing, and it is signed by the testator (first name is sufficient as long as the testator intended that to be her signature). There are, however, issues with respect to whether the document adequately expresses the "material provisions" and whether the document has "testamentary intent." With respect to testamentary intent (the party's intent that this document constitutes his or her will), some jurisdictions require the testamentary intent to be in the handwritten provisions of the document. Here, the word that arguably expresses that intent is "estate" — but there is precedent that "estate" is too ambiguous standing alone to constitute testamentary intent. Under the most recent version of the UPC, however, testamentary intent can be established by extrinsic evidence. If the court accepts Document #3 as the second page of the will, the express use of the word "will" and the overall intent as expressed by the two documents should be sufficient to establish testamentary intent. (One could also try to argue that Document #3 should be considered as page 2 of the will and that the two pages are one will under integration. Integration provides that all pieces of paper that were physically present at the time the will was executed and that the testator intended to be pages of the will constitute the pages of the will. The problem is that here there is no evidence as to which pieces of paper were physically present when Tawny signed the primary document.)

Even assuming, *arguendo*, that the primary document expresses testamentary intent, the problem is that the primary document, standing alone, still does not express the material provisions. The material provisions — that is, who gets what — are expressed in Document #1 and Document #2, found in the bottom drawer of the desk as described by the primary document. The primary document, standing alone, does not constitute a valid will.

Can the primary document be combined with Documents #1 and #2 to create a valid will?

The beneficiaries will attempt to argue that Documents #1 and #2 can be "combined" with the primary document to give the primary document its material provisions — thereby qualifying the primary document as a valid holographic will. There are two doctrines they can invoke. The first is integration (discussed above), but there is no evidence that Document #1 was physically present when the primary document was executed (and the language of the primary document implies just the opposite; the primary document expressly indicates that Documents #1 and #2 are elsewhere — in the bottom drawer of the testator's desk). It is unlikely that a court would give effect to either Document #1 or Document #2 under integration.

The second doctrine the beneficiaries will invoke to try to give effect to the material provisions in Documents #1 and #2 is incorporation by reference. Incorporation by reference permits a court to give effect to testamentary intent expressed in a document other than a will as long as the will expresses the intent to incorporate the document, the will describes the document with reasonable certainty, and the document was in existence when the will was executed. (UPC §2-510). Here, the primary document makes reference to two pieces of paper that can be found in the bottom drawer. In fact, three pieces of paper were found. The first two read as if they are the documents to which the primary document was referring — they indicate to whom Tawny's property should be distributed. The third document, Document #3, reads like a codicil or page 2 of the primary document. As such, one can argue that when the primary document refers to "two pieces of paper" that will make known the testator's wishes for final distribution of her estate, the primary document is (1) expressing the intent to incorporate Documents #1 and #2 by reference, and (2) that the primary document has described the documents being incorporated with reasonable certainty. The courts generally apply a low threshold to the first two requirements of incorporation by reference, so those elements are probably satisfied under these facts.

The problem is the third requirement. The party seeking to incorporate the documents must be able to prove that the documents being incorporated were in existence when the will was executed. Because the primary document is undated, this is a difficult task. The proponents of the holographic will, however, have two arguments. The first is based on the verb tense used in the primary document. The primary document says that the two pieces of paper "are in the bottom drawer" of my desk — not that they "will be" in the bottom drawer. The use of present tense arguably supports the position that Documents #1 and #2 were in existence at the time the primary document was executed. Second, the primary document expressly states that there are "two" pieces of paper in the bottom drawer. The primary document was able to give the exact number because the documents were already in existence. To the extent the court accepts these arguments as sufficient proof that the documents being incorporated were in existence at the time the will was created, the requirements to incorporate Documents #1 and #2 are satisfied.

Tawny's heirs will challenge the incorporation by reference arguments by arguing that: (1) there is not sufficient evidence that Documents #1 and #2 are the documents to which the primary document is referring; (2) there is not sufficient evidence that Documents #1 and #2 were in existence when the primary document was executed; and (3) incorporation by reference permits a will to incorporate another document by reference, but the primary document does not qualify as a will unless the material provisions are incorporated by reference.

Incorporating the material provisions from Documents #1 and #2 into the primary document creates a document that arguably qualifies as a holographic will. It is, however, far from certain that a court would accept the incorporation by reference argument. Most courts take a strict approach to the requirement that the proponent must establish that the documents being incorporated were in existence at the time the will was executed. Here, that evidence is rather thin. If the court were to take the more traditional, strict approach, it is unlikely that the court would find a valid holographic will. The modern trend, however, focuses more on the testator's intent and takes a more lenient approach to the doctrine. If the court were to apply the modern approach, there is a good chance that the court would find a valid holographic will by incorporating the provisions of Documents #1 and #2.

Assuming the requirements for incorporation by reference are otherwise satisfied, Tawny's heirs might argue that it is inappropriate to incorporate the documents because the material provisions of both Documents #1 and #2 are typed, not handwritten. To the extent the documents are being incorporated into a holographic will, and one of the requirements of a holographic will is that the material provisions must be in the testator's handwriting, the heirs will argue that the material provisions of any document being incorporated by reference should have to be in the testator's handwriting as well. The courts, however, have rejected this argument. The material provision is the provision in the will that expresses the intent to incorporate the document. The document being

incorporated into the holographic will does not have to be in the testator's handwriting. Incorporating typed material into a holographic will is
permitted (but a testator cannot integrate typed material into a holographic will — another reason why integration is not helpful to the will
proponents under these facts).

Can Document #3 be probated as a holographic codicil to the primary will?

Assuming that the primary document constitutes a valid will, the beneficiaries under Document #3 have a strong argument that it constitutes a
holographic codicil to the primary document. Document #3 is in writing, it
is signed by the testator, it does a better job of expressing testamentary
intent on its own (talks about the first page "of my will" and then calls
this "Page 2" — thereby arguably establishing that the testator intended
this document to be part of her will). This document also expresses some of
the testator's material provisions ("everything else should be divided
equally among Bob, Shirley, and Ann"). A strong argument can be
made that this document qualifies as a valid holographic codicil to the
primary document.

(To the extent a court might be reluctant to call the primary document a
valid will, one might be able to give effect to the primary document
through incorporation by reference. Here, the primary document makes
reference to two pieces of paper that will be found in the bottom drawer. In
fact, three pieces of paper were found. The first two read as the primary
document indicated they would — they indicate to whom Tawny's property should be distributed. The third document, Document #3, reads like a
codicil or page 2 of the primary document. As such, one can argue that
when Document #3 refers to "my will" it is referring to the primary document. Most courts would hold that this reference adequately expresses
the intent to incorporate the primary document and describes it with
reasonable certainty. The question is whether there is sufficient evidence
to establish that the primary document was in existence when Document
#3 was created. There is only circumstantial evidence to support this claim.
Because it is in the bottom drawer, and because it calls itself page 2 — if the
court concludes that page 1 is the primary document, there is sufficient
evidence. That would permit the primary document to be incorporated by
reference. Then the beneficiaries under Documents #1 and #2 would argue
that the document being incorporated should be permitted to incorporate
yet another set of documents per the arguments above to establish the
material provisions.)

Summary:

A court could go either way on whether there is a valid will here, but a strong argument can be made that (1) the primary document, when combined with Documents #1 and #2, constitutes a valid holographic will; and (2) Document #3 constitutes a valid holographic codicil.

Is Document #1 (the deed) by itself a testamentary document?

Assuming, *arguendo*, that the court rejects the incorporation by reference argument and refuses to give effect to the primary document as a valid holographic will or Document #3 as a valid codicil, can Ann still successfully claim the house under Document #1 — the deed? First, Ann cannot claim the house under the deed because the deed was not delivered *inter vivos*. A properly executed deed does not transfer the property interest until the deed is delivered. Delivery is an abstract concept, but it signifies the grantor's intent to relinquish all dominion and control over the property — to make a present transfer of the property interest in question. Where the grantor retains possession of the actual deed, the assumption is that the grantor has not delivered the deed. Because Tawny retained possession of the deed until she died, and because Tawny continued to live in the house and enjoy the benefits of the property, the deed was not delivered *inter vivos* and will not convey the house to Ann.

Ann may try to argue that the handwritten note attached to the deed constitutes a valid holographic will that incorporates the deed by reference and validly constitutes a testamentary transfer of the house. The note is in Tawny's handwriting, and Tawny validly signed it. But even if the case can be made that the note makes sufficient reference to the deed to permit incorporation by reference (a tough argument, but maybe because the documents are paper-clipped together and the use of the word "this"), there is no evidence of testamentary intent. Testamentary intent requires evidence that the testator intended the document to be taken down and probated as his or her will. There is nothing about Document #1, or the note attached to it, that expresses such intent. On the contrary, the reference to document #1 in the primary document arguably indicates that Tawny intended the primary document to be the will and *not* Document #1 standing alone.

It is unlikely that Document #1 standing alone, or in conjunction with the handwritten note attached to it, can be given effect as a valid deed or can be probated as a valid will.

Assuming all the documents are read together as one integrated will, how should Tawny's estate be distributed?

The gift of "All my money — brother Bob": There are several issues with respect to Tawny's gift to her brother Bob. First and foremost is the line through the gift and the handwritten interlineation "son Sam."

First, the handwritten interlineation does not qualify in its own right as a holographic will. There is not enough in the testator's handwriting to qualify as the material provisions, nor does the document, standing alone, have testamentary intent. The handwritten interlineation can be given effect only as part of the larger set of documents.

The problem is that when a document is incorporated by reference, it is incorporated as it exists on the day the will is executed. Subsequent amendments or modifications to the document cannot be given effect. Although the reference in the primary document is arguably sufficient to indicate that Document #2 was in existence when the primary document was executed, there is absolutely no way of knowing when the handwritten interlineation was made to Document #2. Sam cannot prove that the handwritten interlineation was on the document when the primary document was executed. Under a strict application of incorporation by reference, the handwritten interlineation should not be given effect. Moreover, assuming Document #3 qualifies as a valid codicil, and under republication by codicil, the codicil will re-execute, republish, and generally redate the underlying will, the same problem continues. Document #3, the codicil, is undated, so it is still impossible to prove that the handwritten interlineation was on Document #2 when the codicil was executed. Under strict application of incorporation by reference, the handwritten interlineation of the gift to "son Sam" cannot be given effect.

If, however, the jurisdiction has adopted the UPC's harmless error doctrine, Sam should be entitled to the money. Section 2-503 of the UPC validates a document or writing that doesn't meet testamentary formalities "if the proponent of the document or writing establishes by clear and convincing evidence that the decedent intended the . . . writing to constitute . . . (iii) an addition to or an alteration of the will . . . ." The comment to this section makes it clear that it is designed to cover the situation in which a testator crosses out some text and substitutes new text without a new signature and a new set of witnesses. The change from Bob to Sam probably satisfies this test, though there is no "clear and convincing" evidence that the change was made by Tawny herself rather than by someone else (say, Sam).

Assuming the jurisdiction has adopted UPC §2-503, there is a good chance Sam will take the money. Otherwise, the gift was validly revoked (assuming the jurisdiction recognizes partial revocation by act) and it will fall to the residuary where Ann, Bob, and Sam will share it equally.

The ABC stock: The only issue with respect to the ABC stock is *when* the shares were acquired and *how* they were acquired. Because of the specific reference to ABC stock in Document #2, it is assumed that Tawny owned at least some shares of ABC stock at the time she executed the will. Under the UPC, where the testator makes a gift of stock in the will, and the testator owns matching shares at the time the will is executed, the beneficiary gets all the additional shares of securities in the testator's estate as long as the additional shares were acquired as the result of action initiated by the corporate entity. (UPC §2-605). As long as Tawny either owned all $50,000 at the time Document #2 was executed, or any additional shares were acquired as a result of action initiated by ABC, Shirley will receive all of the ABC stock.

Jewelry: There is a latent ambiguity in the gift. At the time of Tawny's death, she owned no jewelry, but she did own a jewelry box. The issue is whether the court will construe the entry in Document #2 "Jewelry — Ann" as referring to the jewelry box. Because of the ambiguity, extrinsic evidence will be admissible to help determine Tawny's intent (both under the common law approach, which only admits extrinsic evidence if the ambiguity is latent, and under the modern trend approach, which admits extrinsic evidence anytime there is an ambiguity). The key evidence will be the circumstances surrounding Tawny at the time the will was executed. Inasmuch as the date of the primary document is unknown, the court will focus on the date Document #2 was executed: June 1, 1999. If Tawny owned the jewelry box but not any jewelry on that date (or subsequently), Ann has a decent argument that Tawny was referring to the jewelry box. On the other hand, if Tawny owned jewelry on that date, Ann's argument that she is entitled to the jewelry box is weaker. (Though in that event, Ann might be able to convince the court that the gift should be construed as a specific gift and that under the UPC she is entitled to the pecuniary value of the jewelry in question as of the date of its disposal.) If the court were to rule that Ann was not entitled to the jewelry box, it would fall to the residuary clause and be distributed equally to Ann, Bob, and Shirley.

Furniture: Ann might argue that the devise of the house included the furniture within it. (How else could she enjoy the dwelling as much as Tawny?) But furniture in a home is usually considered personal property of the testator or testatrix and is not usually deemed part of the realty. There is no easy answer here, but because there is no clear indication that Tawny intended the furniture to go to Ann, it would probably be included in the residuary estate.

Summary:

This is a tough question with more uncertainty than certainty. At one end of the possibilities is that the court may rule that Tawny died intestate. Under that possible scenario, Ann and Sam would split all of her property equally. At the other end of the possibilities is that the court may rule that the combined documents constitute a holographic will and codicil. Under that scenario, Ann is likely to get the house; Sam is likely to get the money (as long as the jurisdiction has adopted the UPC's harmless error doctrine); Shirley is likely to get the ABC stock; Ann may or may not get the jewelry box (depending on the facts surrounding Tawny at the time the document was executed); and the furniture is likely to pass to Bob, Shirley, and Ann equally under the residuary clause in the codicil.

Answer to Question 18

1. Who is entitled to the trust estate and in what amounts?

Every trust must have a trust res, a trustee, and named or ascertainable beneficiaries. The first two requirements are clearly satisfied by these facts (the assets of Silver's estate constitute the trust res and Thompson is the trustee). The beneficiaries are not named, but can they be ascertained? The answer is "yes." The "employees of the bar and grill" at the time of Silver's death can be ascertained by reviewing the payroll records. Thompson had no discretion as to which employees to designate; any one of them (Able, Baker, or Charley) could enforce the trust.

Silver's heirs will contend, however, that the trust fails because Thompson never designated the amount that each employee would receive. They will argue that a resulting trust would arise in their favor.

In a situation such as this, courts will normally attempt to determine whether the trustee had any real discretion to depart from the testator's mandate in designating the beneficiaries. (Parol evidence is ordinarily admissible upon this point.) In most cases, the courts will decide that the testator did not intend to give the trustee this latitude.

Here, the amount to be allocated to each of the employees was, presumably, to be based upon some verifiable measure (*e.g.*, years worked, position held, dedication, attendance, work attitudes, etc.). If Thompson's successor trustee were unable to determine how the trust assets should be distributed, the court would probably determine that the three employees should share equally. Silver obviously wanted to distribute his estate among his employees. Presumably, he would have preferred an equal distribution among them to distribution to his next of kin in intestacy.

2. What standards determine whether Thompson has breached the duty of trust?

The actions of a trustee are ordinarily judged by the "reasonably prudent investor" standard. Under this doctrine, a trustee must ordinarily act with the same care and prudence toward the trust assets as he or she would with respect to his or her own funds — considering the purposes, terms, distribution requirements, and other circumstances of the trust.

In some jurisdictions, a trustee may make only certain types of investments (government bonds, blue chip stocks, etc.). However, we'll assume that this jurisdiction does not follow this rule and that Thompson was free to operate the bar and to own the stock of Red Company and Blue Company.

Thompson's estate might claim that he was given greater latitude than most trustees in investing assets of the trust, because he was specifically authorized to utilize his "discretion." While it is possible for a settlor to enlarge a trustee's authority to make investments beyond the "reasonably prudent investor" standard, the settlor must express this intent clearly. It is unlikely the word "discretion," without more, would be construed to expand the usual "reasonably prudent investor" standard. Instead, the court will probably conclude that Thompson's discretion was to be exercised in accordance with the "reasonably prudent investor" standard.

Did Thompson breach the "reasonably prudent investor" rule by retaining the bar and grill?

The next of kin will argue that a bar and grill is an inherently speculative investment, even in the hands of a sound operator, and is thus never suitable property for a trust. They will argue that the bar should have been sold immediately. However, modern courts have expanded the notion of what constitutes a suitable trust investment, and are willing to let the possibility of unusually high profits offset unusual risk. Given that the bar was originally part of the trust property, and that it was operating profitably at the beginning, the court would probably not hold that it was a breach of trust for Thompson to try to operate the bar initially.

A better argument is that Thompson should not have retained the bar and grill for a second year (during which time the business lost $15,000). The beneficiaries could argue that the success of this type of establishment requires personalized skill and experience that Thompson may not have possessed. (The facts fail to indicate whether Thompson had any prior background in running a bar and grill.) Thompson's estate will assert in rebuttal, however, that he had successfully operated the bar and grill during the initial year (as evidenced by the $10,000 profit during this period), and that there was no reason to suspect that he would not do at least as well in the second year.

Additional facts are needed to determine whether Thompson's estate will be liable. If, for example, Silver had regularly achieved a $50,000 per year profit prior to his death, there would be a persuasive argument that Thompson should have concluded after his first year of operation of the business that he lacked the skill to run it effectively. On the other hand, if Thompson's estate can show that he did as well as Silver or can identify independent and unforeseeable market factors that reduced the restaurant's profits, the estate should be able to escape liability.

Thompson's estate will also contend that Silver's will implicitly authorized retention of the bar and grill for two years (it was not until the conclusion of that period that the principal and accrued interest were to be distributed). This argument would probably fail. The court would probably determine that Silver's instructions were not intended to override the "reasonably prudent investor" rule, but merely to prescribe an outside date by which the establishment was to be sold.

If it is determined that Thompson breached the "reasonably prudent investor" standard, his estate would be liable for all losses that should have been avoided. That is, the estate would be liable for: (1) the difference between the fair market value of the business at the time it should have been sold and the amount received at the actual sale; (2) the operating losses incurred after the time the business should have been sold; and (3) interest on items (1) and (2) above.

Thompson's estate will argue that any losses computed under this formula should be reduced by the profits ($10,000) earned during Thompson's first year of operations. If the property should have been sold by Thompson promptly, or soon after the *first* year began — so that retaining the business at all was a single breach of trust — then Thompson's estate would probably be entitled to an offset of profits against losses because gains and losses from a single breach of trust may be offset against each other, according to most courts. If, on the other hand, it was reasonable (and not a breach of trust) for Thompson to keep the business during the first year, and the breach of trust arose only after it started to lose money during the second year, then Thompson's estate would probably *not* be entitled to an offset of profits against losses — a trustee may not offset losses from a breach of trust by using profits made from other, reasonable trust investments.

Did Thompson's election to accept Blue Company stock in lieu of the fair market value of Red Company shares violate the "reasonably prudent investor" rule?

The trust beneficiaries will contend that it was imprudent for Thompson to invest in a new, highly speculative business (experimental electronics). Thompson's estate could respond by pointing out (correctly) that the trust deferred any capital gains tax on the Red shares by accepting the stock swap, whereas it would have had to pay these taxes if it had sold the Red Company stock. Tax considerations certainly are taken into account in determining whether a trustee has behaved "prudently." However, the risks from a new speculative electronics investment were so great that the court would probably conclude that these risks far outweighed the benefits from tax deferral, and that a "reasonably prudent investor" would have opted for the sale of Red Company stock instead of the stock swap. Thompson's estate will be liable for the sum of $4,500 (the difference between the fair market value of the Red Company stock and the sale price of the Blue Company stock) less the net capital gains resulting from both transactions, plus interest upon the net after taxes, commencing from the date when the Red Company stock could have been sold for $75 per share.

Did Thompson's failure to sell the bar, and to take the Blue stock, constitute a failure to diversify?

In recent years, courts have begun to hold that an investment strategy is "reasonably prudent" only if it is reasonably *diversified.* See, for example, Restatement 3d of Trusts, §227(b). ("In making and implementing investment decisions, the trustee has a duty to diversify the investments of the trust unless, under the circumstances, it is prudent not to do so.") A trust corpus consisting of only two investments, one of which is completely illiquid (the bar), is almost certainly insufficiently diversified. The fact that these were the sole investments left by Silver to the trust does not matter—the trustee has a duty to sell pre-existing trust assets where it is necessary to achieve diversification, unless the trust instrument explicitly provides otherwise. Therefore, the court will probably hold that Thompson had the obligation to sell part of the Red stock (or part of the Blue stock once he received it in the swap), and perhaps to sell the bar, solely on diversification grounds. If so, the measure of damages would be the difference between the performance of a reasonably diversified portfolio and the actual performance achieved by Thompson here.

Answer to Question 19

1. Was the typewritten document dated September 17, 1985, a valid will?

The answer is "no." The document does not satisfy the formal requirements for a valid will. It was not signed by the testator. It was not acknowledged as a testamentary document before two witnesses. The testator's signature was not witnessed by at least two subscribing witnesses.

2. Did the June 15, 1986, document create a valid holographic will?

The beneficiaries can make a very plausible argument that the June 15, 1986, document created a valid holographic will.

Hoby will contend that the June 15, 1986, document is *not* a valid holographic will because: (1) it is not signed, but merely initialed; (2) it does not specifically incorporate by reference the distribution scheme set forth in the September 27, 1985, writing (and so contains no disposition of Tait's estate); (3) a subsequent document may not incorporate a prior document that is itself invalid as a testamentary document; and (4) even if the September 27, 1985, document were incorporated, there would still be no valid holographic will because the "material provisions"(*i.e.*, those describing the disposition of Tait's estate) are typewritten.

But the beneficiaries will reply as follows. First, the initials of the testator are ordinarily viewed as sufficient to satisfy the signature requirement in a will. Second, the word "adopt" should be construed to mean "incorporate by reference," because Tait obviously intended to give effect to the testamentary scheme in the September 27, 1985, writing. (It would not be helpful for the beneficiaries to argue that the word "adopt" should be read as "republish"; the majority view is that an invalid will *cannot* be republished.) The requirement that "material provisions" must be in the testator's handwriting is arguably satisfied by the words "I adopt"(*i.e.*, "I incorporate by reference") the typewritten draft. There is every reason to interpret the two documents together in this manner because they give effect to Tait's testamentary intentions instead of leaving her intestate. And lastly, the document adequately expresses testamentary intent. The opening reference to "sound mind" coupled with the later phrase "my last will" should be sufficient to indicate that Trisha intended the document to be her will. The case is even stronger when the language from the document being incorporated by reference is included in the analysis.

The beneficiaries should prevail. Therefore, the will (composed of the September 27, 1985, and June 15, 1986, documents together) is valid.

3. Assuming Tait had a valid will, how should her estate be distributed?

Minco stock: Although Sal predeceased Tait, his daughter (Helen) would step into Sal's position under the antilapse provisions. (UPC §2-603(b)). Helen, although adopted, would be treated as Sal's issue. (UPC §§1-201(5), 2-114(b)).

The UPC provides that where a testator devises stock, and at the time the testator executed the will, the testator owned matching shares of stock, if thereafter the stock changes due to action initiated by the corporate entity, the beneficiary receives the benefit of the change — regardless of whether the language of the gift makes it look like a general or specific gift. (UPC §2-605(a)(1)). The facts are a bit ambiguous, but the natural inference from the language in the will is that Tait owned 150 shares of Minco stock when she executed her will. Moreover, the facts do not indicate how Tait acquired the additional shares. Assuming she acquired the additional shares as a result of action initiated by the company, Helen would take all of the additional shares. Therefore, Helen would receive all 300 shares of Minco stock unless Hoby was able to show that the additional shares of Minco stock were actually purchased by Tait from her general funds.

Zebco stock: Hoby will contend that the gift of Oilco stock has been extinguished by ademption, and that, therefore, he is entitled to the Zebco stock via the residuary clause. When a testator devises a gift of *stock*, and he or she owned shares of stock at the time the will was executed that *match* the stock being devised in the will, the devisee is entitled to: (1) any additional or other securities of the same entity owned by the testator at death by reason of action (such as a stock split or stock dividend) initiated by that entity, and (2) any securities *of another entity* owned by the testator as a result of a merger, consolidation, reorganization, or other similar action. (UPC §2-605). Here, the facts are a bit ambiguous, but the natural inference from the language in the will is that Tait owned 500 shares of Oilco stock when she executed her will. As a result of the merger, she acquired 500 shares of Zebco. All 500 shares of Zebco stock in her estate appear to be the result of the merger. Unless Hoby can prove otherwise, Diane is entitled to all 500 shares of Zebco stock.

Abco stock: Bill will contend that the Abco stock passes to him because it was found in the wall safe. But Hoby will argue — probably successfully — that stock is ordinarily not viewed as a "personal effect." The Abco stock should pass to Hoby under the residuary clause.

Jewelry: Tait's personal jewelry will be considered a part of her "personal effects." Because it was found in the wall safe, Bill will argue that the jewelry passes to him. Hoby will assert that because she put her jewelry into the safe only after the will was made, Tait did not intend a specific testamentary act; in any event, the act did not comply with any of the necessary testamentary formalities. Thus, Hoby would contend, the gift to Bill should fail.

However, under the *acts of independent significance* doctrine, a will may dispose of property as a consequence of acts or events that have significance apart from their testamentary effect. (UPC §2-512). Because placing items in a safe has a purpose that is nontestamentary in nature (*e.g.*, the testator may intend simply to prevent the articles from being misplaced or stolen), the fact that Tait's act also had a testamentary effect (effectuating the gift to Bill) would be irrelevant. Thus, Tait's jewelry should pass to Bill.

Bank account: The bank account would pass to Hoby under the residuary clause of Tait's will.

4. If the will is not valid, how would Tait's estate be distributed?

Under intestacy principles, Hoby would receive the entire estate. The reasoning: all of Tait's surviving descendants are also Hoby's descendants and Hoby does not have other surviving descendants who are not descendants of Tait. (UPC §2-102(1)(ii)).

5. Result if Hoby had predeceased Tait, and the latter had then married John:

Hoby's interest would lapse, because he would not be considered a surviving spouse. John would be considered a pretermitted spouse and would take an intestate share. (UPC §2-301). However, John would not get an intestate share of the whole estate — any devises to a child of the testator born before the testator married the surviving spouse (or to a descendant of that child, under UPC §2-603's antilapse provision) would be carved out first, and John would then get his intestate share of the balance. Thus the Minco stock (which goes to Sal's daughter Helen), and the Zebco stock (which goes to Tait's daughter Diane) would be removed from the computation. John would then get the first $100,000 plus one-half of the balance of the estate. (UPC §2-102(4)).

Other gifts would have to be abated to satisfy John's intestate share. The order in which items are abated is set forth in UPC §3-902: first, property not disposed of by will; then, residuary devises; then, general devises; finally, specific devises. Assuming there is no property passing to John outside of the will (the facts don't point to any), residuary devises, which include the Abco stock and the bank accounts (worth a total of $105,000), would be abated first. There are no general devises. The jewelry (the only asset not yet taken into account) is a specific devise; John would take half the value of this jewelry after the first $5,000 in jewelry value.

Answer to Question 20

Was the September 20, 1995, document a valid will?

The September 20, 1995, document does not satisfy the UPC's requirements for a valid attested will. It is not acknowledged by two witnesses, and it is questionable whether it is properly signed. See UPC §2-502(a). However, the document may qualify for probate as a holographic will. To be a valid holographic will, a document need not be witnessed, but it must be in writing, signed by the testator; the "material provisions" must be in the testator's handwriting; and it must have testamentary intent. (UPC §2-502).

Among the beneficiaries, Bessie is the one who would gain the most if Timothy is deemed to have died intestate. She will argue that the September 20, 1995, document was not a valid holographic will because: (1) it was not signed by Timothy, and (2) it did not clearly and unambiguously dispose of Timothy's entire estate. The document refers to "one-half" of something, but it is not clear what that "something" is. Did Timothy mean one-half of the residue after subtracting the stock in the notebook he was keeping (although the facts don't tell us when he started to keep the notebook)? Or did he mean one-half of the entire estate? Or one-half of his stock only? We don't really know, and that strengthen's Bessie's argument that the document should not be accepted because it does not contain a clear dispository scheme.

On the other hand, the Boys Club will assert: (1) by writing his own name in the body of the document, Timothy satisfied the signature requirement (UPC §2-502(b) does not say that the testator's signature must be at the foot of the document); and (2) a reasonable interpretation of the document is that Timothy wanted to divide his estate evenly between Bessie and the Boys Club because Timothy preceded the words "one-half" with the words "I . . . make this will." Given the usual desire of probate courts to effectuate the testator's wishes by accepting documents that display a testamentary intent, the September 20, 1995, document will probably be received as a valid holographic will.

If the September 20, 1995, document was not itself a valid will, was it republished, or otherwise made valid, by the June 30, 1998, document?

Although the June 30, 1998, document reads like a codicil, if the September 20, 1995, document is *not* a valid will, the later document cannot be a codicil. A codicil is a subsequent will that merely amends or supplements a pre-existing valid will. But while the June 30, 1998, document cannot qualify as a codicil (thereby barring application of the republication by codicil to validate the September 20, 1995, document), the latter document may qualify as a valid holographic will, thereby permitting an argument under incorporation by reference to give effect to the testamentary intent expressed in the September 20, 1995, document.

The Boys Club will contend that the June 30, 1998, document was itself a complete and valid holographic will (rather than a codicil to an existing will) that incorporated the September 20, 1995, document by reason of the reference to "my former will." Although Timothy's language does not specifically incorporate the prior document, this argument will probably succeed. Because Timothy obviously believed that the first document was valid (as evidenced by his reference to his "previous will"), this result would effectuate his testamentary intent.

Finally, the Boys Club (as well as Dorothy) will argue that the two documents (September 20, 1995, and June 30, 1998) should be read together as a single will, enforceable under UPC §2-503's provision validating certain documents that don't meet all the testamentary formalities. Under that provision, noncompliance with the formalities is ignored "if the proponent of the document or writing establishes by clear and convincing evidence that the decedent intended the document or writing to constitute (i) the decedent's will [or] (iii) an addition to or an alteration of the will . . . ." The September 20, 1995, document probably qualifies under (i) of this test, and the June 30, 1998, document probably qualifies under (iii).

Summary:

The court will probably accept the argument of the Boys Club (as well as of Dorothy) that the second document is a valid holographic will which incorporates the first by reference, and the court will dispose of Timothy's entire estate under the provisions of the two documents.

Does the black book become part of the testamentary scheme?

Because the black book does not on its face meet any of the testamentary formalities, it cannot by itself constitute either a will or a codicil. However, under the doctrine of incorporation by reference, a writing in existence when a will is executed may be incorporated into the will if the will's language manifests this intent and the will describes the writing sufficiently to identify it. Because (1) the June 30, 1998, document clearly refers to "stocks listed in my black book"; (2) the black book was found in the same safe-deposit box as the 1998 document and contained a handwritten list of stock transactions; and (3) the black book existed on June 30, 1998, the requirements for incorporation by reference are met. Therefore, the black book becomes part of the testamentary scheme because the June 30, 1998, document is part of that scheme. (As to the effect of changes to the black book made after June 30, 1998, see the subsequent discussion.)

What is the effect of the June 30, 1998, document on Timothy's testamentary scheme?

If we conclude that the June 30, 1998, document is an integral part of Timothy's testamentary scheme, we need to determine just what the effect of that document is.

It is unclear from the June 30, 1998, document ("Bessie doesn't need all that") whether Timothy wanted to *revoke* the portion devised to Bessie in the September 20, 1995, document, or intended instead to *reduce* Bessie's one-half share of the entire estate by the value of the stocks listed in the black book.

If the June 30, 1998, document is interpreted as a mere reduction of Bessie's interest, Bessie would get half the estate ($70,000), less the value of the stocks ($40,000), or $30,000. If the document is interpreted as a revocation of Bessie's portion, then the distribution would be as follows: (1) the Boys Club would receive one-half of Timothy's estate ($70,000); (2) Bessie's child, Dorothy, would receive the stocks (value — $40,000). The issue then becomes what happens to the remainder of Timothy's estate ($30,000). Bessie will argue that because the will does not contain a residuary clause, the property in question falls to intestacy and as Timothy's closest heir, she takes the $30,000. (UPC §2-103(3)). (Because Dorothy claims through Bessie, who is still alive, she would take nothing in intestacy.)

The Boys Club will argue, however, that the will should be read as containing only one clause, a residuary clause, and that under the UPC/ modern-trend approach, if part of a residuary clause is revoked or fails, the revoked or failed gift passes to the other residuary clause takers.

A court could go either way on this, and many courts may favor Bessie as a family member over the Boys Club, but under the UPC the Boys Club has the stronger argument and should take the $30,000 if the June 30, 1998, document is construed as a revocation of Bessie's gift. But the better construction of the June 30, 1998, document is that it is merely a reduction ("she doesn't need *all* that" implies the testator is taking away part of it; if he had intended to take away all of it, the will would have simply read "she doesn't need that") so Bessie would still take the $30,000 in question.

What is the effect of the stock transactions that occurred after June 30, 1998?

Bessie will contend that entries in the black notebook made after June 30, 1998 (the date of the second document), should be disallowed. She will argue that Timothy's act in making these entries should not be given testamentary effect because they did not comply with any of the necessary testamentary formalities. Accordingly, the XYZ stock should pass through intestacy.

Although the entries in the black notebook do not constitute a valid will in their own right, Dorothy has two arguments she can use to try to convince a court to give effect to the testamentary intent expressed in the black notebook. At first blush the most applicable argument is incorporation by reference. The clause in the 1998 will that "all stocks listed in my black book go to Bessie's child" meets the requirements for incorporation by reference. The black book was in existence at the time the will was executed, the express reference to it in the 1998 will evidences the intent to incorporate it, and the will describes it with reasonable certainty. The black notebook can be incorporated by reference into the 1998 will.

The problem with Dorothy's invoking incorporation by reference to claim the stocks listed in the black notebook is that strict application of incorporation by reference means that the notebook can be incorporated only as it existed on the day the will was executed. The entries made after June 30, 1998, could not be given effect. Dorothy would not be entitled to the 100 shares of XYZ stock purchased on July 7, 1998. As to the 100 shares of ABC stock that she sold on July 7, 1998, the first issue is whether the gift was originally a general gift or a specific gift. If construed as a general gift, the fact that the stocks were sold would not affect Dorothy's right to the gift. The personal representative would simply have to go out and purchase 100 shares of ABC stock. If the gift is construed as a specific gift, normally ademption would apply to the 100 shares that were sold. Under the UPC approach to ademption, however, the beneficiary of specifically devised property that is no longer in the estate has the right to a pecuniary devise equal to the value of the specifically devised property as of the date of its dispostion. Dorothy could argue that she is entitled to a pecuniary devise under this section. (Dorothy could not claim the XYZ stock under this UPC section as replacement property because the replacement property doctrine is limited to tangible personal property. Dorothy could, however, claim the XYZ stock under UPC 2-503 in that there is clear and convincing evidence that Timothy intended the writing to constitute an addition to his will.)

In the alternative, Dorothy could invoke the doctrine of acts of independent significance to claim the stocks listed in the black book. Under the doctrine of acts of independent significance, the will can make reference to acts outside of the will, which can control either who takes under the will or how much a beneficiary takes as long as the referenced act has its own significance independent of its effect upon the testator's testamentary scheme. (UPC §2-512). Here, Dorothy would claim that the will's reference to the stocks listed in the black book is the act outside of the will that controls what she takes. Her argument is that the act of listing the stock in the black book was not just for testamentary purposes, it was also for general record-keeping purposes to help Timothy keep track of his stock purchases and sales. This argument is strengthened by the fact that almost all of the entries predate the creation of the will. Timothy created this black book not for testamentary purposes but for valid *inter vivos* purposes — to help him with his record keeping.

It is a close call whether a court would adopt the acts of independent significance argument. If it did, Dorothy would get all of the stocks listed in the black book — even the XYZ stock entered on July 7, 1998. Dorothy has a very strong argument under incorporation by reference, but her chances for the XYZ stock depend on whether the jurisdiction has adopted UPC §2-503 and whether the court would apply it to a document being incorporated into a will as opposed to the will directly. And whether Dorothy is entitled to the pecuniary value of the ABC stock that was sold depends on whether the gift is characterized as specific or general. The facts are ambiguous as to that issue.

Summary:

Based on the above analysis, The Boys Club will receive $70,000. Dorothy will receive the ABC stock that is still in the estate ($30,000). She has a decent chance of receiving the XYZ stock under acts of independent significance, and depending on whether the court characterizes the gift of all the stocks listed in "my" black book as a general or specific gift, she has an argument that she is entitled to a pecuniary devise equal to the ABC stock that was sold. If the language in the second document is construed as reducing Bessie's gift, the rest will go to Bessie; if it is construed as revoking Bessie's gift, the rest will probably go to the Boys Club.

Answer to Question 21

1. Did Thor die testate or intestate?

Sandra (who would receive Thor's entire estate if Thor died intestate by virtue of being Thor's only surviving issue) will argue that Thor died intestate because: (1) Will #1 was expressly revoked by the note that was attached to it (*i.e.*, a will may be revoked by a subsequent writing that was executed with the necessary testamentary formalities, and the attached note qualifies as a holographic will); and (2) Will #2 is invalid because it was (a) not in Thor's handwriting (preventing it from qualifying as a holographic will), and (b) not attested by two witnesses (preventing it from qualifying as an attested will).

The takers under the two wills (John, Gil, and Warren) will make the following three arguments that the court should find either Will #1 or Will #2 valid (either will would protect their interests equally):

Doctrine of dependent relative revocation (DRR): Under DRR, where a testator validly revokes a will based upon a mistake, and the testator would not have revoked the will but for the mistake, the court is authorized to ignore the revocation and give effect to the validly revoked will. Where the revocation is by a subsequent will, the courts almost invariably require that the mistake be set forth in the writing and to be beyond the knowledge of the testator. Here, Will #2 was not valid. But when Thor died, the handwritten note found stapled to Will #1 qualified as a valid holographic will that revoked Will #1. The revocation, however, was based upon the mistaken belief that Will #2 was valid. That arguably was the meaning of the reference "I have made a new will"(the note was dated the day after Thor executed what she thought was a valid Will #2). There seems little doubt that Thor revoked Will #1 on the mistaken belief that Will #2 was valid, this mistake is set forth in the revoking instrument, and this mistake was beyond Thor's knowledge. Lastly, inasmuch as Will #2 (what Thor really wanted) is nearly identical to Will #1 (for all practical purposes it is identical, now that Ethel is dead), there is no reason to doubt that if Thor had known of the mistake, she would not have revoked Will #1 (because it is closer to her desired testamentary scheme [Will #2] than it is to intestacy).

Incorporation by reference: Alternatively, the heirs will stake their argument on the doctrine of incorporation by reference. Under this doctrine, a writing that is in existence when a will is made may be incorporated by reference, if the language of the will manifests this intent and describes the writing sufficiently to permit its identification. (UPC §2-510). The heirs might argue: (1) the note that was attached to Will #1 was a valid holographic will because it was in the testator's handwriting and signed by her; and (2) the holographic will, by means of the statement "I have made another will," incorporated Will #2 into the terms of a valid holographic document.

Sandra will contend first that the validity of a holographic will should be judged by looking at the entire document, including the portions incorporated: here, the requirement that a holographic will contain "material provisions" in the testator's handwriting is not met. On the contrary, Will #2, which contains all the material terms, was entirely typewritten. Second, Sandra will argue that the language that is asserted to be the language of incorporation ("I have made another will") does not evidence a clear intent to incorporate Will #2; it is merely a statement of past action that does not specifically refer to Will #2.

In response to Sandra's argument, the takers under Will #2 will argue that the holographic note adequately identifies and expresses the intent to incorporate Will #2 and that the material provisions are in Thor's handwriting. The material provision is the provision incorporating Will #2 by reference ("I have made a new will"). They will also emphasize that applying incorporation by reference is more consistent with Thor's clear intent.

Harmless error: Under UPC §2-503, a document that was not properly executed with full wills act formalities may nevertheless be probated as the testator's will if there is clear and convincing evidence that the testator intended the document to be his or her will. Will #2 was a formal will, properly prepared, signed, and witnessed, except for the fact that there was only one subscribing witness, not two. There is little doubt that Thor intended this to be her will, as evidenced not only by the execution ceremony that she performed (signing the will and having it witnessed by one witness), but also by the fact that the next day she wrote a note revoking his first will because, as she herself wrote "I have a new will." The reference is clearly to her second will, Will #2. There is clear and convincing evidence that Thor intended Will #2 to be her will.

Summary: The takers under Thor's wills have several strong arguments. A court would probably apply DRR under these circumstances and probate Will #1. In the alternative, if the jurisdiction has adopted the UPC harmless error doctrine, there is little doubt that the doctrine would apply and the court would probate Will #2. Even the incorporation by reference argument, the weakest of the arguments made by the proponents of the wills, has a decent chance of success. Inasmuch as there is no practical difference between Will #1 and Will #2 (now that Ethel has died), it does not really matter which doctrine the court applies and which will the court probates. Sandra will lose on her argument that Thor died intestate.

2. Assuming Thor died testate, how should her estate be distributed?

If we assume that Thor died testate, we don't actually need to know whether the operative will is Will #1 or Will #2. Now that Ethel is dead, the two documents are functionally identical.

Was the $10,000 to Robert Rood an outright gift to him, or was it to be held in trust for Carrie?

Carrie will contend that because the $10,000 bequest to Robert Rood was "to be used" for her education, a trust for her benefit was created, and Robert has to spend the $10,000 as prescribed. Robert will argue that no trust was created because the language used was not clear enough. When Thor intended to create a trust, she used language that was clear and unequivocal, as evidenced by the terms "trustee" and "trust" in the second paragraph of both her wills. This is a close call. The language Thor used in the gift to Robert normally would be construed as imposing a legal obligation on him, not just a moral obligation, to use the money for the benefit of his daughter. That is enough to create a trust. But because of the more formal language used in the very next paragraph, there is the possibility that a court would conclude that the language in the gift to Robert was merely precatory. Ultimately this is a question of the decedent's intent, and under these facts it could go either way.

Would Sandra be entitled to receive anything?

Sandra would receive nothing. Ethel's interest under the trust was only a life estate. Ethel had no interest under the trust that she could devise under her will. The property under the trust passes pursuant to the express "gift over" clause that devises the property to Thor's heirs upon Ethel's death.

What shares would John, Gil, and Warren receive?

When a will provides that a decedent's property is to be distributed to his or her "heirs," distribution is usually made according to intestacy principles. Where there is no surviving parent and no descendants of the testator, distribution is made to the descendants of the decedent's parents, by representation. (UPC §2-103(3)). The distribution is made "per capita at each generation," the division of the estate starting at the highest level at which there are living members. (UPC §2-106). The highest level at which there are living members is that shared by John and Gil and by Warren's deceased parent, the child of Thor's deceased sister Bessie. Therefore, the estate is split into thirds. John and Gil take one-third each. Warren takes his parent's one-third by representation. Thus, John, Gil, and Warren would each receive one-third of Thor's remaining estate (after the $10,000 gift to Rood).

3. Assuming Thor died intestate, how should her estate be distributed?

An heir does not have to survive until the close of distribution of an intestate decedent's estate to be entitled to take his or her share. An heir need only survive the decedent by 120 hours (as established by clear and convincing evidence). (UPC §2-104). Here, Ethel, Thor's only descendant, survived Thor by 120 hours and therefore is entitled to take all of Thor's estate as her only surviving descendant. (UPC §2-103). Ethel's interest in Thor's estate vested before Ethel died, making her interest devisable and inheritable. Ethel validly devised her interest to Sandra, her friend. When Thor's estate is finally distributed, Sandra will be entitled to all of it under the terms of Ethel's will.

Answer to Question 22

Was Will #1 valid?

A will is valid even though it was witnessed by an interested person. (UPC §2-505(b)). Because Will #1 was witnessed by two persons, it appears to be valid.

Was Will #1 revoked by Will #2?

Where a testator executes a second will that is inconsistent with his or her earlier will and codicils, the earlier will is cancelled. Thus, Mary and John would argue that, because the testamentary scheme of Will #2 is irreconcilable with Will #1, Will #1 was invalidated.

However, Allen would argue that Will #2 was induced by John's fraud. Fraud in the inducement occurs where the testator understands the provisions of the will he or she is signing, but has been induced to make provisions that he or she would not have made had he or she not been deceived as to underlying facts. Here, Allen can make a strong claim that John's false statements about Allen's criminal activities constituted fraud in the inducement, leading Tom to remove Allen from the revised will.

Courts sometimes deny probate to a will that is the product of fraud in the inducement. However, where only some clauses, rather than the whole will, are induced by fraud, the court usually accepts the will for probate and uses the doctrine of constructive trust (discussed below) to remedy the fraud. Because there is no sign that the entire Will #2 was the product of fraud (*e.g.*, there is no evidence that the removal of the phrase "niece and nephews"—which would have been construed as including David [see discussion below]—was accomplished by fraud), the court will probably admit Will #2, and regard Will #1 as having been revoked by Tom's adoption of Will #2.

Was Will #1 cancelled?

Even if Will #2 is found to be completely invalid for fraud, the court might find that Will #1 was cancelled. Drawing lines through a will with the intention of canceling it will revoke that document. Tom arguably cancelled Will #1 by drawing lines through it. Will #1 might still have been negated.

The takers under Will #1 can argue, however, that Tom's canceling Will #1 was also the result of John's fraud. Although there is no direct evidence of when the lines were drawn, when the revocation is read in conjunction with the provisions of Will #2, a strong argument can be made that the most likely scenario is that the testator revoked Will #1 as part and parcel of the process of executing Will #2 — a process prompted by John's fraud. If the court were persuaded that the revocatory lines were induced by John's fraud, the court could impose a constructive trust on the ultimate takers of Tom's estate in favor of the beneficiaries under Will #1.

In the alternative, the takers under Will #1 can argue that the doctrine of dependent relative revocation (DRR) should apply to permit the court to give effect to Will #1. Under this theory, if one revokes a will under the *mistaken belief* that a simultaneous, alternative will is effective, the earlier will may be reinstated (provided the court believes that this is the result the testator would have wanted).

If Will #1 was revoked upon the belief that Will #2 was valid, but Will #2 was in fact invalid because of John's fraud, Will #1 should arguably be reinstated. However, there is no proof that Will #2 was made simultaneously with the cancellation of Will #1. Nevertheless, the fact that Will #1 was in the same safe deposit box as Will #2 permits an inference that the latter was created concurrently with the cancellation of the first. This result would probably be what Tom would have desired. Thus, Will #1 could possibly be probated.

Disposition under Will #1:

If Will #1 is valid, Mary would receive $80,000 ($50,000, plus one-fourth of the $120,000 residue); John, $45,000 ($15,000, plus one-fourth of the residue); and Allen, $45,000 (same computation as John). David had predeceased the making of Will #1, and therefore was arguably *not* within the class of "nephews and nieces" to which the residuary portion was to be distributed. However, UPC §2-603(b)(2) permits the descendants of a deceased person who is included in a class description to take under the antilapse provision even though the deceased ancestor was dead at the time the will was executed. Thus, David's two children would step up into his share (one-fourth of the $120,000 residue) under the antilapse statute and would receive $15,000 each.

Disposition under Will #2:

If Will #2 is found to be the valid will, the court will need to deal with the fact that John apparently committed fraud and thereby deprived Allen of the share he would have received absent the fraud. The rest of this discussion assumes that the court has concluded that such fraud did in fact occur.

Where a provision of a will is procured by fraud in the inducement, the court will generally attempt to redress the fraud by use of the doctrine of *constructive trust*. That is, the court will leave the legal title to property as the will places it, but will require that the legal holder hold the property in trust for the benefit of the person who would have received it had the fraud not occurred. Usually the court also orders that the legal holder then convey legal title to the beneficiary of the constructive trust.

The court here will have to decide what Tom would have done had the fraud not taken place. The "conservative" approach is to assume that the fraud did not affect Mary's share, only the split between John and Allen. If the court makes this assumption, Mary will get $110,000 (the $50,000 specific bequest plus the same one-half of the $120,000 residue that the will by its terms gives her), and a constructive trust will be used to make Allen and John split the money ($90,000) that the will gives to John alone. That is, the court will declare $45,000 of John's proceeds subject to a constructive trust for the benefit of Allen, and would then compel John to convey this amount to Allen.

Alternatively, the court might conclude that absent the fraud, Tom would have decided to split the $30,000 specific bequest between John and Allen (so far, this is still the same as the "conservative" approach discussed above), but that the residuary would have been split equally among Mary, John, and Allen. This approach has the merit of being similar to the prefraud approach taken by Tom. If the court did this, then Mary would take $90,000 (the $50,000 specific bequest plus one-third of the $120,000 residue), and John and Allen would split $110,000 (the $30,000 specific bequest to John plus two-thirds of the $120,000 residue). This approach, of course, penalizes the "innocent" Mary, but there is good authority and logic for it: Mary's innocence should not lead to her getting something that she would not have gotten absent John's fraud. (UPC §1-106 expressly authorizes any person injured by fraud to obtain relief not only from the perpetrator but also from any-one [other than a bona fide purchaser] who benefited from the fraud, whether innocent or not.)

Disposition if Tom died intestate:

If Will #1 and Will #2 are both invalid (Will #1 because it was cancelled and Will #2 because it was the product of fraud), Tom's brothers and sisters (and the issue thereof by right of representation) would share his estate. The distribution is made "per capita at each generation," the division of the estate starting at the highest level at which there are living members. (UPC §2-106). The $200,000 would be divided into four parts (for Mary, Tom, Allen, and David). Thus, Mary, Tom, and Allen would each receive $50,000, and David's children would share the remaining $50,000.

Answer to Question 23

1. Disposition of Betty's estate:

We will assume that Betty's will was executed with the requisite testamentary formalities (the facts are silent as to this point).

Effect of simultaneous death:

Under UPC §2-702, a beneficiary is not deemed to have "survived" the testator unless the beneficiary lives at least 120 hours following the testator's death. Therefore, for purposes of Betty's will, Wilma did not "survive" Betty. Consequently, the $100,000 goes to "the natural persons who are beneficiaries of Wilma's last will and testament . . ."

Acts of independent significance:

Inasmuch as the provisions of Wilma's last will, not Betty's will, will control who takes Betty's gift of $100,000, the use of Wilma's will to dispose of Betty's probate property must be validated. At first blush, because Betty is referring to the provisions of another document, incorporation by reference might appear to be the most logical doctrine to use. But because Wilma executed a new will in 1992, two years after Betty executed her will, Wilma's 1992 will cannot be incorporated into Betty's will because it was not in existence at the time Betty executed her will. The beneficiaries under Wilma's will have to invoke events of independent significance.

Under the doctrine of acts of independent significance, the will can make reference to acts outside of the will, which can control either who takes under the will or how much a beneficiary takes as long as the referenced act has its own significance independent of its effect upon the testator's testamentary scheme. (UPC §2-512). Here, the referenced act in Betty's will that will control who takes the $100,000 is Wilma's act of executing her last will and testament. That act has its own significance apart from its effect on Betty's will—Wilma's will also controls who takes Wilma's estate. Thus the referenced act has its own significance independent of its effect on Betty's will. Acts of independence significance can be used to validate the provision in Betty's will letting Wilma's will control who takes the $100,000.

Takers under Wilma's will:

Although Wilma's will *may* exclude Bill (based on the codicil), Bill has several arguments to support his claim that he should be permitted to participate in the distribution under Wilma's will. First, Bill could point out that he was one of the three beneficiaries of Wilma's will *as that will was constituted when Betty's will was made* in 1990. Thus, Bill would claim that he is entitled to one-half of the $100,000 gift made by Betty.

Mary would argue, however, that the language in Betty's will should be read literally. Thus, Wilma's "last will and testament"(*i.e.*, the will as it stood at Wilma's death) designated only Mary as a "natural person" beneficiary.

Second, Bill can also argue that where there is an ambiguity in a will, the vague provision will ordinarily be construed in a manner that would effectuate the testator's probable intent. The term "last will and testament" could mean Wilma's will as it existed (1) in 1990 (when Betty's will was made), or (2) when Wilma died. However, Betty obviously wanted to bestow an additional gift upon those particular persons who were the objects of Wilma's bounty. Because Wilma finally decided to reward only Mary, not Bill, Betty would presumably have preferred to do the same.

Lastly, Bill can claim that Wilma's codicil should be ignored under dependent relative revocation (discussed below). Whether Bill will prevail on this argument depends on the evidence.

State University is not a natural person, and therefore would not share in the gift.

In summary, whether Bill is included as a beneficiary under Wilma's will depends on his dependent relative revocation argument. If he is successful, he and Mary will split Betty's gift of $100,000. If he is unsuccessful, Mary would receive the $100,000 bequest.

How should the balance of Betty's estate be distributed?

The balance of Betty's estate is left "to my children, share and share alike." Because both "children" predeceased Betty, the following issues arise: (1) does the gift fail completely, and (2) if not, how should the residue be distributed among Betty's descendants?

Does the gift fail?

The gift does not fail — it will be saved either by the antilapse provision, UPC §2-603(b), or by the Uniform Probate Code provision covering class gifts to family members where the form of distribution is not specified, UPC §2-708.

Alice will argue that the gift should be saved by the antilapse provision. There are two different provisions of the UPC antilapse doctrine that may apply, but the result here is the same under both provisions. First, assuming that the gift to Betty's "children" qualifies as a class gift (the gift is described in the aggregate; the beneficiaries are not named individually but collectively; the beneficiaries share a common characteristic and no one else with that characteristic is excluded; and it appears that her overall testamentary scheme was to treat her children equally), the applicable provision is §2-603(b)(2), which states: "Each deceased devisee's surviving descendants who are substituted for the deceased devisee take by representation the share to which the deceased devisee would have been entitled had the deceased devisee survived the testator." Notice that under this language, the first division is made at the level of the deceased devisee (because of the last clause,"had the deceased devisee survived the testator"). Applying that provision to the facts here, Betty's children, Charles and Jane, would have split the residue of her estate 50-50 ($200,000 each). Therefore, Charles's 50 percent would be split equally by his surviving descendants, George and Fred (so each would take 25 percent of Betty's residue or $100,000 each). Jane's 50 percent would pass to her surviving descendant, Alice, who would take the whole share (50 percent of Betty's residue, or $200,000).

In the alternative, there is a slight chance (but not a good chance) that a court might construe the gift to Betty's "children" not as a class gift but rather as a nonclass gift to a group of individuals: Betty's children. Under that construction, UPC §2-603(b)(1) would apply. It provides in pertinent part that if "the deceased devisee leaves surviving descendants, a substituted gift is created in the devisee's surviving descendants. They take by representation the property to which the devisee would have been entitled had the devisee survived the testator." Notice again that under this language, the first division is made at the level of the deceased devisee (because of the last clause "had the deceased devisee survived the testator"). Betty's children, Charles and Jane, would have split the residue of her estate 50-50 ($200,000 each). Charles's 50 percent would be split equally by George and Fred ($100,000 each), and Jane's 50 percent would pass to her surviving descendant, Alice (all $200,000). The result here is the same as under the class gift provision above.

George and Fred will argue, however, that UPC §2-708 should apply. Section 2-603(b)(2) of the UPC expressly excludes class gifts to "'issue,' 'descendants,' 'heirs of the body,' 'next of kin,' 'relatives,' or 'family,' or a class described by language of similar import." Class gifts of such nature are excluded from antilapse protection because they already express the idea of representation under which a deceased class member's descendants are already substituted for him or her pursuant to sections 2-708, 2-709, and 2-711 of the UPC. Under such provisions, if all of the class members are deceased, the property is distributed in the same manner as if the testator had died intestate. (UPC §2-708). Although the property passes to the surviving descendants of the deceased devisees, the first division of the property would be at the first generation where there is a living descendant. (UPC §2-709(b)). Under this approach, George, Fred, and Alice would each take one-third of the residue ($133,333.33 each). George and Fred are better off under this approach.

Alice's argument, however, should prevail. The antilapse provisions of the UPC apply to class gifts unless the class is composed of family members of the testator and the express language describing the class implicitly includes reference to multiple generations. Here, Betty's use of the word "children," while constituting a class of family members, does not constitute a reference that implicitly contains multiple generations. The antilapse provisions should apply (UPC §2-603(2) most likely), and Alice should take $200,000, George and Fred $100,000.

[There is a small chance that a court might construe the language "share and share alike" in Betty's devise to her "children" to mean that in the event the children should predecease Betty (and the antilapse doctrine should come into play), that Betty wanted the grandchildren to also "share and share alike." While this argument is plausible, the language is not clear enough to overcome the statutory scheme created by the express provisions of the UPC. It is unlikely that a court would find that the phrase "share and share alike" here is express enough to constitute the testator's intent to apply a different distribution scheme than the default scheme applied by the UPC provisions.]

2. Disposition of Wilma's estate:

We will assume that Wilma's will and codicil were executed with the requisite testamentary formalities (the facts are silent as to these points).

A factual mistake that induces a testator to make a particular disposition is ordinarily **not** a basis for invalidating a will. However, some states may deny probate of a will if (1) the mistake appears upon the face of the document, *and* (2) the alternative disposition that the testator would have desired is inferable from the will. Generally and historically, extrinsic evidence of an error is not admissible. Because the mistake here does not appear on the face of the will, the codicil deleting Bill because of his "ingratitude" is valid.

Dependent Relative Revocation (DRR): Bill will argue dependent relative revocation. Under the doctrine of dependent relative revocation (DRR), where the testator validly revokes his or her will because of a mistake, and the testator would not have revoked the will but for the mistake, the doctrine of DRR authorizes the court to ignore the valid revocation and probate the will. Where the valid revocation is by writing, invariably the courts require the writing to set forth the mistake and the mistake must be beyond the testator's knowledge. Here, Wilma validly revoked her will in writing when she executed the valid codicil. The revocation was based upon a mistake — she thought her son was being ungrateful. The codicil expressly recites the mistake, the mistake clearly caused Wilma to revoke the gift to Bill, and the mistake was beyond Wilma's personal knowledge. There appears little doubt that if Wilma had known of the mistake, she would not have revoked the gift to Bill. The key is if Bill can prove to the court's satisfaction that the revocation was based upon a mistake. If the "thank you" letter can be found, there is a good chance that Bill will be successful under DRR and the codicil will be ignored. On the other hand, if the claimed "thank you" letter cannot be found, the court may conclude that Bill's self-serving testimony that he wrote and mailed a "thank you" letter is insufficient to overcome the express terms of the codicil.

[If Bill is successful on his DRR claim, Betty's gift of $100,000 to the natural persons who are beneficiaries of Wilma's last will and testament would be split 50-50 between Mary and Bill.]

Was Wilma's gift to her children a class gift?

It is a bit unclear whether Wilma's gift to her children was (1) a class gift, or (2) a gift to each of her children, individually. If it was an individual gift to each child, then the codicil would simply cancel the gift to Bill. Assuming the clause in Wilma's will devising her estate between her children and State University were construed to constitute a residuary clause, under the modern trend and UPC approach the revoked gift would not fall to intestacy but rather would be distributed pro rata to the other beneficiaries in the residuary clause. Mary would take half of the gift to Bill, and State University would take the other half. (If the jurisdiction still followed the traditional common law "no residue of a residue" approach, Bill's one-fourth would fall to intestacy where he and Mary would split it (Bill would end up with one-eighth of Wilma's residuary estate in that event). This "individual gifts" interpretation is at least weakly buttressed by the codicil's statement, "I delete the gift to my son, Bill" (as opposed to, say, "I modify the gift to my children to include only Mary . . .").

If, however, "my children" was intended to set up a class gift (with the class being Wilma's children), Mary would take the entire one-half of the estate.

Unfortunately for Bill, the term "children" is ordinarily viewed as denoting a class gift (*i.e.*, Wilma did *not* state something like, to "Bill and Mary, my children"). This ordinary construction probably outweighs the small countervailing weight to be given to the "I delete the gift to my son Bill" language. Thus, if the court does not apply DRR, Mary and State University will probably share Wilma's estate equally; if the court does apply DRR, Mary and Bill will split 50 percent of Wilma's estate and State University will take the other 50 percent.

Answer to Question 24

1. Was the trust effectively terminated by Ball during his lifetime?

Under the traditional, and still majority rule, an *inter vivos* trust is ordinarily irrevocable unless the settlor expressly reserves the power to revoke the trust. The modern trend, as evidenced by the Uniform Trust Code (UTC), is to reverse the default rule and to presume that an *inter vivos* trust is revocable unless the trust expressly provides that it is irrevocable. (UTC § 602(a)). Here, Ball expressly reserved the power to revoke the trust so the *inter vivos* trust is revocable under either approach.

Thus, the question becomes whether that power was effectively exercised? Although the trust provided that this power was to be exercised only by a writing that was (1) signed by Ball, and (2) delivered to the trustee, Sam will argue that Ball's oral communication to the trustee was sufficient to accomplish a revocation. However, a power to revoke is ordinarily narrowly construed — it can be exercised only in strict accordance with its terms. See Restatement 2d of Trusts, §330 and Comment j thereto. Therefore, Ball's phone call probably was not effective to revoke the trust during his lifetime.

[The modern trend, as evidenced by the UTC and the Restatement Third of Trusts, is to make it easier for a settlor to revoke a revocable trust. The UTC and the Restatement Third of Trusts permit revocation even if the settlor only "substantially complied" with the method provided for in the will (UTC §602(c)(1); Restatement 3d. Trusts §63, Comment i). And they provide that if the method in the trust is not expressly made exclusive, as long as there is clear and convincing evidence that the settlor intended to revoke the trust, the trust is revoked. (UTC §602(c)(2); Restatement 3d. Trusts §63, Comment h). The facts here are unclear as to whether the trust "expressly" made the method of revocation exclusive. Assuming it did, the argument can be made that Ball's oral statement was substantial compliance. This is a tough argument to make, however, because substantial compliance in the wills context has been construed as requiring not only clear and convincing evidence of the person's intent but also as requiring sufficient steps to be taken towards the requirements that one could conclude that the actor has "substantially complied" with the requirements. Here, a mere telephone call arguably is not enough — but the equities of the facts (he died unexpectedly the very next day before being able to write the letter) may be enough for a court under the modern, intent-based approach.

The rest of the analysis of this question will assume that the trust was *not* validly revoked.]

2. Is the trustee obligated to pay Pearl past or future alimony out of the income and, to the extent necessary, the principal of the trust?

A spendthrift trust is one in which, by statute or the terms of the trust, the beneficiary is unable to voluntarily or involuntarily transfer his or her interest in the trust. Spendthrift trusts are valid in almost all jurisdictions, and bar creditors of a beneficiary from reaching his or her interest in the trust to satisfy a claim. However, in many states (and under the Second Restatement of Trusts) an ex-spouse or child of a trust beneficiary can override the spendthrift clause for the purpose of securing support. See Restatement 2d of Trusts, §157(a); see also Uniform Trust Code §503. In other states, there are statutes that protect the interest of beneficiaries in a spendthrift trust, but only to the extent necessary to secure their proper care, maintenance, and support.

Therefore, the trustee would probably be obliged to pay Pearl for past and future alimony out of the trust's income. Because Sam has only an *income interest* in the trust, and because even those states allowing the beneficiary's children or ex-spouse to reach the trust limit the invasion to the beneficiary's interest, the trustee cannot be compelled to pay Pearl out of the principal.

3. Do Sam and Pearl have the legal power to terminate the trust?

The interests in the trust are an equitable life estate in Sam and a contingent remainder in Carol, subject to open for other children who may be born to Sam. The contingency is that Carol must survive Sam (*i.e.*, Carol's interest does not vest until Sam's death).

The majority rule is that beneficiaries may compel termination of a trust if (1) all of the beneficiaries are legally competent and join in the request to terminate, and (2) termination will not defeat a material purpose of the settlor in creating the trust. See Restatement 3d of Trusts, §65; see also Uniform Trust Code §411.

The first problem is that all beneficiaries must not only consent but have legal capacity to consent. While Sam is competent, Carol is a minor and, therefore, incompetent. A guardian *ad litem* might be appointed to represent Carol's interests. Neither Sam nor Pearl, however, can be appointed as guardian *ad litem*, because they have interests that are adverse to Carol (*i.e.*, to the extent Sam or Pearl receive income from the trust, the trust res, which would ultimately be distributed to Carol, is diminished). Assuming that a guardian other than Sam or Pearl was appointed, valid consent could be given by all three present beneficiaries.

The second, bigger problem is the requirement that *all* beneficiaries consent. The class of Sam's children is open until Sam dies. Thus, the interests of potential, unborn children cannot be determined or adequately represented at this time. Therefore, the "consent by all beneficiaries" requirement probably cannot be satisfied at this time, and the trustee probably cannot be compelled to terminate the trust.

There is a last, probably fatal (depending on whether the court takes the traditional approach or the modern approach), difficulty: termination of the trust would violate a material purpose of the settlor in creating the trust. The choice of a spendthrift trust by Ball evidences his intention to provide a lifetime income interest to Sam, free from Sam's improvidence. This purpose would be defeated if the trust was revoked. See Restatement 2d of Trusts, §337, Comment l. (The Uniform Trust Code offers an *optional* provision that the presence of a spendthrift clause is not presumed to constitute a material purpose. Section 411(c) of the UTC and Comment e of the Restatement 3d of Trusts, §65, say that a spendthrift clause is not enough, by itself, to automatically conclude that termination of the trust would defeat a material purpose.)

Answer to Question 25

Which, if any, of the documents found in Taylor's safe-deposit box may be admitted to probate?

Because the typewritten document bears no signature and is not witnessed, it lacks the requisite testamentary formalities. Thus, this document, standing alone, is *not* a valid will and, therefore, may not be admitted to probate. The handwritten document, however, is signed and evidences a testamentary intent (*i.e.*, it states, "this is the way I want my property to go"). It would therefore arguably qualify as a holographic will.

The beneficiaries could then argue that the doctrine of *incorporation by reference* should be applied to provide the necessary material provisions (the "who gets what"). Under this doctrine, a writing that was in existence when a will was made and that is incorporated by the will becomes part of the will (even though the separate writing was not created with the requisite testamentary formalities). (UPC §2-510). Here, the typewritten document obviously preceded the handwritten one (because the latter makes reference to the former), and the handwritten one clearly refers to the typewritten one (by the language, "The attached is the way I want my property to go . . ."). Therefore, the typewritten document should be incorporated into the valid holographic writing.

In response to this argument, Doris (who would prefer Taylor to have died intestate) could contend that the incorporation by reference doctrine should not be applied here, because to do so would nullify the requirements for a valid holographic will. To be valid as a holographic will, a document must be signed by the testator, and contain "material provisions" in the testator's handwriting. (UPC §2-502(b)). Doris would argue that because the bulk of the provisions of the two documents taken together are typewritten, and the only one in handwriting is the residuary clause, the "material portions in the testator's handwriting" requirement is not satisfied if incorporation by reference is used.

However, the residuary clause is certainly a material provision, as is the clause incorporating the typewritten document into the holographic will. Therefore the material provisions arguably *are* in the testator's handwriting. Thus the court will probably hold that the handwritten note was a valid holographic will that successfully incorporated the typewriting.

Alternatively, the two documents together could be validated under UPC §2-503's "harmless error" provision, by which a document that is shown by "clear and convincing evidence" to have been intended by the decedent as his or her will can be admitted to probate even though it does not meet testamentary formalities.

In summary, the two documents found in Taylor's safe-deposit box probably together constitute her will.

What is the effect of the destruction of the home on the gift to Aunt Marie?

The devise of the home to Aunt Marie is a "specific" devise. Under the Uniform Probate Code, where the subject of a specific devise is no longer in the testator's probate estate, the specific devisee has the right to "any proceeds *unpaid* at death on fire or casualty insurance" on the specific devise. (UPC §2-606(a)(3)). This clause does not help Marie, however, because here the proceeds had already been paid to Taylor prior to her death.

Aunt Marie might be able to benefit from UPC §2-606(a)(6), which provides that "unless the facts and circumstances indicate that ademption of the devise was intended by the testator or ademption of the devise is consistent with the testator's manifested plan of distribution, [the specific devisee has the right to] the value of the specifically devised property to the extent the specifically devised property is not in the testator's estate at death and its value or replacement is not covered by [other paragraphs of §2-606(a)]." Because Taylor never conveyed the house to anyone else (which would have weakened Marie's case that Taylor wanted her to have the house's value), and because the house was "transformed" into insurance proceeds only very recently, through no voluntary act by Taylor, Marie will probably convince the court that under §2-606(a)(6), ademption should not apply and she should get the insurance proceeds (plus any other money needed to make up the value of the house before destruction).

What is the effect of the stock split upon the gift to Al of XYZ stock?

Under the UPC, a beneficiary of a gift of securities under a will is entitled to any accretion of that stock resulting from action initiated by the corporation as long as the testator owned matching shares of the stock at the time he or she executed the will. (UPC §2-605(a)(1)). Here, although the facts are a bit ambiguous, the natural inference is that Theresa owned 200 shares of XYZ stock when she executed the will. Assuming that is the case, Al would receive all 400 shares of XYZ stock.

What is the effect of the bequest of 20 shares of IBM to Frank?

A gift of stock when no such shares are owned by the testator is usually held to be a general bequest. This is especially true where, as here, the form of the gift is "100 shares of XYZ" rather than "*my* 100 shares of XYZ." Where the gift is found to be a general one, the executor is normally required to use the estate's cash to buy the specified property and pay it to the beneficiary. Thus, Taylor's executor must purchase 20 shares of IBM stock from the residuary portion of the estate and give those shares to Frank.

What is the effect of Sarah's death prior to Taylor?

A gift to a beneficiary who predeceases the testator ordinarily lapses. However, under the UPC's antilapse statute, if the beneficiary is the testator's grandparent, or a lineal descendant of the testator's grandparent, who died leaving descendants, the descendants take in place of the beneficiary as long as the testator does not express a contrary intent. (UPC §2-603(b)(1)). Although Sarah was a lineal descendant of Taylor's grandparents, she had no issue. Thus, the gift to Sarah will lapse. Where the lapsed gift is a gift of the complete residuary, the property involved passes by intestate succession.

Who takes the property passing by intestate succession?

Under the UPC, where the decedent is not survived by a spouse, the intestate succession is to the deceased's descendants. In this case, that would be Doris, Taylor's daughter. See UPC §2-103(1). The question is whether the language "to my daughter Doris — NOTHING" affects the intestate distribution.

At common law, a testator could not use words in the will to prevent a person from taking her intestate share of property not covered by the will — the only way to disinherit someone was to bequeath all property to others under the will. But UPC §2-101(b) changes this result: "A decedent by will may expressly exclude or limit the right of an individual or class to succeed to property of the decedent passing by intestate succession." The Comments to this provision make it clear that testamentary language stating that X gets nothing suffices, even if the language does not expressly mention intestacy. Thus the language "to my daughter Doris — NOTHING" is sufficient to disinherit Doris. Instead, the residuary will go by intestate succession to the next in line, Taylor's brother Ben. See UPC §2-103(3).

Multiple-Choice Questions

1. Rosa died intestate. She was survived by her husband Bill and their children, Tim and Tammy. Her net estate available for distribution is separate property of $200,000. How should her estate be distributed?

   A. $50,000 to Bill; $75,000 each to Tim and Tammy.

   B. $125,000 to Bill; $37,500 each to Tim and Tammy.

   C. $100,000 to Bill; $50,000 each to Tim and Tammy.

   D. $200,000 to Bill.

2. On July 1, Jim Williams died intestate from injuries received in an automobile accident. His wife Wanda died the next day from injuries received in the same accident. Jim and Wanda were survived by one child, Bob, and two grandchildren, who are the children of the deceased daughter of Jim and Wanda. Jim's net estate available for distribution is $200,000. How should Jim's estate be distributed?

   A. $125,000 to Wanda's estate; $37,500 to Bob; and $18,750 each to the two grandchildren.

   B. $125,000 to Wanda's estate; $25,000 each to Bob and the two grandchildren.

   C. Nothing to Wanda's estate; $100,000 to Bob; $50,000 each to the two grandchildren.

   D. Nothing to Wanda's estate; $66,666 each to Bob and the two grandchildren.

3. Leonard and Evelyn were married ten years ago. They had no issue. Five years ago, Leonard executed a will leaving everything to Evelyn, if she survived him; if she failed to survive him, the estate was to go to Leonard's mother and father in equal shares. Leonard's sister Sue and his brother-in-law Ken witnessed this will. Last year, Leonard and Evelyn were divorced. Leonard died recently without ever expressly revoking his will. He was survived by Evelyn, his sister Sue, and a brother, Ted. Both of Leonard's parents died in an automobile accident three months before his death. How should Leonard's estate be distributed?

   A. All to Evelyn.

   B. Half to Sue and half to Ted.

   C. All to Ted.

   D. All to Sue.

4. One year ago, Dan, an unmarried 19-year-old who was illiterate and without issue, asked his friend to write the following:

   > I, Dan Smith, do hereby declare that this is my will. I want everything I have to go to my mother. My brother, Les, is not to get anything I own.

X

Witnessed:

Ben Jones ... Thorp Curry

The mark "X" that appeared at the bottom of the will was made by Dan in the presence of Ben Jones and Thorp Curry, who signed as witnesses. Dan died, survived only by his brother, Les, and by his grandmother, Ann Smith. Dan's mother predeceased him by one week. How should Dan's estate be distributed?

A. All to the estate of Dan's mother.

B. All to Dan's grandmother, Ann Smith.

C. Half to Dan's grandmother, Ann Smith; half to Dan's brother, Les.

D. All to Les.

5. Ellen Morris recently died intestate. Her husband Ed had predeceased her. Ellen and Ed adopted a daughter, Lisa, and they also had a natural-born son, Tom. One year ago, Ellen gave Tom $10,000 to invest in a fast-food franchise, telling him orally that it would be deducted from his share of her estate, unless it was repaid prior to her death. A friend of Ellen was present when the conversation with Tom took place and is prepared to testify as to Ellen's statement. Ellen's net estate available for distribution is separate property of $150,000. How should her estate be distributed?

A. $75,000 each to Lisa and Tom.

B. $80,000 to Lisa; $70,000 to Tom.

C. $150,000 to Tom; nothing to Lisa.

D. $150,000 to Lisa; nothing to Tom.

6. Laura, a single woman, executed a valid will in 1990 leaving her entire estate to her mother. Two years later, she married Edward. Laura died two years after her marriage. She was survived by her mother and Edward. How should her estate be distributed?

A. To her mother.

B. To Edward.

C. The first $200,000, plus three-fourths of the balance of the estate to Edward; the remaining one-fourth to her mother.

D. The first $200,000, plus three-fourths of the balance of the estate to her mother; the remaining one-fourth to Edward.

7. John created an *inter vivos* trust naming his children as income beneficiaries and his grandchildren as beneficiaries of the corpus.

John's sister Ann then executed a valid will that contained the following bequest:

I leave the sum of $100,000 to those persons who are the income beneficiaries, at the date of my death, under an *inter vivos* trust created by my brother, John.

At Ann's death, John had two children, Adrian and Kimberly. Ann was survived by her mother Rita, by her brother John, and by a sister, Lisa. How should Ann's bequest be distributed?

A. To Adrian and Kimberly, in equal shares.

B. To the trustee of the trust created by John with the income to be paid to Adrian and Kimberly and, at their death, the $100,000 to be paid to John's grandchildren.

C. To Rita.

D. One-half to Rita; one-fourth each to John and Lisa.

8. Bill executed a valid will that contained the following bequest:

I leave the sum of $500,000 to those persons who are the residuary legatees under my mother's last will and testament.

At the time Bill executed his will, his mother had executed a valid will that left her residuary estate to Bill's uncles, Tom and Tim. Thereafter, she revoked that will and executed a new one, naming State University as her residuary legatee.

When Bill's mother died, her residuary estate was paid to State University. When Bill died, he was survived by his wife Ann, and by one child, Emily, both of whom were provided for in his will. Bill's residuary estate was left to the American Red Cross. To whom should the $500,000 bequest be paid?

A. To Tim and Tom, in equal shares.

B. To State University.

C. To the American Red Cross.

D. To Ann as intestate property.

9. Carly executed a valid will devising her condominium to her brother Tom, and the residue of her estate to Lighthouse University, her alma mater. Several years later, Carly bought a house and entered into an installment land sales contract with Buyer for the sale of the condominium.

Carly placed the $10,000 initially paid by Buyer as a down payment on the condominium in a separate savings account entitled

"Condominium Proceeds Account." All subsequent payments have also been deposited in that account.

At Carly's death, the account contained $15,000; the unpaid balance under the contract of sale was $100,000. Carly was survived by her parents and her brother Tom.

Assuming that neither the will nor the surrounding circumstances indicate anything further about how Carly would have wanted the account and the unpaid balance of the installment sales contract to be distributed, how should these two items be distributed?

A. The account to Lighthouse University and the balance of the installment sales contract to Tom.

B. The account and the balance of the installment sales contract to Tom.

C. The account to Carly's parents and the balance of the installment sales contract to Tom.

D. The account and the installment sales contract to Lighthouse University.

10. Kathy executed a valid will disposing of her entire estate. One of the dispositive provisions was as follows:

> I give all of my 100 shares of ABC Corp. stock to my good friend Edna. The remainder of my stocks, I give to my mother Kay.

At the time the will was executed, Kathy owned exactly 100 shares of ABC Corp. stock. Shortly after execution of the will, the stock of ABC Corp. split three for one, so that Kathy now owned 300 shares. One year later, ABC Corp. declared a 10 percent stock dividend so that Kathy received 30 additional shares of stock. XYZ Corp. then made a "two for one" tender offer for all of the outstanding shares of ABC Corp., and Kathy received 660 shares of XYZ Corp. in exchange for her ABC Corp. stock. One month later, she purchased 40 shares of XYZ Corp. for cash. Thus, at her death, Kathy owned 700 shares of XYZ Corp. stock. Kathy was survived by her son Bill (who was alive when her will was made), her friend Edna, and her mother Kay.

What disposition should be made of the XYZ Corp. stock owned by Kathy at her death, assuming that the residue of the estate is devised to Bill?

A. The XYZ Corp. stock should be distributed to Edna.

B. One hundred shares of the XYZ Corp. stock should be distributed to Edna and the balance should be distributed to Kay.

C. Six hundred and sixty shares of the XYZ Corp. stock should be distributed to Edna, and the balance should be distributed to Kay.

D. All of the XYZ Corp. stock should be distributed to Bill as part of the residue of the estate.

11. Larry, a widower, executed a valid will that included the following three bequests:

1. I give, devise and bequeath my home to my son Ron.
2. I give, devise and bequeath the sum of $100,000 to my daughter Carolyn.
3. I give, devise and bequeath my residuary estate, in equal shares, to my son Ron and my daughter Carolyn.

At the time that Larry executed his will, he owned a home worth approximately $100,000. One year later, he conveyed this home to his son Ron by a simple quitclaim deed that made no reference to the will. At the same time, he made a gift of $50,000 in cash to his daughter Carolyn. Shortly before his death, Larry purchased a home for $200,000, which he paid in cash. Larry recently died. His estate consists of $100,000 in cash and his home. He is survived only by Ron and Carolyn. How should his estate be distributed?

A. To Ron and Carolyn equally.

B. The home to Ron; the cash to Carolyn.

C. The home to Ron and Carolyn, equally; $100,000 in cash to Carolyn.

D. The home to Ron; $75,000 in cash to Carolyn; $25,000 in cash to Ron.

12. Bert died on July 1 from multiple gunshot wounds received in the course of a family dispute. His wife, Sofia, was convicted of murdering Bert. The conviction was affirmed on appeal. Bert left a will disposing of all of his property to Sofia, if she survived him. His estate consists of $100,000 in cash, a life insurance policy payable to Sofia as the primary beneficiary (with Bert's issue as secondary beneficiaries), and a home held in the name of Bert and Sofia as joint tenants with right of survivorship. Bert was survived by Sofia and three grandchildren. How should Bert's estate be distributed?

A. The cash should be distributed to Sofia pursuant to the will. The insurance proceeds should be payable to Sofia pursuant to the beneficiary designation, and the joint tenancy is extinguished leaving title in Sofia alone.

B. The cash should be distributed to the three grandchildren equally. The insurance proceeds should be payable to Sofia pursuant to the beneficiary designation, and the joint tenancy is extinguished leaving title in Sofia alone.

C. The cash should be distributed to the three grandchildren equally. The insurance proceeds should be payable to Sofia pursuant to the beneficiary designation, and the joint tenancy is severed with the half owned by Bert passing to the three grandchildren equally.

D. The cash and insurance proceeds should be distributed to the three grandchildren equally. The joint tenancy is severed and the half owned by Bert should pass to the three grandchildren equally.

13. Jamir executed a valid will disposing of his entire estate to his father. One year later, Jamir executed a second will that revoked the first will and disposed of his entire estate to his mother. Six months later, Jamir tore up the second will, stating to his friend Steve, who was present at the time, "This will take care of my estate so that my father gets it under the other will that I executed." At Jamir's death, the first will was found among his papers. He was survived by his parents and two sisters. How should Jamir's estate be distributed?

A. To his father under the first will.

B. To his mother under the second will.

C. Equally, to his mother and father by intestate succession.

D. Equally, to his sisters by intestate succession.

14. Suppose that, under the facts in Question 13, (1) Jamir's second will had provided that $1,000 was to go to his mother, with the remainder of his estate to go to his father, and (2) at the time he tore up the second will, Jamir said only, "Wills are for wimps." How should Jamir's estate be distributed?

A. To his father under the first will.

B. $1,000 to his mother, and the remainder to his father under the second will.

C. Equally, to his mother and father by intestate succession.

D. Equally, to his sisters by intestate succession.

15. Edgar validly executed Will #1, which disposed of his entire estate to his brother Tom. One year later, Edgar validly executed Will #2, which disposed of his entire estate to his sister Wilma. Will #2 did not contain a revocation clause. Six months later, Edgar validly executed Will #3, which expressly revoked Will #2 and left Edgar's estate to the American Red Cross. Will #3 made no reference to Will #1. One year later, Edgar revoked Will #3 by physical act. At Edgar's

Start Here

OK
Read answers
Review

Harmless clear
Error — evid. of Will
Con. evid. to
in fact

death, Will #1 was found among his important papers with an unsigned and undated note on it which read, "This is my will." Edgar was survived only by his brother Tom and his sister Wilma. How should Edgar's estate be distributed?

A. To Tom under the terms of Will #1.

B. To Wilma under the terms of Will #2.

C. To The American Red Cross under the terms of Will #3.

→ **D.** To Tom and Wilma by intestate succession.

16. Kristin executed a valid holographic will that contained the following provision:

> Within the next few days, I will prepare a list of some personal items that I wish to be given to the persons named thereon.

Several days later Kristin prepared and signed the following handwritten list:

> Mother's diamond ring — Laura; Dad's diamond stickpin — Larry; My ruby ring — Samantha

OK

Kristin died and was survived by her children, Rusty and Rosa. Under the will, the residue of her estate, after providing for Rusty and Rosa, was given to the American Red Cross. Laura, Larry, and Samantha are friends of Kristin. How should the rings and stickpin be distributed?

A. To Laura, Larry, and Samantha.

B. To the American Red Cross as part of the residuary.

C. To Rusty and Rosa, as part of their bequests under the will.

D. To Rusty and Rosa under intestate principles.

17. Cary executed a valid will that made, among others, the following bequest:

> I give, devise, and bequeath my grand piano to my sister Roberta, with the hope that she will realize her dream of becoming a concert pianist.

The residue clause of Cary's will reads as follows:

> I give, devise, and bequeath the remainder of my estate to my brothers and sisters, share and share alike.

At the time he executed the will, Cary had one brother, Ted, and three sisters, Roberta, Edwina, and Judy. Ted predeceased Cary and was survived by his wife and one child. Roberta predeceased Cary and was survived only by her parents. Edwina and Judy survived Cary. How should Cary's estate be distributed?

A. The piano and one-fourth of the residuary to Roberta's parents. One-fourth of the residuary each to Edwina, Judy, and Ted's child.

B. One-third of the estate each to Edwina, Judy, and Ted's child.

C. One-half of the estate each to Edwina and Judy.

D. One-sixth of the estate each to Ted's wife and child. One-third of the estate each to Edwina and Judy.

18. Tim executed a valid will disposing of his real estate to "my nephew Albert" and devising the remainder of his estate "to my brothers and sisters, share and share alike." Tim specifically disinherited his own children. When he died, Tim was survived by Albert, two brothers, one sister, and his (Tim's) three children. Albert has one child, a son. After Tim's death, Albert filed a valid, written statement renouncing his interest in Tim's estate. How should Tim's estate be distributed?

A. Real estate to Albert; residue to Tim's brothers and sister.

B. The entire estate to Tim's brothers and sister.

C. The entire estate to Tim's children.

D. The real estate to Albert's son; residue to Tim's two brothers and sister.

19. Tom executed a valid will disposing of "all my real estate to my sister Joan" and "the rest, residue, and remainder of my estate to my brother Bill." The will also contained a provision stating that "My executor is hereby directed to pay all of my just debts." At the time Tom executed his will, he owned Blackacre, which was worth $100,000, and stock worth $100,000. One year before his death, Tom borrowed $90,000 from ABC Bank and gave the bank a mortgage on Blackacre to secure payment of the debt. He then lost all of the borrowed money gambling in Las Vegas. Blackacre is now worth $125,000 and the unpaid mortgage is still $90,000. The stock is worth $300,000. How should Tom's estate be distributed?

A. Blackacre, encumbered by the mortgage, should be distributed to Joan; the stock should be distributed to Bill.

B. Blackacre should be distributed to Joan free and clear of the debt; the stock remaining after payment of the debt should be distributed to Bill.

C. Blackacre and $90,000 worth of stock should be distributed to Joan; the remainder of the stock should be distributed to Bill.

D. Because Tom's testamentary scheme was to treat Joan and Bill equally, Blackacre and the stock should be sold, the debt to ABC Bank paid and the remainder distributed equally to Joan and Bill.

20. John and Betty met in Hawaii, where both were vacationing. They spent much of their time together. After they returned to their homes, Betty discovered that she was pregnant. After her child, Jennifer, was born, Betty, who had never married John, sued John to establish paternity. Although John denied that Jennifer was his child, the jury found by clear and convincing evidence that John was the father. The court entered judgment accordingly. Thereafter, John refused to acknowledge Jennifer as his child or to spend any time with her, but did pay the support ordered by the court. When John died, his will (executed prior to the birth of Jennifer) left his entire estate to ABC Charity. John was survived by Betty, Jennifer, and his parents. How should his estate be distributed?

A. To Jennifer.

B. To ABC Charity.

C. Half to Jennifer, and the remainder to ABC Charity.

D. Half to Jennifer, and the remainder to John's parents, in equal shares.

21. Suppose that, in Question 20, Jennifer was the one who died, and that she was survived by her mother Betty, her father John, and two sisters. Assume further that Betty married John after the paternity suit described in Question 20 (but he continued to refuse to acknowledge Jennifer as his child), and the two sisters were conceived by Betty during her marriage to John. If Jennifer died without a will, how should her estate be distributed?

A. To John and Betty, equally.

B. To Betty.

C. One-half to Betty; the other one-half to Jennifer's sisters.

D. To Jennifer's sisters in equal shares.

22. Jane had two children, Will and Mark, by her first marriage. After the death of her first husband, she remarried and had one child, Kane, by her second husband, Steve. Jane then died. One year later, Mark died intestate. Mark was survived only by Will and Kane. Steve is still alive. How should Mark's estate be distributed?

A. To Will.

B. To Will and Kane, in equal shares.

C. One-third each to Steve, Will, and Kane.

D. One-half to Steve; one-fourth each to Will and Kane.

23. Ted died in an automobile accident. He was survived by his wife Judy and their daughter Lisa. Judy has a child, Amy, by reason of an earlier marriage. Shortly after Ted's death, Judy discovered that she was two months pregnant. Judy gave birth to a son, Ted Jr., seven months after Ted's death. Assuming that Ted died intestate, how should his estate be distributed?

A. The first $150,000, plus one-half of the balance of the intestate estate to Judy; the remaining one-half to Lisa.

B. The first $150,000, plus one-half of the balance of the intestate estate to Judy; the remaining one-half to be divided between Lisa and Ted Jr., equally.

C. One-half of the intestate estate to Judy; the remaining one-half to be divided between Lisa and Ted Jr., equally.

D. One-half of the intestate estate to Judy; the remaining one-half to Lisa.

24. Suppose that, in Question 23, Lisa and Amy were Ted's children by reason of an earlier marriage, and that only Ted Jr. was the child of both Ted and Judy. How should Ted's estate be distributed?

A. The first $100,000, plus one-half of the balance of the intestate estate to Judy; the remaining one-half to be divided among Lisa, Amy, and Ted Jr., equally.

B. The first $100,000, plus one-half of the balance of the intestate estate to Judy; the remaining one-half to be divided between Lisa and Amy, equally.

C. One-half of the intestate estate to Judy; the remaining one-half to be divided among Lisa, Amy, and Ted Jr., equally.

D. One-half of the intestate estate to Judy; the remaining one-half to be divided between Lisa and Amy, equally.

25. When Lisa was seven years old, her parents were killed in an automobile accident. The night of the accident, her aunt and uncle, Harvey and Ann, arrived and told Lisa that she was going to go live with them and "be our little girl." Several years later, they told Lisa, "You're going to court with us, so that you can be our little girl

forever." Harvey and Ann held Lisa out as their daughter. She participated in every way as a member of their family. Harvey had a son, Bob, by reason of a previous marriage. When Harvey died intestate, Ann claimed his entire estate. After consulting an attorney, Lisa found out that, while Harvey and Ann had obtained legal custody of her, there had been no formal adoption. Harvey was survived by Ann, Lisa, Bob, and Harvey's parents. How should his estate be distributed?

A. The first $200,000, plus three-quarters of the balance of the estate to Ann; the remaining one-quarter of the estate to Harvey's parents.

B. The first $100,000, plus one-half of the balance of the intestate estate to Ann; the remaining one-half to be divided between Bob and Lisa, equally.

C. One-half of the intestate estate to Ann; the remaining one-half to be divided between Bob and Lisa, equally.

D. The entire intestate estate to Ann.

26. Patricia was preparing for a trip to the Caribbean. She wrote the following and signed it in her own handwriting:

> I am getting ready to take a cruise. If I don't return from the cruise, I want my entire estate to go to the County Art Museum.
>
> /s/ Patricia

Patricia took the cruise and returned. One month later, she died. She was survived by her mother and a brother. How should her estate be distributed?

A. To her mother, because the holographic will was not dated.

B. To her mother and brother, equally.

C. To the County Art Museum.

D. One-half each to the County Art Museum and her mother.

27. Arnold and his father, Clay, orally agreed that Clay could live in Arnold's house, that Arnold would provide Clay with food and clothing, and that Clay would make a will leaving his entire estate to Arnold at Clay's death. When Clay died, he left a valid will that (1) made no reference to the agreement with Arnold, and (2) disposed of his entire estate to Anne. How should Clay's estate be distributed, assuming that (1) Clay was survived by Arnold and Arnold's brother, Tom, and (2) Anne also wishes to take the estate?

A. Anne.

B. Arnold.

C. Arnold and Tom, equally.

D. One-half to Anne and one-half to Arnold and Tom, equally.

28. Suppose that, in Question 27, Arnold and Clay had put their agreement in writing and that Clay moved into Arnold's home and has lived there until the present. (For this question only, assume that Clay is still alive.) Several years ago, after signing the agreement, Clay transferred one-half of his assets to Tom. What remedy, if any, can Arnold obtain against Clay or Tom while Clay is still alive?

A. Specific performance to require Tom to transfer the assets to Arnold.

B. Anticipatory breach of the agreement, with damages paid to Arnold.

C. An injunction preventing Clay from transferring his assets and requiring Tom to reconvey the assets to Clay.

D. Anticipatory breach of the agreement, with a constructive trust being imposed upon the assets transferred to Tom.

29. Two years before her death, Toni, a widow, executed and took home with her a valid will in which she gave her entire estate to her church, First Baptist. At her death, the will could not be found. Her attorney, Agnes, has a conformed copy of the will and can testify that she had a conversation with Toni the week before her death in which Toni affirmed that her will, as executed, still represented her testamentary wishes. Toni was survived by her two children, Rob and Adam, both of whom were born prior to the making of the will, and her parents. To whom is it likely that the estate will be distributed?

A. To the First Baptist Church.

B. Half of the estate to the First Baptist Church; half to Rob and Adam, equally.

C. To Rob and Adam.

D. Half of the estate to Toni's parents; half to Rob and Adam, equally.

30. Parker, a widower, executed a valid will that disposed of his entire estate to "the children of my best friend, Sam Riley." At the time the will was executed and at Parker's death, Sam Riley had no children. After Parker's death, Sam had three children, Bob, Sally, and Ellen. Parker was survived by his sister, Ann, and his parents. To whom should Parker's estate be distributed?

A. To Bob, as Sam's first-born child.

B. To Bob, Sally and Ellen, at Sam's death.

C. To Ann.

D. To Parker's parents.

31. Suppose that, in Question 30, the gift was "to the children of my best friend, Sam Riley" and that at the time Parker died, (1) Bob, Sam's eldest child, was already alive, and (2) Sally and Ellen were born after Parker's death. To whom should Parker's estate be distributed?

A. To Bob.

B. To Bob, Sally, and Ellen.

C. To Ann.

D. To Parker's parents.

32. Suppose that, in Question 30, the gift was "to the children of my best friend, Sam Riley, who reach the age of 25." When Parker died, Bob, the eldest child, was 15. Prior to Bob's reaching age 25, Ellen was born. Sally was born after Bob reached age 25. How should Parker's estate be distributed?

A. To Bob.

B. One-half each to be held for Bob and Ellen until they reach age 25, and then paid to them; but if either dies before reaching age 25, remainder to the one who survives.

C. One-third to Bob; remainder to be held until Ellen and Sally reach age 25, and then distributed to them equally. If they fail to reach age 25, the remainder to be split among the other members of the class who reach age 25.

D. One-third to Bob, Ellen and Sally, immediately.

33. Suppose that, in Question 30, the only gift was "$10,000 each to the children of my best friend, Sam Riley" and that at the time Parker died, Sam Riley had no children. Bob, Sally, and Ellen were born after Parker's death. To whom should Parker's estate be distributed (assuming that the will made no other gifts)?

A. $10,000 to Bob; one-half of the remainder to Ann; the balance to Parker's parents.

B. $10,000 each to Bob, Sally, and Ellen; the balance to Parker's parents.

C. To Parker's parents.

D. To Ann, entirely.

34. Edward and Mary validly executed joint and reciprocal wills in which each disposed of his or her property to the survivor; upon the death of the survivor, all property was to go to their children. Mary died, her will was probated and her property was distributed to Edward. Thereafter, Edward executed another valid will, leaving all of his property to his friend, Ann. When Edward died, he was survived by one child, Tim, and by two grandchildren who were the issue of Lisa, the predeceased daughter of Edward and Mary. How should Edward's estate be distributed?

   A. One-half to Tim, and one-fourth each to the grandchildren pursuant to Edward's original will.

   B. One-half to Tim, and one-fourth each to the grandchildren by intestate succession.

   C. All to Tim by intestate succession.

   D. All to Ann.

35. Bill executed a last will and testament. It made two bequests, as follows:

   1. $10,000 to my son, Jim.
   2. All the rest, residue and remainder of my estate to my daughter, Elizabeth.

The will also explicitly revoked a prior valid will that had expressly disinherited Jim and left everything to Elizabeth. Bill was survived by his two children (Jim and Elizabeth) and his parents. It is admitted by all parties that Bill's first will was valid. Assuming that there are grounds for opposing the probate of Bill's second will, who may contest probate of the will?

   A. Jim only.

   B. Jim or Elizabeth.

   C. Jim or Elizabeth or Bill's parents.

   D. Elizabeth only.

36. John and Beth Askew were married for many years. During the course of their marriage, a son, Clay, was born. Clay was the only child John ever had. Although he had no rational basis for his suspicions, John believed that Clay was conceived as the result of a relationship between Beth and another man. Although Beth denied this, John persisted in his belief. Several tests showed that Clay had the same blood type as John. Beth died when Clay was four. When

Clay was six, John executed a holographic will (the only will he ever made), reading as follows:

> My wife has betrayed me. She gave birth to a child by another man. The child is not mine, although I have provided a home for him. I therefore disinherit Clay. I leave everything to my aunt, Matilda Askew.
>
> /s/John Askew

John died without changing his belief or the will. Should the will be admitted to probate?

A. No, if John was suffering from an insane delusion.

B. Yes, if the will was validly executed.

C. No, because John had been unduly influenced in his beliefs.

D. Yes, because John has the absolute right to disinherit his son.

37. Assume the same facts described in Question 36, except that (1) there was a rational basis for John's belief that Clay was the product of an illicit relationship, and (2) the final sentence of John's holographic will (leaving everything to Aunt Matilda) was omitted.

John died without changing (1) his belief that Clay was the product of an illicit relationship, or (2) the purported will. Should the document be admitted to probate?

A. No, because the purported will is not a valid testamentary document.

B. No, because a natural father cannot disinherit his son.

C. Yes, because the writing constitutes a valid holographic will.

D. No, because John's belief about Clay's parentage was mistaken, although rational.

38. Fred Jones, an attorney, had represented Ellen Morris for many years. Ellen requested that Jones prepare a will for her and that a bequest of $10,000 to Jones be included in the will. Jones, sensing that it would be improper for him to draw a will in which he was a legatee, asked his associate Michael Fox to prepare the will. Fox did so and returned the will to Jones for execution by Ellen. When Ellen died, Jones filed an application to probate the will. Assuming that Ellen's son, Thad, who received the residue of the estate, wishes to contest the will, upon what basis is he most likely to be successful?

A. Undue influence.

B. Fraud.

C. Lack of testamentary capacity.

D. Violation of the Rules of Professional Conduct applicable to lawyers.

39. Robin Thomas was married to Hal Thomas. One month after they agreed to a "trial" separation, Robin met Craig Jones (a very wealthy businessman) at a bar in another city. When Craig proposed to Robin two months later, Robin accepted. When Robin and Craig applied for a marriage license, Robin represented that she was single. One week after they were married, Craig signed a valid will that left one-half of his estate to "My beloved wife, Robin," and one-half to his Aunt Martha. In his will, Craig explicitly stated that although he had two children from a previous marriage, he wanted them to receive nothing (because they had sided with his previous wife). Aunt Martha, however, had stood by him.

Craig died one month later, survived by Robin, Aunt Martha, and his two children. His children requested that the will be denied probate. What action is the court likely to take?

A. Admit the will to probate, because Craig can leave his estate to whomever he wishes.

B. Admit the will to probate, but impose a constructive trust upon Robin's share in favor of Aunt Martha.

C. Deny the will to probate, because it was procured by fraud.

D. Deny the will to probate, because Craig was mistaken as to Robin's marital status.

40. John executed a will giving his friend, Ted, a power of appointment over the residue of John's estate. The residuary clause reads as follows:

I give, devise, and bequeath the rest, residue, and remainder of my estate to such person or persons as my friend, Ted, may appoint either by deed during Ted's lifetime or by his will; if my friend, Ted, does not exercise this power of appointment, at Ted's death the residue of my estate shall be distributed to my heirs.

The power of appointment given to Ted is classified as a:

A. General power presently exercisable.

B. Special power presently exercisable.

C. General testamentary power.

D. Special testamentary power.

41. Suppose that, in Question 40, Ted fails to exercise the power during his life, but executes a will that disposes of his property as follows:

I give $10,000 to my only son, Bill. All the rest, residue, and remainder of my estate, I give to my wife, Ann.

How should the property over which Ted was given a power of appointment under John's will be distributed?

A. To Ann.

B. The first $50,000, plus one-half of the balance to Ann; the remainder to Bill.

C. To John's heirs.

D. To Ted's heirs.

42. Suppose that, in Question 40, at the time he executed his will, John had three children, Art, Bob, and Charles. Art died before John without a spouse or issue. Art left a will devising all his property to the American Red Cross. At John's death, Bob and Charles were living; however, both predeceased Ted. Bob left no issue, but was survived by his wife, Sally, to whom he left his entire estate by will. Charles was survived by his wife, Marcy, to whom he left his entire estate by will, and by one child, Ned.

Assuming that Ted failed to exercise the power of appointment (during his lifetime or by his will), how should the property be distributed?

A. One-third to the American Red Cross; one-third to Sally; one-third to Marcy.

B. One-half to Sally; one-half to Marcy.

C. One-half to Marcy; one-half to Ned.

D. All to Ned.

43. Suppose that, in Question 40, Ted exercised the power of appointment by his will, and that the main provision read as follows:

I give, devise, and bequeath all of my property, including any property over which I hold a power of appointment, as follows:

1. The property over which I hold a power of appointment to John's children, Art, Bob, and Charles, in equal shares; and
2. The rest, residue and remainder of my property I give to my wife, Ann.

Suppose further that (1) all of John's children predeceased Ted, and (2) none of them left surviving spouses or issue. Ted was survived by

Ann and Bill, his son by reason of a previous marriage. John's only heirs were his two brothers. How should the property that was subject to Ted's power be distributed?

A. To John's brothers, in equal shares.

B. To Ann.

C. The first $100,000, plus one-half of the balance, to Ann; the remainder to Bill.

D. To Bill.

Questions 44–47 are based upon the following fact situation:

Ten years ago, T purchased 300 shares of the stock of Rex, Inc., a family corporation. Nine years ago, T executed a valid will, which provided as follows:

1. I give 300 shares of Rex, Inc., stock and $1,000 to my brother-in-law Ben.
2. I give the sum of $15,000 to my son Mike.
3. I give the residue of my estate to my wife Doris.

Liz, T's second child (by Doris), was born after T executed his will and on the very day T was seriously injured in a heated altercation with his brother-in-law, Ben. T subsequently sold his Rex stock for $15,000 and invested the proceeds in municipal bonds.

Doris obtained a valid final judgment of divorce from T nine months ago. T married Kay six months ago.

One week ago, T died as a result of the injuries he received in the altercation with Ben. Ben was arrested for voluntary manslaughter, tried, and convicted.

T died without revising his will. T's estate, entirely his separate property, consisted of the municipal bonds now worth $20,000 and cash of $110,000 on deposit at City Bank. T is survived by Ben, Mike, Liz, Kay, and Doris.

44. How much of T's estate will Doris receive?

    A. One-half.

    B. The entire estate, less the gifts to Mike and Ben.

    C. Nothing.

    D. None of the above.

45. How much of T's estate will Kay receive?

    A. One-half.

    B. The entire estate, less the gifts to Mike and Ben.

    C. Nothing.

    D. None of the above.

46. How much of T's estate will Liz receive?

    A. One-fourth.

    B. One-third.

    C. Nothing.

    D. None of the above.

47. How much of T's estate will Ben receive?

    A. Nothing, because the gifts to Ben were adeemed by extinction.

    B. Nothing, because he killed T.

    C. The value of the stock when it was sold, plus $1,000.

    D. $21,000 (the value of the bonds at T's death, plus $1,000).

48. Ralph devised property to Sam in trust to pay the income to Linda for life, and on Linda's death to distribute the principal to such of Linda's issue as Linda should appoint by will. If Linda did not exercise the power of appointment, at Linda's death Sam was to distribute the principal to Linda's then living issue, the issue to take per stirpes.

Prior to Linda's death, she delivered a written letter to Sam stating that she released all rights that she might have as donee of the power of appointment that Ralph had given to her. Thereafter, Linda executed a will that disposed of all the property she owned, including any property "over which I hold a power of appointment," to her son Adam. When Linda died, she was survived by two children, Adam and Ron, and by a grandchild, Martha, the issue of a predeceased daughter, Karen. How should Sam distribute that part of Ralph's property subject to appointment?

    A. To Adam, Ron, and Martha, in equal shares.

    B. To Adam.

    C. To Adam and Ron, in equal shares.

    D. To Ralph's heirs.

49. Suppose that, in Question 48, prior to Linda's death, she entered into a contract with Adam, one of her children. The terms of the agreement were that, in exchange for the payment of $10,000 to Linda by Adam, Linda agreed to exercise the power of appointment in favor of Adam. Adam paid the $10,000. However, at Linda's death, her will provided for exercise of the power in favor of Adam, Ron, and Martha, equally. How should the court distribute the property?

A. To Adam, pursuant to the contract.

B. To Adam and Ron, equally, as Linda's children.

C. To Adam, Ron, and Martha, pursuant to the exercise of the power.

D. To Adam, Ron, and Martha, as takers in default of the power.

50. Alice transferred $1,000,000 to her brother Jim; the transfer was carried out without any statement of conditions by Alice. Two weeks later, Alice told Jim, "That $1,000,000 I gave you is to be held by you for the benefit of all of my children. If you don't agree, I want it all back." Jim responded by telling Alice, "You gave me that money, I'll use it the way you want me to." Alice later heard that Jim had told other people that he wasn't going to give Alice's children a penny. Alice filed suit against Jim to recover the money, but died before the case came to trial. Assume that:

(1) Alice died survived by two children, Bill and Penny, and

(2) Alice's will left everything to Bill and Penny.

How should the court order distribution of the money?

A. To Jim, outright.

B. To Penny, outright.

C. To Jim in trust for Bill and Penny.

D. To Bill and Penny, outright.

51. Stephanie executed a will that gave all her property to her son Rick. Thereafter, she wrote and delivered to her brother, Sam, a letter that read as follows:

Dear Sam: As you know, I am leaving for Europe in two weeks. When I return, it is my intent that my farm, on which you now reside, shall be placed in trust for the benefit of your children. I have given the rest of my estate to Rick. All my love, Stephanie.

Stephanie died while on her European trip. She was survived by Sam, Sam's daughter Tina, Stephanie's mother Ann, and Rick. How should the court dispose of the farm?

A. Because a valid trust was created upon delivery of the letter to Sam, the farm should be distributed to Sam as trustee for Tina.

B. No valid trust was created, and so the farm should be distributed to Rick pursuant to the will.

C. Although no valid trust was created at the time of delivery of the letter, a trust came into being upon Stephanie's death, and so the property should be distributed to Sam as trustee for Tina.

D. No valid trust was created, and so the farm should be distributed to Rick under intestacy principles.

52. Ralph gave property to Sam in trust. Sam was directed to pay the income to Linda for life, and on Linda's death to distribute the principal to any one or more of Linda's issue as Linda should appoint by her will. If Linda did not exercise the power of appointment, at Linda's death Sam was to distribute the principal to Linda's then living issue, by right of representation. The power of appointment bestowed upon Linda is:

A. A general power, presently exercisable.

B. A general testamentary power.

C. A special power, presently exercisable.

D. A special testamentary power.

53. Christina executed a valid will that made the following bequest:

I give, devise, and bequeath to my friend John, as trustee, the sum of $15,000. I direct that he invest this money and, once each year, use the income therefrom to throw a party for the persons who are my three best friends at the time of my death.

At Christina's death, John advised the court that he was willing to carry out the terms of the trust. He also stated that it was unclear who Christina's three best friends were at the time of her death, but that if he had to guess, he'd say that they were Ann, Barbara, and Cary. The residue of Christina's estate was bequeathed to her mother. How should the court distribute Christina's estate?

A. Fifteen thousand dollars to John, as trustee to be used for the purpose stated in the will; remainder of the estate to Christina's mother.

B. Fifteen thousand dollars to John, as trustee of a trust for *all* of Christina's friends; remainder of the estate to Christina's mother.

C. Five thousand dollars each to Ann, Barbara, and Cary; remainder of the estate to Christina's mother.

D. All to Christina's mother.

54. T was feeling very weak. After T signed her typed will in front of X and Y, Y left the room to obtain a glass of water for T. While Y was away, X signed the will as a witness. When Y returned, she signed the will in front of X and T. Which of the following statements is correct?

A. T has a valid holographic will.

B. T has a valid formal will.

C. T's will is invalid, because the witnesses did not sign in each other's presence.

D. T's will is invalid, if the will was undated.

55. T was in a hospital, feeling increasingly weak. T announced to X and Y that the document that he was about to ask them to witness was a will. After T signed the typewritten will, he began to cough continuously. Dr. Debbie rushed into T's hospital room and asked X and Y to leave. They left the room and signed T's will as witnesses in the hospital lobby. Which of the following statements is correct?

A. T has a valid holographic will.

B. T has a valid formal will.

C. T's will is not valid, because the witnesses did not sign in his presence.

D. T's will is not valid, if X and Y did not actually read the document.

56. Bruce made the following bequest in his will:

> I give, devise, and bequeath the sum of $10,000 to my friend, Selma, as trustee, the income and such portion of the corpus as may be necessary to be used by her to provide care and shelter for my dog, Rusty.

The remainder of Bruce's property was bequeathed to the Humane Society in the city where Bruce lived. At Bruce's death, Selma declared that she was willing to carry out the terms of Bruce's trust. How would Bruce's estate be distributed in most U.S. jurisdictions under traditional trust principles?

A. Ten thousand dollars to Selma to be held in trust for Rusty; the remainder to the Humane Society.

B. Ten thousand dollars to Selma free of trust; the remainder to the Humane Society.

C. All to the Humane Society.

D. None of the above.

57. Elaine made the following bequest in her will:

> I give, devise, and bequeath the sum of $1,000,000 to my husband Will, if he survives me, as trustee, the income from such trust to be paid to my husband so long as he remains unmarried. In the event that my husband shall remarry, or upon his death, whichever shall first occur, I appoint my brother Tom, as successor trustee, to pay the income to my children, so

long as they remain unmarried. In the event they marry, or upon their deaths, whichever first occurs, to pay all accrued income and principal to my alma mater, State College.

Elaine was survived by her husband Will, her brother Tom, and her children, Bob and Ellen. Will, Bob, and Ellen have petitioned the court to strike the conditions that they not marry and distribute the property in other respects in accordance with the trust. How should the court distribute Elaine's estate?

A. The court should strike the conditions as to all beneficiaries and distribute $1,000,000 to Will, as trustee.

B. The court should strike the conditions as to Will, but not as to Bob and Ellen and distribute $1,000,000 to Will, as trustee.

C. The court should strike the conditions as to Bob and Ellen, but not as to Will, and distribute $1,000,000 to Will as trustee.

D. The court should declare the trust invalid and distribute the property pursuant to the residuary clause of the will, or by intestate succession, whichever is appropriate.

58. Judith made an unconditional bequest of $200,000 in her will to her brother Earl. The bequest was preceded by a conversation between Judith and Earl, in which Earl agreed to hold the property in trust for Judith's friend Grace. The residue of Judith's estate was bequeathed to her "brothers and sisters, in equal shares." At Judith's death, Earl advised Grace, as well as his brothers and sisters, that the $200,000 was his, outright. Judith was survived by Grace, Earl, one other brother and two sisters. What of the following should guide the court in regard to the bequest to Earl?

A. The oral agreement to hold the funds in trust is enforceable by Grace as an express trust.

B. The oral agreement to hold the funds in trust is unenforceable as an express trust, but the court will impose a constructive trust in favor of Grace.

C. The oral agreement to hold the funds in trust is unenforceable as an express trust, but the court will impose a resulting trust, and the property will pass under the residuary clause to Judith's brothers and sisters.

D. The bequest passes to Earl alone.

59. Suppose that, in Question 58, the bequest by Judith in her will was to "my brother, Earl, in trust for someone mentioned to him during my lifetime." If Earl refuses to perform the trust, what action should the court take in regard to the bequest to Earl?

A. The oral agreement to hold the property in trust may be enforced as an express trust by Grace.

B. The oral agreement to hold the property in trust may be enforced as a constructive trust by Grace.

C. The oral agreement to hold the property in trust may be enforced as a resulting trust by Judith's brothers and sisters.

D. The bequest passes to Earl, outright.

60. Amy Jones deposited $10,000 in a bank account at First Bank. The account was created as "Amy Jones, Trustee for Karen Smith." Karen Smith is Amy's friend. Amy used this account as her checking account, depositing her monthly paychecks into the account and paying her bills from it. Karen Smith had no knowledge of the account. After creating this account, Amy executed a will in which she left all of her property to her brother, Ed Jones. Amy recently died and was survived by her parents, her friend Karen, and her brothers, Ed and Warren Jones. The balance in the account at Amy's death was $35,000. How should the bank account be distributed?

A. To Karen Smith.

B. To Ed Jones.

C. To Karen, Ed, and Warren, in equal shares.

D. To Amy's parents, in equal shares.

61. Suppose that, in Question 60, Karen Smith predeceased Amy Jones, and that (1) Amy never changed the designation on the bank account, and (2) Karen was survived by her daughter, LeeAnn, and her husband Mike Smith. Suppose further that Karen, after the birth of LeeAnn, executed a valid will disposing of all of her property to her husband Mike. How should the bank account be distributed?

A. To Mike Smith.

B. To LeeAnn.

C. To Ed Jones.

D. To Amy's parents, in equal shares.

62. Able created a revocable *inter vivos* trust with Blackacre (a farm) as the trust res, Baker as the trustee, and Carl as the beneficiary. Baker, as trustee, was directed to pay the income from the trust (*i.e.*, profits from operation of the farm) to Carl, until Carl reached age 45, and then to deed Blackacre to Carl in fee simple absolute. The trust

contained no statement regarding Carl's right to alienate his interest in the trust. Carl, in order to satisfy a debt he owed to Sam, made a written assignment of "all my right, title, and interest in Blackacre" to Sam. Under these circumstances:

A. Sam acquires no interest in Blackacre.

B. Sam acquires a right to the income interest only.

C. Sam may require the trust to terminate, and Baker to convey Blackacre to him (because Carl no longer owns any interest in the property).

D. Sam may require the trustee to pay the income to him until Carl reaches age 45, and then to deed Blackacre to him when Carl reaches age 45.

63. Suppose that, in Question 62, subsequent to the assignment to Sam, (1) Carl assigned his interest in the trust to Ted, and, (2) Ted was the first to notify Baker of the assignment. As between Sam and Ted, who has the greater right?

A. Sam, because the first assignment has priority.

B. Sam, but only if Sam gave present consideration in exchange for the transfer.

C. Ted, because the first assignee to notify the trustee of his assignment prevails.

D. Ted, if he gave present consideration for the transfer.

64. Lucille is the life income beneficiary of a trust created by her mother. The trust res includes Blackacre. Lucille receives quarterly distributions of income from the trust. At her death, the remainder interest in the trust will go to her children. However, Lucille is presently unmarried and has no children. Caleb obtained a final judgment against Lucille arising out of an automobile accident in which Caleb was injured. The marshal has delivered a writ of execution to the trustee of Lucille's trust. Under these circumstances:

A. The writ of execution, a legal remedy, is ineffective against an equitable interest in the trust.

B. The marshal may order Blackacre sold at public sale in satisfaction of Caleb's judgment. The remainder of the proceeds, if any, would then be returned to the trustee.

C. The trustee must pay the income to the marshal for application against the judgment until it is fully satisfied or Lucille dies, whichever occurs first.

D. The trustee must deed Blackacre to Caleb, outright.

65. Alice created a trust in her will that provides that the income shall be paid to her children during their lifetimes, and upon the death of her last child, the principal shall be divided among her grandchildren. The trust contains the following clause:

> My children shall not, by way of present or future anticipation, assign their interest in this trust under any circumstances. The income interest of my children shall not be subject to the claims of their creditors, whether by voluntary or involuntary transfer.

After Alice's death, one of her children, Beatrix, directed that her income installments be paid to her sister, Karen, in satisfaction of a debt that Beatrix owed to Karen. Under these circumstances:

A. The transfer of Beatrix's income interest is void.

B. The transfer of Beatrix's income interest is valid, and the trustee must pay Beatrix's income interest to Karen.

C. The transfer of Beatrix's income interest is valid to the extent (1) the trustee decides to honor the purported transfer, and (2) Beatrix, the beneficiary, does not revoke the transfer.

D. Although the transfer of Beatrix's income is void, the debt owed to Karen by Beatrix is deemed to be satisfied, because Karen knew the transfer was void.

66. Suppose that, in Question 65, the United States obtained a judgment against Beatrix for unpaid income taxes. Under these circumstances:

A. The judgment of the United States takes priority over a spendthrift clause, and the trustee must pay the income to the United States.

B. The judgment of the United States takes priority over a spendthrift clause, and the trustee must deliver principal sufficient to satisfy Beatrix's income tax delinquency to the United States.

C. The spendthrift clause is valid against the judgment of the United States; but, the trustee may pay the income to the United States until Beatrix objects.

D. The spendthrift clause is valid against the judgment of the United States, and so the trustee may not pay any of Beatrix's income to the United States.

67. John, a widower, made the following bequest in his valid will:

> I give, devise, and bequeath the sum of $1,000,000 to my friend Ted, in the hope that he will use such funds for his children.

At the time that John made the bequest, Ted had two children, Andy and Lon. John's will gave his residuary estate to his father, Bill. John was survived by Bill. Ted contends that he has no obligation to use any of the money for the benefit of his children. What action, if any, should the court take in relation to this gift?

A. It should declare the property to be held in trust for Ted's children, remove Ted as trustee and appoint a successor trustee.

B. It should find a resulting trust in favor of John's father, Bill.

C. It should find a constructive trust in favor of John's father, Bill.

D. It should declare the property to belong to Ted outright.

68. In her will, Kathy created a trust by transferring stocks and bonds worth $1,000,000 to National Bank as trustee, for the following purpose:

> The trustee shall distribute to my grandchildren such amounts of income as it, in its sole and complete discretion, deems appropriate for their comfortable support and maintenance. At the death of the last of my children to die, the trustee shall distribute all unpaid income and the principal of this trust to my grandchildren then living, per capita.

After Kathy's death (but before the death of her children) one of Kathy's grandchildren, (Larry), incurred a debt that he could not pay. The creditor obtained a judgment against Larry. Under these circumstances:

A. The creditor may levy against Larry's income interest in the hands of the trustee.

B. The creditor may obtain a lien against (but not a sale of) Larry's remainder interests in the hands of the trustee.

C. The creditor may levy against Larry's income and remainder interests in the hands of the trustee.

D. The creditor may not levy against Larry's income or remainder interests in the hands of the trustee.

69. Ted created an *inter vivos* trust by transferring $500,000 to First National Bank, as trustee. The declaration of trust provided that the income of the trust was to be paid to Ted during his lifetime. At his death, the principal was to be distributed to Ted's daughter, Mae. The trust provides as follows:

> No beneficiary of this trust may, by way of present or future anticipation, assign his or her interest in this trust, under any circumstance. The income

interest of any beneficiary shall not be subject to the claims of creditors, whether by way of voluntary or involuntary transfer.

Several years after this trust was created, Ron obtained a judgment against Ted in the sum of $400,000. This obligation arose after the trust was created. Under these circumstances:

A. The income interest of Ted is exempt from his creditors.

B. Ron may not levy on Ted's interest in the hands of the trustee, but may levy on any income actually received by Ted.

C. Ron may levy on Ted's income interest, but not on the remainder interest.

D. Ron may levy on both the income and remainder interests.

70. Leslie created a trust of $250,000, with the First Bank as trustee, for the following purpose:

The principal of this trust, together with all accrued income therefrom, shall be paid over to the person who discovers a cure for cancer.

This trust is:

A. Valid, because its purpose is to promote medical research.

B. Invalid, because it will benefit a limited number of persons.

C. Invalid, because it is not certain to vest within the allowable period of the Rule Against Perpetuities.

D. Invalid, because it is not certain ever to vest.

71. Suppose that, in Question 70, the trust had the following purpose:

The principal of this trust, together with all accrued income therefrom, shall be used for charitable purposes.

This trust is:

A. Invalid, because the beneficiaries are unascertainable.

B. Invalid, because the trust violates the Rule Against Perpetuities.

C. Valid, with the trustee authorized to pay over the proceeds to any charity that the trustor had supported during his lifetime.

D. Valid, with the trustee authorized to use the trust funds to support any recognized charity.

72. Lynn created a testamentary trust that provides as follows:

I give, devise, and bequeath the sum of $1,000,000 in trust to First National Bank, as Trustee. The trustee shall pay from the income the sum of $100 to each person who is convicted of possession but has less than one ounce of marijuana. It is my belief that this law is an unconstitutional invasion of privacy and that these people should not suffer for their transgression. Perhaps this trust will wake our legislators up to the need for a revision of the law. The trustee shall have the sole and exclusive right to ascertain which persons should receive payments from the trust income.

Lynn was survived by her son, Max, to whom she devised the residue of her estate. Under these circumstances:

A. The trust may be sustained as a valid charitable trust for the promotion of health.

B. The trust may be sustained as a valid charitable trust for the advancement of education.

C. The trust may be sustained as a valid trust for general charitable purposes.

D. The trust is invalid as a charitable trust and the trust res should be distributed to Max.

73. Maura created a testamentary trust that provides as follows:

I give, devise, and bequeath the sum of $1,000,000 in trust to First National Bank, trustee; the income therefrom to be paid to International University to provide scholarships for children of low-income families.

International University is a privately owned, profit-making corporation that educates persons for technical jobs in industry. It has an outstanding reputation.

Maura was survived by her son, Will, to whom she devised the remainder of her estate. Under these circumstances:

A. The trust is a valid charitable trust for education.

B. The trust is a valid charitable trust to mitigate poverty.

C. The trust is a valid charitable trust only if the recipients of the scholarships are indigent.

D. The trust is invalid as a charitable trust, and so the trust property should be distributed to Will.

74. Terry created a testamentary trust that provides as follows:

I give, devise and bequeath the sum of $500,000 to my alma mater, Normal University, the income therefrom to be used to provide scholarships for worthy students from the state of Arizona.

Terry was a graduate of Normal University. After Terry's will was executed, Normal University ceased to operate as a university. Its facilities were sold to Welcome University, a privately owned, profit-making school. Terry devised the remainder of her estate to her parents. Terry died recently. Under these circumstances:

A. The charitable gift should be distributed to Welcome University.

B. The charitable gift should be distributed to another nonprofit university chosen by the court.

C. The charitable gift should fail and be distributed to Terry's parents.

D. The charitable gift should fail and be distributed to Terry's heirs.

75. Settlor made a testamentary, charitable gift of $1,000,000 to Delphi University for the following purposes:

> The income from this gift shall be used to provide scholarships for the education of white, male students at Delphi University who regularly attend their respective churches, temples, or synagogues. Women, and minority students probably receive sufficient aid already. I do not wish to spend my money on atheists.

Delphi is a nonprofit, nonsectarian, coeducational institution. It has prided itself on educating disadvantaged persons, regardless of race or creed. It desperately needs money to provide additional scholarships for its students. However, Delphi is prohibited by its charter from accepting a gift with racial restrictions. Settlor recently died. Under these circumstances a court would probably:

A. Strike all of the restrictions, and sustain the entire gift to Delphi.

B. Substitute another institution that can adhere to the restrictions.

C. Strike the racial restriction only and sustain the gift to Delphi with the other restrictions attached.

D. Void the gift and distribute the funds to the residuary legatees or trustor's heirs.

76. Edward is the trustee of an *inter vivos* trust created by his father. The trust res consists of an office building that produces revenue that is equivalent to a 4.5 percent return on investment. In order to increase income resulting from the trust, Edward purchased the office building from the trust for $200,000 and caused the trust to invest the proceeds in higher-yield assets. The trust instrument made no mention of a power to sell or mortgage trust assets. Under these circumstances, the most likely result under traditional trust principles is:

A. Edward violated his fiduciary duty by selling the trust asset.

B. Edward violated his fiduciary duty in purchasing the trust asset for himself, regardless of whether he paid the fair market value of the property.

C. Edward violated his fiduciary duty in purchasing the trust asset for himself, but only if he paid less than the fair market value for this asset.

D. Edward did not violate his fiduciary duty.

77. Suppose that, in Question 76, Edward had, in his capacity as trustee, elected to borrow funds, using the office building as security for the debt, and had then invested the borrowed funds in higher-income-yielding assets. Under these circumstances, the most likely result under traditional trust principles is:

A. Edward breached his fiduciary duty.

B. Edward breached his fiduciary duty, if the net income of the trust is reduced by his actions.

C. Edward breached his fiduciary duty by borrowing funds, if he has the power to sell the asset.

D. Edward did not breach his fiduciary duty.

78. Claire created a testamentary trust as follows:

> The trustee shall pay so much of the income as she shall, in her sole, absolute, and uncontrolled discretion, determine is necessary for the care, maintenance, and support of my children, until my youngest child shall reach the age of 25 years, at which time all accrued income and principal shall be distributed to my children, share and share alike.

At Claire's death all of her three children were minors. The trustee thereafter paid all of the income annually to the oldest child. When the youngest child reached the age of 25, the two youngest children sued the trustee, claiming that the trustee had breached her fiduciary duty by not previously paying any of the income to them. Under these circumstances:

A. The court has no power to review the "sole, absolute, and uncontrolled" discretionary decisions of the trustee.

B. Although the court has the power to review discretionary decisions of the trustee, the trustee will be presumed to have acted reasonably under these circumstances.

C. The court has the power to review the discretionary decisions of the trustee and to impose liability for those decisions made arbitrarily or in bad faith.

D. The court has the power to review the discretionary decisions of the trustee and to impose liability for those decisions the court believes were not sound.

79. Ted is the trustee of an *inter vivos* trust. The trust res is composed of $300,000 in cash. The beneficiaries are Ted's nephews and nieces. Ted recently located a parcel of unimproved property that is available for sale. The price of the property is $300,000, and Ted projects that the property will increase in value to $500,000 within two years. Under these circumstances, the best statement of Ted's rights and duties is that he may:

A. Invest in this property, if a prudent investor would do so.

B. Invest in this property, if he obtains an appraisal showing that the value of the property is now at least $300,000.

C. Not invest in this property, regardless of what the trust instrument authorizes.

D. Not invest in this property, unless the trust instrument specifically authorizes real estate investments.

80. Able and Baker were appointed cotrustees of a trust created by Mabel Schultz. In the course of administering the trust, they initiated a lawsuit against a real estate agent who they felt had defrauded the trust. The case was tried and judgment was rendered in favor of the real estate agent. Both Able and the trust's attorney believe the case was wrongly decided. Able wishes to appeal the judgment but Baker refuses to do so. Under these circumstances:

A. Able may appeal the judgment unilaterally; but if the appeal is unsuccessful, Able is personally responsible for all costs of appeal.

B. Able may appeal the judgment without Baker's consent.

C. Able may not appeal the judgment without Baker's consent.

D. Baker may not refuse to join in the appeal, because to do so would be a breach of his fiduciary duties.

81. Karl, a college professor, is the trustee of a trust created by his father-in-law for the benefit of Karl's children. Karl accepted a visiting professorship at Cambridge University for an academic year. Because he was going to be out of the country, Karl retained Edward, a stockbroker, to act as the substitute trustee for that year. Karl

executed a document authorizing Edward to "exercise all powers and fulfill all duties that I now possess as trustee." Under these circumstances:

A. Karl is effectively relieved of his duties as trustee during the year, and is not liable for any breach of fiduciary duties that might occur.

B. Karl is not relieved of liability for any breach of fiduciary duties, but properly delegated the powers of the trustee to Edward.

C. Karl is not relieved of liability for any breach of fiduciary duties, but Edward may exercise all discretionary powers of the trustee under the trust.

D. Karl has breached his fiduciary duty and is liable for all damages resulting from Edward's acts or omissions.

82. Suppose that, in Question 81, Edward was employed by Karl to make investment decisions pertaining to trust assets. Karl unquestioningly adhered to Edward's suggestions, which were based upon Edward's judgment alone. One of the securities purchased for the trust at Edward's suggestion dropped in value, causing a significant loss to the trust estate. Under these circumstances, the most likely result under traditional trust principles is:

A. Karl is liable to the trust, if (and only if) a prudent investor would not have purchased the stock.

B. Karl is liable to the trust, without regard to whether a prudent investor would have purchased the stock.

C. Karl is liable to the trust only if Edward failed to act as a competent stockbroker.

D. To determine if Karl is liable to the trust it is necessary to determine if he utilized reasonable care in selecting Edward to make investment decisions.

83. Suppose that, in Question 81, Karl loaned trust funds to himself at a higher rate of interest than the prevailing market rate for similar loans. Karl used the loan to invest in several new stocks, which he later sold at a substantial profit. Upon selling the stocks, Karl repaid the loans to the trust, together with all accrued interest. Under these circumstances, Karl:

A. Breached his fiduciary duty to the trust, but no damage has occurred.

B. Breached his fiduciary duty to the trust, and must remit the profits he made on the sale of the stock to the trust.

C. Has not breached his fiduciary duty to the trust, but would have been liable for any losses that the trust might have suffered in this type of transaction.

D. Has not breached any duty to the trust, because he had promised to pay and did pay a higher rate of interest than the market rate.

84. Amy is the trustee of a testamentary trust that consists of $300,000 in cash. The trust instrument provides that Amy is entitled to receive trust income that is "necessary to her proper support, maintenance, and education." The principal passes to Amy's children upon her death. Amy recently purchased a business for the trust for $100,000. However, because she failed to research the new business carefully, she subsequently learned that there were several lawsuits pending against it. As a consequence, the business was actually worth only $25,000. The trust document has a provision that states: "The trustee shall not be liable for negligence in administering the trust assets, or any activity undertaken on behalf of the trust." Under these circumstances:

A. Amy would not be liable for any losses that occurred, under any circumstances.

B. Amy is liable for the loss incurred by the trust corpus, but not for any loss of income.

C. Amy is liable for the loss of trust income, but not the loss of corpus.

D. Amy would not be liable for the losses, unless her actions amounted to gross negligence.

85. Laura is the trustee of an *inter vivos* trust, the ABC Trust. She signed a contract with Xavier whereby Xavier was to perform certain accounting services for the trust. (Laura signed the contract, "Laura, as trustee for the ABC Trust.") A *bona fide* dispute arose concerning whether Xavier had adequately performed the services. Laura refused to pay (or have the trust pay) for the services. Xavier sued Laura personally on the contract. Under traditional trust principles, if Xavier prevails on the merits:

A. Laura will be personally liable for breach of contract, but may indemnify herself from trust assets (assuming she acted in good faith).

B. Laura will not be personally liable for breach of contract, because she may be sued only in her capacity as trustee.

C. Laura will be personally liable for breach of contract, and may not be indemnified from trust assets.

D. Laura will be personally liable for breach of contract, and may not be indemnified from trust assets unless the trust instrument specifically contains an exculpatory clause.

86. Bill, the trustee of an *inter vivos* trust having a trust res of $500,000, negligently struck Phyllis while driving his car. At the time, he was on his way to a meeting with the trust's investment adviser. Phyllis sued Bill, individually and as trustee of the trust, for her damages ($300,000). Under traditional trust principles, under these circumstances:

   A. Bill is personally liable for any judgment, but may indemnify himself from the trust's assets.

   B. Bill is not personally liable for any judgment, but may be sued in his capacity as trustee of the trust.

   C. Bill is personally liable for any judgment and may *not* be indemnified from trust assets.

   D. Bill is personally liable for any judgment and may not be indemnified from trust assets, unless the trust instrument specifically contains an exculpatory clause.

87. Suppose that, in Question 86, (1) the tort was committed by an employee of the trust who was hired by Bill, while on trust business, and (2) the damages sustained by Phyllis were $600,000. Under traditional trust principles, under these circumstances:

   A. Bill is personally liable for the damages, but may seek indemnity from the trust and, to the extent not satisfied therefrom, may seek indemnity from the beneficiaries.

   B. Bill is personally liable for the damages, and may seek indemnity from the trust, but only to the extent of the trust assets.

   C. Bill is not personally liable for the damages, but must pay such damages from the trust assets.

   D. Neither Bill nor the trust assets are liable for the woman's damages, but she can recover from Bill's employee.

88. Ben created a testamentary trust by bequeathing 300 shares of Bloomfield, Inc., common stock to Adams National Bank, as trustee. The trustee was instructed to pay the income to Ben's children for life, and the remainder to his grandchildren at the death of the last

survivor of his children. Bloomfield has a net profit for the current year. However, due to plans to expand its facilities, it does not wish to declare cash dividends. It has decided to declare a stock dividend of one share for each four shares of stock currently owned by shareholders. The trust created by Ben will receive 75 shares of Bloomfield, Inc., common stock. Under traditional trust principles, under these circumstances:

A. Add the stock dividend shares to the corpus of the trust.

B. Distribute the stock dividend shares to the income beneficiaries.

C. Distribute half of the stock dividend to the income beneficiaries, and the other half to the corpus of the trust.

D. Distribute stock equal in value to the cash dividend that would have been declared but for the expansion plans to the income beneficiaries, and add the remainder of the stock to the trust corpus.

89. Taft Trust company is the trustee of a trust created by Marlon Cando. Marlon transferred certain real estate to the trust with instructions to use the income therefrom "for the relief of the poverty of American Indians." After 20 years, the trust corpus is to be paid to the Animal Welfare League. Taft has determined that, of the three properties conveyed to it as trustee, two are unproductive, in that they produce no current income. Under these circumstances, the most likely result under the modern trend is:

A. Taft is not obligated to sell the two properties; but if it does so, all proceeds are allocated to the corpus of the trust.

B. Taft is not obligated to sell the two properties; but if it does, the trustee must apportion the proceeds between the income beneficiaries and the principal.

C. Taft is obligated to sell the two properties, and all proceeds must be allocated to corpus.

D. Taft is obligated to sell the two properties; and when the sale is made, the trustee must apportion the proceeds between the income beneficiaries and the principal.

90. Louise is the trustee of a trust created by her mother. The income beneficiaries of the trust are Louise and her two brothers. The remaindermen are Louise's two sisters. The corpus of the trust consists of two income-producing properties. During the course of each year, the trust must pay for maintenance, real estate taxes, and insurance on the properties. Under traditional trust principles, under these circumstances:

A. Maintenance is charged to the income beneficiaries; but taxes and insurance are chargeable against the corpus of the trust.

B. Maintenance and taxes are charged to the income beneficiaries; but insurance is chargeable against the corpus of the trust.

C. Taxes and insurance are chargeable against the income beneficiaries; but maintenance is chargeable against the corpus of the trust.

D. Maintenance, taxes, and insurance are chargeable to the income beneficiaries, exclusively.

91. Ellen created an *inter vivos* trust by transferring $100,000 in trust to First National Bank, as trustee, for the benefit of her children for life, with the remainder to her grandchildren. The trust document did not state whether Ellen retained the power to revoke or modify the trust. After the creation of the trust, Ellen delivered a letter to the trustee, advising it that she wished to revoke the remainder gift to the grandchildren and to substitute her nephews as remaindermen. The trustee rejected Ellen's modification of the trust. Angered by the trustee's response, Ellen delivered a second letter to the trustee, revoking the trust in its entirety. The trustee rejected this letter also. Under traditional trust principles, under these circumstances Ellen is entitled to:

A. Modify the trust by revoking the gift to the remaindermen and substituting her nephews, but cannot revoke the trust in its entirety.

B. Revoke the trust in its entirety, but cannot modify it.

C. Modify and revoke the trust.

D. Neither revoke nor modify the trust.

Multiple-Choice
Answers

1. **D** When a decedent dies *intestate*, survived by a spouse and surviving descendants who are also descendants of the surviving spouse and there is no other descendant of the surviving spouse who survives the decedent, the surviving spouse takes the entire estate. (UPC §2-102(1)(ii)). Because Rosa is survived by her husband Bill and two children who are descendants of Rosa as well as of Bill, Bill takes the entire estate. Choices **A**, **B**, and **C** are all incorrect under the rules for intestacy contained in the UPC.

2. **C** An heir who does not survive the decedent by *120 hours* is deemed to have predeceased the decedent. (UPC §2-104). Because Wanda is deemed to have predeceased Jim, her estate takes nothing. The deceased daughter's grandchildren are entitled to take their parent's share of the estate by right of representation. (UPC §2-103(1)). Thus, the estate is split into two shares of $100,000 each. Bob takes one share and the grandchildren split the other share. Choices **A** and **B** are incorrect, because they assume that Wanda is entitled to take a share of the estate. Choice **D** is incorrect, because it assumes that Bob and the grandchildren take *per capita* instead of by representation.

3. **B** If after executing a will, the testator is *divorced*, the divorce *revokes any testamentary disposition* to the former spouse, unless the will provides otherwise. (UPC §2-804(b)). Because Leonard and Evelyn were divorced, her gift was revoked (even though she survived him). The gift over to Leonard's mother and father fails because they did not survive him. Leonard's sister and brother take in place of Leonard's parents pursuant to the antilapse statute, because they are descendants of a beneficiary related to the testator. (UPC §2-603(b)). Although Sue was a witness to the will, the will is valid and the gift to her is also valid so long as there is no showing of undue influence by her. (UPC §2-505). Choice **A** is incorrect because it presumes the gift to Evelyn was not revoked by the divorce. Choice **C** is incorrect because it assumes Sue cannot take because she was an interested witness. Choice **D** is incorrect; there is no basis for precluding Ted from inheriting.

4. **B** This is an unusually tricky question, so follow closely. Any person 18 or older who is of sound mind may make a will. Every nonholographic will must be in writing signed by the testator and by two other persons each of whom witnessed either the signing or the testator's acknowledgment of either (a) the signature or (b) that the document is a will. A mark made by the testator suffices as a

signature. The will was valid because Dan was 19, he signed the document with a mark, and the execution of the will was witnessed by two witnesses. Because Dan's mother predeceased him, the gift to her fails.

Under the antilapse statute, Les would normally take his mother's share, as her sole descendant — but this would happen as a "substitute gift," not by having Dan's property pass through the mother's estate. (UPC §2-603). However, the antilapse doctrine applies only "[i]n the absence of a finding of a contrary intention, ..." (UPC §2-601). A court would probably conclude that the language in the will disinheriting Les manifests Dan's intent not to have the antilapse provision apply. If so, the estate would pass by intestacy because all bequests would have failed. Here, too, Les would ordinarily take, under UPC §2-103(3). But again, the UPC honors the testator's wishes: UPC §2-101(b) protects a decedent's choice to "expressly exclude or limit the right of an individual . . . to succeed to property of the decedent passing by intestate succession." The disinheritance language here would certainly meet this test. Consequently, the estate would go to the next in line — the decedent's grandmother. (UPC §2-103(4)).

Choice **A** is incorrect, because Dan's mother predeceased him. Choices **C** and **D** are incorrect. Les takes nothing for the reasons described above.

5. **A** An adopted child is treated as a natural-born child for purposes of inheritance. (UPC §2-114(b)). Lisa will inherit equally with Tom because she was adopted by Ellen. The $10,000 will not be treated as an advancement, because the only evidence of Ellen's intent was oral. (Section 2-109(a) requires that if an individual dies intestate, advancements must be established as such either in a writing contemporaneous with the gift signed by the testator or in a written acknowledgment by the heir.) Because the condition upon Tom's gift was oral and not written, Lisa and Tom will each take $75,000. Choice **B** is incorrect because it assumes that the $10,000 will be treated as an advancement against Tom's share of the estate. Choice **C** is incorrect because it assumes that Lisa is not treated as Ellen's child for purposes of inheritance. Choice **D** is incorrect because it fails to provide for inheritance by Tom.

6. **C** A spouse who married the testator after the making of the testator's will takes an intestate share unless: (1) it appears from the will or other evidence that the will was made in contemplation of the testator's marriage to the surviving spouse; (2) the will expresses the intention that its terms should be effective notwithstanding any subsequent marriage; or (3) the testator provided for the spouse by

transfer outside the will, and the intent that the transfer be in lieu of a testamentary provision is shown by the testator's statements or can be reasonably inferred from the amount of the transfer or other evidence. (UPC §2-301). None of these conditions appears to be satisfied here; therefore, Edward takes an intestate share. If no descendant of the decedent survives the decedent, but a parent of the decedent survives the decedent, the spouse's intestate share is the first $200,000, plus three-fourths of any balance of the intestate estate. (UPC §2-102(2)). So Edward gets this amount, with the remaining one-fourth going to Laura's mother. Choice **A** is incorrect in that it does not provide for Edward at all. Choice **B** is incorrect in that it does not provide for Laura's mother. Choice **D** is incorrect in that it misstates the respective shares of Edward and Laura's mother.

7. **A** A writing that is in existence when a will is executed may be *incorporated by reference*, if the language of the will manifests the intent to incorporate and describes the writing sufficiently to permit its identification. (UPC §2-510). In this case, the will relies upon an extrinsic document (John's *inter vivos* trust) to identify the devisees. The trust was executed prior to Ann's will and is described sufficiently to allow incorporation. Because Adrian and Kimberly were the only income beneficiaries at the time of Ann's death, they take equally. Choice **B** is incorrect because (contrary to the facts) it indicates that Ann intended to put the bequest in trust. The trust was incorporated merely to identify the beneficiaries under Ann's will. The devisees are given Ann's estate free of trust. Choices **C** and **D** are incorrect. Rita, John, and Lisa do not take any part of the $100,000 bequest.

8. **B** A will may dispose of property by *reference to acts and events that have significance apart from their effect upon dispositions made by the testator* in his or her will (whether they occur before or after the execution of the will, or before or after the testator's death). The execution or revocation of a will of another person is such an event. (UPC §2-512). The will of Bill's mother is an event of independent significance because the statute expressly provides for the execution or revocation of another individual's will. Because State University was the residuary legatee in the will of Bill's mother, it will get the $500,000 bequest. Choice **A** is incorrect because Bill's mother revoked the will under which Tim and Tom would take. Choice **C** would be correct only if the gift to State University had failed. Choice **D** is incorrect. If the gift to State University had failed, the money would have passed under the residuary clause to the American Red Cross.

9. A A specific devisee has the right to *any balance* of the purchase price owing from a purchaser by reason of the testator's sale of the property, together with any security agreement by the purchaser. (UPC §2-606(a)(1)). The devise of the condominium was specific; it can be identified as against all other assets of the testator's estate. Although a gift of specifically devised property is ordinarily adeemed when the property is sold during the testator's lifetime, the balance due and owing to the decedent from the buyer is not adeemed. Choice **B** is incorrect because it gives the account to Tom. Tom's best argument that he is entitled to the account is under UPC §2-606(a)(6), which rejects the identity approach to ademption and adopts the intent approach. But UPC §2-606(a)(6) applies only if the specifically devised property is not in the testator's estate and its value or its replacement is not covered by the provisions of paragraphs (1)-(5). Here, provision (a)(1) applies to give Tom the outstanding balance of the installment sales contract, so provision (a)(6) is not applicable. Choice **C** is incorrect because any property not transferred as a specific or general gift passes via the residuary clause, not intestacy, so the account passes under the residuary clause to Lighthouse University. Choice **D** is incorrect because Tom is entitled to the outstanding balance under the installment sales contract under UPC §2-606(a)(1).

10. C When a testator devises a gift of *stock*, and he or she owned shares of stock at the time the will was executed that *match* the stock being devised in the will, the devisee is entitled to (1) any additional or other securities of the same entity owned by the testator at death by reason of action (such as a stock split or stock dividend) initiated by that entity, and (2) any securities *of another entity* owned by the testator as a result of a merger, consolidation, reorganization, or other similar action. (UPC §2-605). When ABC split its stock and declared a stock dividend (actions initiated by ABC), the additional shares became part of the bequest of stock to Edna. When XYZ made a tender offer, the shares of XYZ stock received by Kathy took the place of the ABC shares. The final 40 shares of XYZ stock were purchased subsequently by Kathy, and so were not part of the original bequest of ABC stock. Choice **A** is incorrect because the 40 shares of XYZ subsequently purchased by Kathy are not included in the devise to Edna. Choice **B** is incorrect because the shares resulting from the stock split and stock dividend, as well as the XYZ shares received in the merger, pass to Edna. Choice **D** is incorrect. Even if none of the XYZ shares were to pass to Edna, they would be distributed to Kay under the terms of Kathy's will, not to Bill.

11. **B** Generally, a will is construed in light of the circumstances surrounding the testator when the will is executed. Consistent with that principle, Larry's gift of "my home" to his son Ron will be construed to mean the home that he owned when he executed the will. When Larry later conveyed this home to Ron, the specific gift of "*my* home" was adeemed. When Larry subsequently purchased the second home, Ron has two arguments to support his claim that he is entitled to the second home as well. First, under UPC §2-606(a)(5), any real property owned by the testator at death that the testator acquired as a replacement for specifically devised real property goes to the devisee of the specifically devised property. Larry arguably acquired the second home as a replacement for the first home, so Ron, the specific devisee, is entitled to the second home. In the alternative, Ron can claim "acts of independent significance." Under acts of independent significance, UPC §2-512, a will may dispose of property by reference to acts and events that have significance apart from their effect upon the disposition made in the will. Under acts of independent significance, Ron will argue that he is entitled to the second home because Larry transferred the first home and purchased the second for reasons independent of the effect upon the dispositions under the will, and therefore, he should be entitled to the second home under the terms of the will.

The issue then becomes whether the conveyance of the first home to Ron, and/or the cash gift to Carolyn, acted as a full or partial satisfaction of the specific bequests to them. A lifetime gift of property to a devisee is treated as a satisfaction only if: (1) the will provides for deduction of the gift; (2) the testator declares in a contemporaneous writing that the gifts are in satisfaction of the devise or that their value is to be deducted from the value of the devise; or (3) the devisees acknowledge in writing that the gifts are in satisfaction of the devise or that their value is to be deducted from the value of the devise. (UPC §2-609). None of these conditions was satisfied as to either the house transfer to Ron or the cash gift to Carolyn. Larry's estate will therefore be distributed according to the terms of his will.

Choice **A** is incorrect because it assumes satisfaction of both gifts. Choice **C** is incorrect because it assumes satisfaction of the gift to

Ron. Choice **D** is incorrect because it fails to distribute all of the cash to Carolyn.

12. **D** A person who kills another intentionally and feloniously loses any right to benefit financially from his or her victim's estate, whether the assets are part of the probate estate or pass outside the estate. This principle is codified in UPC §2-803(c)(1), which provides that the felonious and intentional killing of the decedent "revokes any revocable ... disposition ... of property made by the decedent to the killer in a governing instrument, ..." Both wills and insurance policies are covered by the definition of "governing instrument." (UPC §1-201 (18)). The bequest to Sofia and the designation of her as policy beneficiary, are both cancelled. Therefore, the cash and insurance proceeds pass into Bert's intestate estate.

Under UPC §2-803(c)(2), the felonious and intentional killing also "severs the interests of the decedent and killer in property held by them at the time of the killing as joint tenants with the right of survivorship, transforming the interests of the decedent and killer into tenancies in common." Therefore, Bert's intestate estate holds a one-half interest in the home as tenant in common; this tenancy then passes to the grandchildren equally.

Choice **A** is incorrect in that it assumes the conviction of murder has no effect upon any of the assets owned by Bert. Choice **B** is incorrect in that it assumes that the conviction affects distribution of probate assets only, not the insurance policy or the joint tenancy in the home. Choice **C** is incorrect in that it also assumes the conviction does not affect an insurance policy.

13. **A** When a second will — which revoked the first will — is thereafter revoked by physical act, the first will is *revived* if the testator *intended the first will to take effect* as executed and that intent is evident from (1) the *circumstances* under which the second will is revoked, or (2) the testator's contemporary or subsequent *declarations*. (UPC §2-509(a)). Although the second will expressly revoked the first will, the statements of Jamir that his father should take the estate under the first will evidenced an intent to revive the first after destruction of the second will. Choice **B** is incorrect because the second will was revoked by physical act. Choice **C** is incorrect because the first will was revived and is in effect. Choice **D** is incorrect because (1) the first will is revived and is in effect, and (2) even if the first will were not revived and Jamir died intestate, his

mother and father, not his sisters, would take by intestate succession.

14. **C** As in Question 13, the tearing up of the second will was a "revocatory act" that revoked that will. (UPC §2-507(a)(2)). Under these new facts, there are no direct statements by Jamir supporting revival of the first instrument. On the contrary, we have Jamir's statement deriding all wills. That being so, the first will remains revoked by the second will. Therefore, Jamir's estate passes by intestate succession (*i.e.*, to his mother and father equally). Choices **A** and **B** are incorrect because neither will survives and Jamir died intestate. Choice **D** is incorrect because Jamir's father and mother (rather than his sisters) would take by intestate succession.

15. **D** A will is *revoked* by a subsequent will that is *inconsistent* with the former instrument. (UPC §2-507). Will #2 revoked Will #1 by inconsistency. Because Will #3 revoked Will #2, but gave no indication that revival of the first will was intended, revival of Will #1 will *not* occur. See UPC §2-509(c). Thereafter Edgar validly revoked Will #3 by physical act. Under the revival doctrine, where a later will validly revokes a prior will, and thereafter the testator validly revokes the latter will by act, the earlier will is revived as long as the testator intended to revive it and that intent is evident from (1) the circumstances under which the latter will was revoked, or (2) the testator's contemporaneous or subsequent declarations. (UPC §2-509(a)). There was nothing about the circumstances surrounding Edgar's revocation of Will #3 that evidences his intent to revive will #1.

The tough issue is whether the unsigned and undated handwritten note found on Will #1 after Edgar died, which read "This is my will," can be used to validate Will #1. The revival doctrine provides that where the testator revoked the latter will by act, as long as the testator evidences the intent to revive the earlier will, and that intent is expressed contemporaneously with or subsequent to the revocation, the earlier will is revived. The problem is that the handwritten note cannot be used to evidence the testator's intent to revive Will #1 because it cannot be proven that it was a contemporaneous or subsequent declaration by Edgar — it is undated (it may have been written before Edgar revoked Will #3, and the revival doctrine requires that it be a contemporaneous or subsequent declaration). The unsigned and undated writing cannot be used to give effect to Will #1 under incorporation by reference because the writing would have to qualify as a holographic will. A holographic will requires a writing, signed by the testator, with the material provisions in the testator's handwriting, and testamentary intent. (UPC §2-502(b)). The writing found on the will was not signed. (The unsigned and undated writing cannot be validated as a will under the harmless error doctrine [UPC §2-503] because there is no clear and convincing evidence that the decedent intended that writing to be his last will. There were too many executed wills and revocations, and because the unsigned writing was undated, it is impossible to prove by clear and convincing evidence that Edgar intended this writing to be his last will). Thus, Edgar died intestate and his estate should be divided between Tom and Wilma.

Choice **A** is incorrect because it assumes revival (or incorporation by reference) of Will #1 and that did not occur for the reasons stated above. Choice **B** is incorrect because Will #2 was expressly revoked by Will #3. Choice **C** is incorrect because the facts stipulate that Will #3 was revoked by physical act.

16. **A** A will, including a holographic will, may refer to a written statement or list to dispose of tangible personal property not otherwise specifically disposed of by the will. To be admissible, the writing must (1) be signed by the testator, and (2) describe the items and the devisees with reasonable certainty. (UPC §2-513). Even though the list could *not* be incorporated by reference (*i.e.,* it was created after the will) and has no significance apart from its testamentary effect (so acts of independent significance does not apply), inclusion of the list is permitted under the tangible personal property list doctrine. (An argument could also be made that the handwritten list qualifies as a holographic codicil, though it might be difficult to establish testamentary intent, but this argument is unnecessary because it qualifies under the tangible personal property list doctrine). Choice **B** is incorrect because the bequest is effective as written and the items do not fall into the residue. Choice **C** is incorrect; there is no indication that this property was specifically devised to Rusty and Rosa. Choice **D** is incorrect because if the bequests listed in the writing failed, they would pass as part of the residuary gift, not in intestacy.

17. **B** Where a gift (residuary or other) is given to a beneficiary who is the decedent's grandparent or a lineal descendant from the decedent's grandparents, and the beneficiary predeceases the decedent, the beneficiary's issue take the beneficiary's gift unless the instrument

expresses a contrary intent. (UPC §2-603). Here, both Roberta and Ted predeceased the decedent. Roberta was not survived by issue, so her gifts (the piano and her share of the residuary) lapse and pass through the residuary to the other residuary takers. Ted was survived by a son, so he takes Ted's share of the residuary, along with Edwina and Judy. Choice **A** is incorrect because Roberta's gifts lapsed and no one can take through her. (Roberta died without descendants). Choice **C** is incorrect because Ted's child is entitled to share in the residue as Ted's descendant. Choice **D** is incorrect because the antilapse statute applies only if the predeceased beneficiary is survived by a *descendant*, not a *spouse*.

18. **D** A person who is a devisee under a testamentary instrument may *disclaim* the right to take any property or interest therein by filing a *written* disclaimer (UPC §2-1105). Because Albert renounced his gift, he is treated as though he had predeceased the testator. If Albert had predeceased Tim, the antilapse statute would have come into play: because Albert is a descendant of a grandparent of the testator and was himself survived by a descendant, that descendant (Albert's son) would take the real estate under the antilapse statute. Consequently, Albert's disclaimer means that his son takes the real estate. The remainder of the estate is divided among Tim's brothers and sister. Choice **A** is incorrect because a devisee is permitted to disclaim his or her interest in a devise, and Albert validly did so here. Choice **B** is incorrect because the antilapse statute applies when a devisee is deemed to have predeceased the testator. Choice **C** is incorrect because Tim's children would take the real estate only if the whole will were to fail, which it does not here.

19. **A** A specific devise passes the property, subject to any mortgage interest existing at the date of death, without right of exoneration (regardless of a general directive in the will to pay debts). (UPC §2-607). Even though this may result in an unequal distribution of assets on these facts, there is no specific directive by Tom to pay the debt secured by the mortgage from the general assets of the estate. Choice **B** is incorrect because there is no specific directive by Tom to pay the debt secured by the mortgage. Choice **C** is incorrect because there is no provision for a gift of stock to Joan in the will. Choice **D** is incorrect. The court must distribute Tom's estate in accordance with terms of the will, not according to its conjectures about Tom's possible motives.

20. **A** Because paternity was established prior to John's death, Jennifer is treated as his child (UPC §2-114(a)). Jennifer is a pretermitted child (Jennifer was born after John had made his will). A pretermitted child (the UPC refers to an "omitted" child) takes as if her parent had died intestate. (UPC §2-302). When testator is unmarried and leaves only one child, that child's intestate share is the entire estate. (UPC §2-103(1)). Therefore, Jennifer receives the entire estate. Choice **B** is incorrect because Jennifer's claim to the intestate share as a pretermitted child supersedes the devise to ABC. Choices **C** and **D** are incorrect because they do not state Jennifer's share correctly — Jennifer is entitled to the entire estate.

21. **B** Normally, when a decedent dies intestate without a spouse or descendants, the estate is split between the decedent's parents, if both survive. (UPC §2-103(2)). However, the fact that paternity is established against a father is ineffective to qualify him or his heirs to inherit from or through the child born out of wedlock, unless the father has (1) openly treated the child as his, *and* (2) has not refused to support the child. (UPC §2-114(c)). Although John supported Jennifer, he refused to treat her as his own child. Thus, he is disqualified from inheriting from or through her. Because Jennifer has no surviving spouse and no issue, Betty, as Jennifer's only parent entitled to inherit from her, inherits Jennifer's entire estate. Choice **A** is incorrect because John is *not* qualified to inherit. Choices **C** and **D** are incorrect because Betty takes Jennifer's entire estate under the principles governing intestacy. (UPC §2-103(2)).

22. **B** Relatives of the half-blood inherit the same as if they were of the whole-blood. (UPC §2-107). Although Kane is a half-brother of Mark (*i.e.*, they share only one common parent), he is entitled to inherit from Mark just as if he were a whole-blood brother. Mark died without surviving issue or parents. (Steve is not Mark's "parent," because that term "excludes any person who is only a step-parent." [UPC §1-201(32)].). Therefore, Will and Kane as Mark's brothers share Mark's estate equally. (UPC §2-103(3).) Choice **A** is incorrect since Kane is entitled to inherit equally with Will. Choices **C** and **D** are incorrect because Steve is not related to Mark in the degree required by the principles governing intestacy.

23. **B** An heir of the decedent conceived before his death, but born thereafter, *inherits in the same way as if born in the decedent's lifetime.* (UPC §2-108). Because Ted left descendants and a surviving spouse *and* the surviving spouse has one or more surviving descendants

who are not descendants of the decedent, Judy, as surviving spouse, takes the first $150,000 plus one-half of the balance of the estate. (UPC §2-102(3)). Because Ted Jr. was conceived prior to Ted's death and was born after Ted's death, he shares the remaining one-half with his sister Lisa. (UPC §2-103(1)). Choice **A** is incorrect in that it excludes Ted Jr. from his inheritance. Choice **C** is incorrect in that it misstates Judy's share. Choice **D** is incorrect in that it misstates Judy's share and excludes Ted Jr. from any inheritance.

24. **A** The facts here differ in that two of Ted's descendants were not also descendants of his wife Judy. If there are surviving descendants of the decedent, one or more of whom are *not* descendants of the surviving spouse, the intestate share of the surviving spouse is $100,000, plus one-half of the balance of the estate. (UPC §2-102(4)). Because Ted left descendants, at least one of whom is not a descendant of Judy, Judy's intestate share is $100,000, plus one-half of the balance of the estate. Because Ted Jr. was conceived prior to the death of Ted and was born after Ted's death, he is treated as having survived Ted, and he therefore takes one-third of the remainder, along with Lisa and Amy. Choice **B** is incorrect in that it excludes Ted Jr. from any inheritance. Choice **C** is incorrect in that it misstates Judy's share. Choice **D** is incorrect in that it misstates Judy's share and excludes Ted Jr. from any inheritance.

25. **B** Foster children do not ordinarily inherit from their foster parents. Section 1-201(5) of the UPC defines "child" so as to exclude a "foster child." However, most jurisdictions recognize "equitable adoption/adoption by estoppel" when there is an unperformed agreement to adopt. In this case, the statement made to Lisa could reasonably have been interpreted by her as a promise of adoption. Taken together with the fact that Harvey and Ann "held Lisa out as their daughter," most jurisdictions would probably treat Lisa as an adopted child by estopping Harvey's estate from denying that an adoption existed. If there are surviving descendants of the decedent, one or more of whom are not descendants of the surviving spouse, the intestate share of the surviving spouse is $100,000, plus one-half of the balance of the estate. (UPC §2-102(4)). Because Harvey left a descendant, Bob, who is not a descendant of Ann, Ann's intestate share is $100,000, plus one-half of the balance of the estate. Because Lisa would probably be considered Harvey's adopted child and his descendant, she takes one-half of the remainder along with Bob. Choice **A** is incorrect because it would control

the distribution only if Harvey had no descendants. Choice **C** is incorrect in that it misstates Ann's share. Choice **D** is incorrect. It applies only if all of the decedent's surviving descendants were also descendants of the surviving spouse. Here, Harvey had a son by a previous marriage.

26. **C** A holographic will requires a writing, signed by the testator, with the material provisions in the testator's handwriting, and testamentary intent. (UPC §2-502(b)). Here, there is a writing, signed by Patricia, which sets forth the material provisions. The intent that this constitute her will, though a bit ambiguous, is evidenced by the phrase "if I don't return . . . ." The issue is whether the will was intended to be valid *only* if she did not return from the cruise.

    In most jurisdictions, a testator's explanation of her motives in making a testamentary document will not ordinarily be interpreted as a condition to the effectiveness of the document. *In re Taylor's Estate; Eaton v. Brown.* The inference here would be that Patricia was prompted to make her will at this time because she was about to make the trip, not that she wished her will to be ignored if she returned. The writing is a valid holographic will that devises her estate to the Country Art Museum.

    Choice **A** is incorrect because there is no requirement in the UPC that a holographic will be dated to be enforceable. Choice **B** is incorrect because the will is effective, and, in any event, if the will were not effective, Patricia's mother would inherit the entire estate. (UPC §2-103(2)). Choice **D** is incorrect. There is no interpretation under which the two would share. Either the Art Museum would take (if the will is valid) or the mother would take (if the will is not valid), but *not* both.

27. **A** A contract to make a will or testamentary gift, or not to revoke a will or testamentary gift, can be established only by: (1) provisions of a will stating material provisions of the contract; (2) an express reference in the will to an agreement and extrinsic evidence proving the terms of that contract; or (3) a writing signed by the decedent evidencing the contract. (UPC §2-514). (Note that this section does not preclude one from recovering in *quantum meruit* for the value of services rendered.) Because the agreement here is not evidenced in writing (either in Clay's will or in a separate document signed by Clay), it cannot be enforced by Arnold against Clay's estate. Therefore, Anne will take under the will. Choice **B** is incorrect because the agreement with Arnold was oral and not referred to in Clay's will;

therefore, it cannot be proved. Choice **C** is incorrect. Even if the agreement could be proved, Arnold would take to the exclusion of Tom. Choice **D** is incorrect. The will, which is effective, leaves Clay's entire estate to Anne.

28. **D** A contract to make a testamentary gift is generally not enforceable during the testator's lifetime. If the testator, however, either orally or by his actions, repudiates the contract after the promisee has substantially performed or acted in reliance on the contract, the promisee may ordinarily sue for anticipatory breach and seek to impose a constructive trust upon the assets in the hands of a third party. Because Clay has transferred a substantial portion of his assets after promising to leave his entire estate to Arnold, his conduct will probably be viewed as an anticipatory breach. Arnold may sue to have a constructive trust imposed on the assets transferred by Clay to Tom. Tom would probably *not* be deprived of their use during Clay's lifetime, but would be ordered to transfer the assets to Arnold at Clay's death (pursuant to Clay's agreement with Arnold). Choice **A** is incorrect because Arnold has no right to possession of the assets until Clay's death. Choice **B** is incorrect. The assessment of damages before Clay's death would be speculative and difficult. Arnold might die before Clay. Choice **C** is incorrect because Arnold has no right to control Clay's assets until Clay's death.

29. **A** Most jurisdictions recognize revocation by presumption. Under revocation by presumption, if a will that was last in the testator's possession, cannot be found after the testator's death, and the testator was competent until death, a rebuttable presumption arises that the reason why the will cannot be found is that the testator revoked the will by act. Here, the will was last in Toni's possession, she was competent until death, and the will cannot be found after her death. A rebuttable presumption arises that she revoked it by act. However, the conversation Toni had with her attorney just the week before her death, in which she affirmed her will, saying that it represented her wishes, is probably sufficient to overcome the presumption. Even though the will cannot be found, it was not revoked.

A will, the original of which cannot be produced in court, can nevertheless be probated as a "lost" will if its execution and terms can be proven. (UPC §3-402(a)). Most jurisdictions require clear and convincing evidence to prove up the lost will. Here, because Toni's attorney has a conformed copy of the will and the attorney can testify that just a week before she died Toni affirmed that the will, as executed, represented her testamentary wishes, the will should be probated as a lost will.

Answer **B** is incorrect because either the will is probated and First Baptist takes it all, or the will is revoked and First Baptist takes nothing. Under no scenario does First Baptist share the estate with Toni's children. Answer **C** is incorrect because it assumes that the will was revoked and Toni's estate passed through intestacy; but the will is only lost and can be probated. Answer **D** is incorrect because (1) it assumes that the will was revoked (which it was not), and (2) if the will were deemed revoked, under intestacy only Toni's children would take, not her parents.

30. **B** If no members of a class are in existence when a will is executed or at the testator's death, the members of the class (whenever born) ordinarily do not receive their gifts when the designated ancestor of the class dies (this is an exception to the rule of convenience). We can assume that Parker knew that his best friend had no children and that he wanted the distribution to Sam's children postponed until all of the class members could be determined. Choice **A** is incorrect in that it does not include all of Sam's children. Choice **C** is incorrect because Parker did not provide for Ann and was not required to provide for her. Choice **D** is incorrect because Parker's estate would pass to his parents only if the will was invalid. (UPC §2-103(2)).

31. **A** Under the *Rule of Convenience,* a class closes the moment one member of the class is entitled to claim possession of his or her share. Although the doctrine is a rule of construction, not a rule of law, courts generally follow and apply it. Here, because Sam's eldest son, Bob, was alive when Parker died, Bob was entitled to claim his share the moment Parker died and Parker's will became effective. Bob takes the entire estate under Parker's will. Choice **B** is incorrect. Under the Rule of Convenience, the class closed at Parker's death (after-born class members do not participate). Choice **C** is incorrect because Parker was not required to provide for Ann. Choice **D** is incorrect because Parker's estate would pass to his parents only if the will was invalid. (UPC §2-103(2)).

32. **B** Although Parker's class gift would be completely invalid under the common law approach to the Rule Against Perpetuities, the UPC has adopted the "wait and see" approach to the Rule Against Perpetuities, using a fixed period of 90 years. (UPC §2-901(a)). Under

the Rule of Convenience, the class closes when the first member of the class is entitled to distribution. The class would close when Bob reached age 25; only Bob and Ellen were alive when Bob reached 25. Bob's and Ellen's shares would be retained until each reached 25, and would be distributed to him or her as he or she reached that age. If either died before reaching age 25, his or her share would be distributed to the survivor of them. Choice **A** is incorrect because Ellen is a prospective member of the class. Choice **C** is incorrect because Sally was born after the class closed (when Bob reached 25) and therefore is not a member of the class. Choice **D** is incorrect because Bob and Ellen must reach age 25 before he or she takes, and Sally is not a member of the class.

33. C When a testator makes specific *per capita* bequests to members of a class and there are no members of the class living at the testator's death, the gift fails. The bequests fail because the amount of each bequest does not vary and the total cannot be determined. Because there were no takers at Parker's death, the gift fails altogether. When no residuary clause is expressed in the will, property not disposed of by the will passes by intestate succession. Here, the entire estate passes by intestacy. Choice **A** is incorrect because (1) it gives property to one of the class members (Bob), but they are not entitled to take; and (2) it gives property to the testator's sister, Ann, who is not entitled to take under either the will or intestacy. Choice **B** is incorrect because it gives property to the class members (Bob, Sally, and Ellen), but they are not entitled to take. Choice **D** is incorrect because it gives property the testator's sister, who is not entitled to take, because under the rules governing intestacy only the decedent's parents would take.

34. D The mere execution of joint wills or reciprocal wills does not create the presumption of a contract by either testator not to revoke his or her will. There is no evidence of a contract between Edward and Mary not to revoke the original wills. Edward was therefore free to execute a new will. Choice **A** is incorrect in that Edward's first will was revoked by the inconsistent disposition made in his second will. Choice **B** is incorrect in that the second will is valid and that Edward did not die intestate. Choice **C** is incorrect because (1) Edward's second will is valid, and (2) even assuming, *arguendo*, that Edward had died intestate, his estate would have passed by representation one-half to his son, Tim, and one-half to his grandchildren (the issue of his predeceased daughter Lisa).

35. D In most states, only "interested parties" may contest a will. An interested party is one who is *adversely affected* by the will's admission to probate. If the second will here is probated, Jim gets $10,000 more than he would have received under the prior will. Because he is not adversely affected, he cannot contest. Only Elizabeth has standing, because she takes everything under the first will, but suffers a $10,000 reduction under the second will. Choices **A** and **B** are incorrect because Jim's interest is not adversely affected under the second will (*i.e.*, he gets more than he would have if the first will remained in effect). Choice **C** is incorrect because neither Jim nor either of Bill's parents is adversely affected by the second will. Bill's parents take nothing under either will, and the first will is conceded to be valid.

36. A When a will provision is the product of an insane delusion of the testator, that provision will not be given effect by the probate court. An insane delusion is sometimes described as "a belief that is the product of the imagination and is held tenaciously against all evidence and reason to the contrary." (Haskell, p. 42). John's belief about Clay's illegitimacy would seem to qualify: there is no evidence that Clay was conceived as the consequence of an illicit relationship; in fact, the evidence (the blood typing) is to the contrary. The will establishes that John was driven to make his will disinheriting Clay by his irrational belief. On the other hand, there is no evidence that John was otherwise irrational or incompetent to make a will. The court will attempt to admit the will to probate without enforcing the clause relating to Clay. However, because excision of the clause will not remedy the wrong to Clay (Clay still won't get anything), the court will probably refuse to admit the whole will to probate on these facts. This will produce a more just result (Clay takes in intestacy). Choice **B** is incorrect. Compliance with correct formalities is assumed when a will is admitted to probate, but a will (or a provision of the will) will not be enforced when the testator is laboring under an insane delusion. Choice **C** is incorrect because there is no indication that anyone unduly influenced John. Choice **D** is incorrect. Although a testator may disinherit a child, the court will intervene to prevent an inequitable bequest when it is prompted by the testator's insane delusion. Although John may have the legal right to disinherit Clay, his insane delusion prevented him from executing a document that will be admitted to probate.

37. C Under UPC §2-101(b), a decedent "by will may expressly exclude or limit the right of an individual or class to succeed to property of the decedent passing by intestate succession." "Will" is defined in UPC §1-201(55) to include "any testamentary instrument that merely . . . expressly excludes or limits the right of an individual or class to succeed to property of the decedent passing by intestate succession." So a document that does nothing more than disinherit an individual can nonetheless be a valid "will." The document here is entirely in the testator's handwriting, it was signed by him, and it expresses testamentary intent (the intent that it be his will — as indicated by his intent to disinherit his child), so it is a valid holographic will. (UPC §2-502(b)). Therefore, it will be admitted to probate. Choice **A** is incorrect because the document is a valid will for the reasons just discussed. Choice **B** is legally incorrect (a natural father may disinherit his child). Choice **D** is incorrect because a mistake in the "inducement" to a will (*i.e.*, a mistake as to the surrounding facts or circumstances) will not be cause to refuse probate, unless the mistake is evident on the face of the will or is the product of an insane delusion, neither of which circumstance applies here.

38. A When an attorney prepares a will in which he or she is a beneficiary and supervises its execution, the majority view is that a rebuttable presumption of undue influence arises. Although there is no showing that Jones actually influenced Ellen, the facts that (1) the attorney-client relationship is a confidential one, and (2) the lawyer who prepared the will was employed by Jones, raise a presumption that must be rebutted. Choice **B** is incorrect. The question asks which argument is most likely to be successful. Because the party asserting fraud bears the burden of proof, fraud would be more difficult to establish under these facts. A presumption of undue influence arises in many jurisdictions anytime an attorney takes a gift from his client's will (as is the case here). In contrast, there is no evidence that the attorney misrepresented any facts to the testator (as would be necessary to prove fraud in the inducement) or that the attorney fraudulently inserted the gift into the will (as would be necessary to prove fraud in the execution). Choice **C** is incorrect. There is no evidence that Ellen lacked testamentary capacity. Choice **D** is incorrect. A probate judge would not be likely to invalidate a will for this reason. The judge might refer Jones to the proper disciplinary authorities, but he or she would be more likely to use undue influence as the basis for rejecting the will.

39. B Fraud occurs when the testator is willfully deceived as to facts that are material to his or her testamentary scheme, and these facts actually induce him or her to make, alter, or refrain from making, a testamentary gift. Robin had a duty to obtain a divorce before she remarried, and Craig had a right to believe that Robin was in fact divorced. When she declared her marital status as single, she committed a fraud upon Craig. The fraud will only matter, for probate purposes, if the court concludes that the fraud "caused" the gift; that is, that the gift would not have been made had the fraud not been committed. Because the gift was made to Robin as "my wife," there is at least strong evidence that the gift was the product of Robin's fraud, so the court will probably conclude that the requisite causal connection between fraud and gift is established. The best remedy in light of Craig's dispositive language is to probate the will and impose a constructive trust upon Robin's share in favor of Aunt Martha. Otherwise, Robin's one-half would be distributed by intestacy. This would result in Craig's children taking part of his estate — a result that he obviously did not want. Answer **A** is incorrect. Although a true general statement, it does not provide for the effect of fraud by a beneficiary. Answers **C** and **D** are incorrect. Both would result in Aunt Martha's receiving nothing and in the distribution of Craig's entire estate to his children, a result Craig expressly did not want.

40. A A general power of appointment is one that is exercisable in favor of the donee, his or her estate, his or her creditors, or the creditors of his or her estate. There are no limits on the persons to whom Ted can appoint, and so the power is a general one. Because there is no condition precedent, Ted is authorized to exercise the power during his lifetime by deed, and it is therefore "presently exercisable." Choice **B** is incorrect because Ted is not prohibited from appointing to himself, his estate, his creditors, or the creditors of his estate. Choice **C** is incorrect because Ted can exercise the power by deed during his life. Choice **D** is incorrect both (1) because Ted can appoint to himself, and (2) because Ted can exercise the power by deed.

41. C Where (1) a testator holds a power of appointment, and (2) the instrument creating the power does *not* require that the exercise of the power reference the power, a general residuary clause in a will exercises the power only if: (a) the power is a general power and the instrument creating the power does not contain an express gift in the event the power is not exercised, or (b) the will manifests the intent to include the property subject to the power. (UPC §2-608). Ted's power was a general power, and John's will contains a gift to John's heirs if Ted failed to exercise the power, so test (a) is not satisfied. Further, Ted's will did not refer at all to the power of appointment bestowed upon him in John's will or the property subject to the power, so test (b) is not satisfied either. The residuary clause of Ted's will will probably not be construed as an exercise of the power. John's estate consequently passes to John's heirs. Choice **A** is incorrect; the residuary clause did not exercise Ted's power. Choices **B** and **D** are incorrect. The property subject to Ted's power passed to John's heirs by virtue of Ted's failure to exercise the power.

42. B The word "heirs" is usually taken to refer to those persons who, at the decedent's death, are entitled to succeed to the estate under the rules of intestate succession. (UPC §2-711). Art predeceased John and was not survived by issue. Thus, his share lapsed (and antilapse does not apply to save the gift because Art has no surviving descendants to take his share). (UPC 2 §2-603(b)(1)). Bob and Charles (John's "heirs") both survived John. Their shares *vested at John's death*, subject to being divested by Ted's exercise of the power over John's estate. Because Ted did not exercise the power, their shares passed by their wills to their wives. Choice **A** is incorrect because Art predeceased John. Art was not within the class of "heirs" at John's death. Choice **C** is incorrect, because (1) Bob's share vested prior to his death, and Bob's wife was entitled to his share under his will, and (2) Charles's share passed to Marcy by will. Choice **D** is incorrect because the interests of Bob and Charles vested at John's death. They could dispose of their shares to their wives by will.

43. B Under the *capture* doctrine, whereby the donee of a general power of appointment makes an ineffective appointment, the property not effectively appointed will go to the donee's estate, not the default takers, *if* the donee manifested an intent to assume control over the appointive property for all purposes (and not simply for the limited purpose of the attempted appointment). The most common evidence of the donee manifesting an intent to assume control over the appointive property for all purposes is when the donee's will has a *blending* residuary clause—a residuary clause that blends the appointive property with the donee's own property. Here, Ted's will contains a *blending* residuary clause that purports to combine the rest of his property with the property over which he has the general power of appointment. Inasmuch as the attempted appointment is ineffective (the appointed beneficiaries are dead and anti-lapse does not apply because none left surviving descendants), and inasmuch as Ted's blending residuary clause shows his intent to exercise control over the appointive property for all purposes, the appointive property becomes part of Ted's residuary clause and will be distributed to Ann. Choice **A** is incorrect because it assumes the capture doctrine does not apply, but it does. Although Choice **C** applies the capture doctrine, it is nonetheless incorrect because it assumes that the appointive property would pass under intestacy to Ted's heirs. While the part of the residuary clause trying to appoint the appointive property was ineffective, the part giving the rest of his estate to Ann is valid and effective. Where only part of a residuary clause is invalid, the property is distributed to the other takers in the residuary clause, not through intestacy. (UPC §2-604(b)). Choice **D** is invalid because Bill has no right to all of the appointive property under either the will or intestacy.

44. C If, after executing a will, the testator is divorced from the spouse who is a beneficiary under the will, the divorce revokes any disposition made by the will to the former spouse. (UPC §2-804(b)). The divorce automatically revoked the gift to Doris, and therefore, she will receive nothing. Choices **A, B,** and **D** are all incorrect because Doris takes nothing from T's estate.

45. D When a spouse marries the testator after the testator makes his or her will, the will is treated as a premarital will and the spouse is treated as an "omitted" spouse. The omitted spouse will receive his or her intestate share of that portion of the estate that the testator did not bequeath to his or her children from another marriage or relationships, unless: (1) it appears from the will or other evidence that the will was made in contemplation of the marriage; (2) the will expresses the intent that it should be effective notwithstanding any subsequent marriage; or (3) the testator provided for the spouse outside the will, and that gift was intended to be in lieu of the spouse taking under the will. (UPC §2-301(a)). T's total estate was $130,000. After first deducting the specific bequest of $15,000 to Mike, Kay's share will be $100,000 plus one-half of the balance of $15,000, for a total of $107,500. The bequests to Ben will not be honored (see Answer 47 below). Choice **A** is mathematically incorrect. Choice **B** is incorrect both because it is mathematically incorrect and because the bequest to Ben will not be honored. Choice **C** is incorrect because Kay is an omitted spouse.

46. **D** If one or more children of the testator were living when he or she executed his or her will and the will devised property to one or more of those children, then a pretermitted child would be entitled to a pro-rata share of the gifts to such child or children. (UPC §2-302(a)(2)). Because Liz was born after the will was executed, she is a pretermitted child and she will receive one-half of the $15,000 gift to Mike ($7,500). Choices **A** and **B** are mathematically incorrect under the required formula. Choice **C** is incorrect because Liz is a pretermitted child.

47. **B** Any person who *kills* another *feloniously* and *intentionally* is not entitled to any benefit under the victim's will, and the decedent's estate passes as if the killer had disclaimed all provisions. (UPC §2-803(c)). A person who commits *voluntary* manslaughter is deemed to have intended to kill or seriously injure the decedent (in contrast to a person who commits involuntary manslaughter). Therefore, Ben satisfies the "feloniously and intentionally kills" definition, and will receive nothing from T's estate. Choice **A** is incorrect. Even though the gift of Rex, Inc., stock was adeemed, the $1,000 gift was not, but Ben is not entitled to it because of the homicide doctrine. Choices **C** and **D** are incorrect because Ben receives nothing from T's estate.

48. **A** *Powers of appointment* are generally *releasable*. Upon the release of a power of appointment, the property passes to previously designated takers in default; in this case, to Linda's living issue, per stirpes. Linda's release of the power was effective when delivered to Sam. Her attempt to exercise the power in her will was ineffective. The result is that the property held by Sam in trust passes to Linda's surviving issue, per stirpes. Choice **B** is incorrect because the attempted exercise of the power is ineffective after the power has been released. Choice **C** is incorrect because Martha is entitled to Karen's share under the per stirpes approach. Choice **D** is incorrect because Ralph provided for default takers in the event the power was released or not exercised by Linda, so the property in question does not pass through intestacy.

49. **C** A testamentary power may not be encumbered by or made subject to a contract with the holder of the power. Because contracts encumbering a *testamentary* power of appointment are unenforceable, Linda's exercise of the power is valid. Thus, Adam, Ron, and

Martha take equally. Choice **A** is incorrect because the contract between Linda and Adam is unenforceable. Adam may, of course, sue Linda's estate for restitution. Choice **B** is incorrect because Martha was specifically included among the appointees. Choice **D** is incorrect because Linda exercised the power through her will.

50. **C/A** A trust is created only if (1) the settlor has the intent to create a trust *when the property is transferred to the trustee*, and (2) the settlor appropriately manifests his or her intent to the outside world. Although the key is the settlor's intent at the moment he or she transfers the property in question, evidence of the intent can include acts or statements that occur *after* the act that purportedly creates the trust. (Restatement 3d of Trusts, §13, Comment b). Here, Alice made no statement when she initially transferred the property to Jim, but only two weeks later she clearly expressed her intent that the property was being transferred in trust. Alice's subsequent statements are relevant to the issue of her intent at the time of transfer and would be considered by a court. The magnitude of the gift, Alice's subsequent unequivocable assertion that the property was to be held in trust, Jim's initial acquiescence to Alice's trust assertion, and the fact that Alice has surviving children — all of these considerations support a finding that Alice intended a trust when the initial transfer occurred. The key, however, is what Alice intended *at the time of the transfer*; a subsequently formed intent would not count. This is a close call. If the court were to conclude that Alice had the intent to form a trust at the time of the transfer, Choice **C** would be correct. Choices **A, B, and D** would all be incorrect because they all assume that no valid trust was created. If, however, the court were to conclude that Alice did not have the intent to form a trust when she transferred the money to Jim, Choice **A** would be correct. (Choice **B, C, and D** would be incorrect because if there is no trust, Jim gets to keep the property and no one else has any right to it.)

51. **B** When a trustor manifests an intent that a trust take effect at some *future point in time*, no trust is created. (Restatement 3d of Trusts, §15, Comment b). Because Stephanie manifested an intent that the trust be created only upon her return from Europe, no valid trust was created. The farm was still part of her estate and passed to Rick pursuant to the will. Choice **A** is incorrect, because no trust was created by the letter to Sam. The letter expressed only an

intent to create a trust in the future. Choice **C** is incorrect. Stephanie's death did not in itself have any testamentary effect. No trust was ever created because the letter to Sam manifested only the intent to create one in the future. Choice **D** is incorrect in that the farm passed pursuant to Stephanie's will, not by intestacy.

52. **D** A special power is one that prevents the donee from appointing to himself or herself, his or her estate, his or her creditors, or the creditors of his or her estate. Because Linda can appoint only to her issue, her power is a special (rather than a general) power. Because Linda is limited to appointment by will, the power is testamentary. Choice **A** is incorrect because Linda's power is neither general nor presently exercisable. The power cannot be exercised (1) in favor of Linda, her estate, her creditors, or the creditors of her estate, and (2) until her death. Choice **B** is incorrect in that the power cannot be exercised in favor of Linda, her estate, her creditors, or the creditors of her estate. Choice **C** is incorrect in that the power can be exercised only by Linda's will.

53. **D** A trust must *identify the beneficiaries* or provide a standard by which the beneficiaries can reasonably be ascertained. If the beneficiaries are indefinite, and there is no reasonable way to identify them, the trust fails. (Restatement 3d of Trusts, §46). The designation of "my three best friends" is probably an insufficient description of the beneficiaries, as evidenced by the fact that John, who was also Christina's friend, was unsure who her three best friends were. Thus, the trust probably fails, and Christina's entire estate passes to her mother. Choices **A** and **B** are incorrect because the trust failed. Choice **C** is incorrect. Christina never manifested any intent that Ann, Barbara, and Cary should take anything outright.

54. **B** A formal will must ordinarily be signed by the testator and at least two persons, each of whom witnessed either the signing of the will or the testator's acknowledgment of his or her signature or the will. (UPC §2-502). Although at common law and under many state statutes the witnesses must sign in the presence of each other, the UPC does *not* require that the two witnesses sign in each other's presence. The UPC does require, however, that each witness sign within a reasonable time of witnessing the testator sign or acknowledge the will. Although X and Y did not sign the will in front of each other, because each signed shortly after having witnessed T execute her will, T has a valid testamentary writing. Choice **A** is incorrect because the will was typed, and the "material provisions" were not

in the testator's handwriting. Choice **C** is incorrect because there is no requirement under the UPC that the witnesses sign the will in each other's presence. Choice **D** is incorrect because there is no requirement that an attested will be dated to be valid.

55. **B**   Because T signed and acknowledged the will in the presence of X and Y, and they signed within a reasonable time thereafter, the writing is valid. (UPC §2-502). Choice **A** is incorrect because the will was typed, and the "material provisions" were not in the testator's handwriting. Choice **C** is incorrect because there is no requirement under the UPC that witnesses sign the will in the testator's presence. Choice **D** is incorrect because there is no requirement that witnesses actually read, or know the provisions of, the testator's will.

56. **C/A** The traditional and general rule is that to be valid, a trust must have (among other requirements) a named or *ascertainable beneficiary* capable of enforcing the trust. Traditionally, in most states, this beneficiary must be a *human* (or organization), not an animal. Although the modern trend is to recognize honorary trusts (a trust with no definitely ascertainable human beneficiary and with only a specific noncharitable purpose), the traditional approach to the law of trusts does not recognize honorary trusts. Trusts for the care of specific animals are honorary trusts. Under the traditional approach to the law of trusts, the trust for Rusty's care will fail. (Note that the UPC has optional provisions, §2-907(a) and (b), and the Restatement Third of Trusts has a provision, §47, which validate a trust for a "designated domestic or pet animal." [UPC §2-907(b)]. The trust is enforceable by a trustee designated in the trust instrument or one appointed by the court. In a jurisdiction with this provision in force or that adopts the Restatement Third of Trusts approach, the correct answer would be Choice **A**.) Choice **A** is incorrect in most jurisdictions; there must be a named or reasonably identifiable *individual* who could enforce the trust. Choice **B** is incorrect because Bruce manifested no intent that Selma take the property in her own right. Choice **D** is incorrect because there is a right answer — Choice **C**.

57. **C**   A condition in a trust unreasonably restraining marriage is usually not enforced. (Restatement 3d of Trusts, §29, Comment j). A gift over to an alternate beneficiary upon *remarriage* of the settlor's **surviving spouse** is usually viewed as only a *partial*

restraint upon marriage. (*Id*). On the other hand, the condition imposed upon the children that they not marry constitutes a *complete* restraint on marriage and is likely to be deemed unreasonable. This condition should be stricken, and the gift for their benefit should be without this restraint. (Restatement 3d, §29, comment i). The condition imposed upon Will that he not receive anything if he remarried is probably enforceable. Choice **A** is incorrect because the condition that Will forfeit his interest if he remarried is probably enforceable. Choice **B** is incorrect. The court is likely to find the condition imposed upon Will reasonable and enforceable. On the other hand, the conditions imposed upon the children will be deemed unreasonable and will be stricken. Choice **D** is incorrect. If a condition is deemed invalid, it is stricken and the trust is otherwise enforced.

58. **B** A secret trust arises when a will makes an outright gift in reliance upon the devisee's *oral promise* to hold the property as trustee for others. The agreement here is unenforceable as an express trust, because the oral agreement did not comply with the statutory formalities for wills (*e.g.*, the requirement that the terms be in writing). However, a *constructive trust* may be imposed in favor of the intended beneficiary to prevent the devisee's unjust enrichment, provided that the court is convinced by extrinsic evidence that the decedent relied on the devisee's promise to hold the property in trust for another. Here, Judith relied upon Earl's oral promise to hold the funds in trust for Grace. Although Earl's promise is unenforceable as an express trust, it may be enforceable as a constructive trust to prevent Earl from being unjustly enriched. Choice **A** is incorrect in that a testamentary express trust cannot be created orally; it must be executed in accordance with the requisite formalities of a valid will. Choice **C** is incorrect; a resulting trust could not result because there was no *express* intention on the face of the will to create a trust. Choice **D** is incorrect; a majority of states would impose a constructive trust in this situation.

59. **C** Where the express language of a will expresses the intent to create a trust, but the trust fails for want of adequate terms (*i.e.*, failure to identify the beneficiary or failure to set forth the terms of the trust), the failed attempt at a testamentary trust is called a *semisecret* trust. The traditional and still majority rule is to impose a *resulting trust* on the failed trust, and the property in question falls to the residuary clause of the will. Because Judith indicated in the will that the gift

was made in trust, but failed to name the beneficiary in the will, the trust is a resulting one for the residuary legatees. A constructive trust will ordinarily not be imposed, because the will indicates on its face that Earl is taking the property as trustee and there's no opportunity for unjust enrichment by him. Choice **A** is incorrect. Grace will probably not be permitted to enforce the trust because the trust fails for want of ascertainable beneficiaries — she was not specifically named in the will. Choice **B** is incorrect because the majority rule is to impose a resulting trust where the failed testamentary trust is a semisecret trust; a constructive trust is imposed, as a general rule, where the failed trust is a secret trust (though there is a modern trend to apply the constructive trust to both the secret and the semisecret trust — in which case Choice B would be the correct choice). Choice **D** is incorrect because Judith's will expressly stated that Earl was to take the bequest in trust, not outright, so the failed trust is a semisecret trust and a resulting trust is the appropriate remedy to keep Earl from taking the bequest.

60. A A bank or savings account in the name of "X, in trust for Y" is called a "Totten trust," and is viewed as a type of informal will. Upon the death of X, the funds in a Totten account will be deemed to belong to Y. See UPC §6-212(b) and the Comment thereto; see also §6-201(8)(ii). This construction will not apply where there is clear evidence that X did not intend a death benefit to Y, but there is no such evidence here. Therefore, Karen takes the funds in the account. Choice **B** is incorrect because there was a valid Totten trust. If no trust existed, Choice **B** would be the correct answer because Amy left all her property to Ed. Choices **C** and **D** are incorrect because the account is a valid Totten trust in favor of Karen alone; and even if the trust were invalid, the account would pass under the residuary clause of Amy's will to only Ed.

61. C A Totten trust is automatically revoked upon the death of the beneficiary prior to the death of the settlor. See UPC §6-212(b)(2), last sentence. The contents of the account then belong to the settlor free of the trust. Therefore, the trust res passes to Ed under the terms of Amy's will. Choice **A** is incorrect in that the interest of Karen was divested when she predeceased Amy. Karen could not dispose of the account by her will. Choice **B** is incorrect because Karen's interest in the Totten trust was extinguished by her death before Amy. No one could take any interest in the account through Karen. Choice **D** is incorrect because Amy's will disposed of her estate to Ed.

62. D The beneficial interest in a trust is *alienable*, unless the trustor specifically imposes some restraint upon alienation. Because no restraint upon the alienation of Carl's interest was stipulated in the trust, the assignment was valid. However, Carl could assign only his own equitable interest in the trust (*i.e.*, the trust continues in accordance with its terms). Choice **A** is incorrect; Carl's interest was alienable because the trustor did not specifically restrain his right to alienate. Choice **B** is incorrect; both income and remainder interests are alienable. Choice **C** is incorrect; although Carl's interests may be assigned, the assignee can receive only an interest that is coextensive with that enjoyed by Carl as the beneficiary-assignor.

63. A In most jurisdictions, the first assignee in point of time prevails, regardless of who first gives notice to the trustee. (Restatement 3d of Trusts, §54). Because Carl's interest is an equitable one, he retained no interest that he could assign subsequently (but if Ted could successfully assert estoppel against Sam, Ted would prevail under the Restatement Third of Trusts approach. [Restatement 3d of Trusts, §54]. But it is unclear whether Ted could prevail under these facts.) Choice **B** is incorrect; consideration is not a pertinent factor here (the bona fide purchaser rule is not applicable in this context). Choice **C** is incorrect as a statement of law (priority of ownership is ordinarily not based upon the order of notification to the trustee). Choice **D** is incorrect in that consideration is not pertinent on these facts.

64. C The vested, equitable interest of a beneficiary in a trust can ordinarily be reached by a writ of execution against the beneficiary. However, only the debtor's interest can be levied upon. Lucille owns only a right to the income from the trust res. The trustee must, therefore, pay the income to the marshal (for application against the judgment) until (1) the judgment is satisfied, or (2) Lucille dies, whichever first occurs. Choice **A** is legally incorrect. In most states, a writ of execution will reach an equitable interest that is *not* contingent. Choices **B** and **D** are incorrect, because Lucille holds only a life interest. The courts will not usually order sale or conveyance of the entire property to satisfy a judgment against one who is solely a life tenant. (Haskell, p. 226).

65. C Although the existence of a spendthrift clause makes it impossible for a beneficiary to make a legally binding transfer of his or her interest, (1) the trustee *may* choose to honor the beneficiary's purported assignment, and (2) the beneficiary can revoke the transfer at any time as to future payments. (Uniform Trust Code [UTC] §502). Here, assuming the trustee decides to honor the purported transfer, the direction is valid, but revocable by Beatrix. The trustee may pay the income to Karen until such time as (1) the trustee decides to recommence distributions to the beneficiary Beatrix, or (2) Beatrix revokes the transfer (as to future payments only). Choice **A** is incorrect because the transfer is not *per se* void — it is valid to the extent the trustee decides to honor it and the beneficiary does not revoke it. Choice **B** is incorrect because the phrase that the trustee "*must*" pay the income to Karen fails to recognize (1) that trustee does not have to honor the purported transfer, and (2) that the beneficiary can revoke the purported transfer (as to future payments). Choice **D** is incorrect because (1) the purported transfer is not *per se* void, and (2) the debt to Karen is not satisfied until completely paid.

66. **A** Under the majority rule, and the newly adopted Uniform Trust Code, UTC §503, certain classes of creditors are not restrained by a spendthrift clause. The claims of the federal government for unpaid taxes under the Internal Revenue Code are usually within this group. (UTC §503(b)(3)). Choice **B** is incorrect; Beatrix's interest is only an income interest, which does not enable the government or any one else to reach the trust principal. Choices **C** and **D** are incorrect because a spendthrift clause is *not* valid against a judgment by the United States.

67. **D** In the absence of words clearly expressing a trust intent, the court will rarely find such intent. John's will expressed only "the hope," instead of the mandate, that Ted would use the funds for his children. The court is unlikely to impose duties of trust on these facts. Words such as "hope," "wish," and "desire" are called precatory language; they are not usually enough to impose a trust. Choice **A** is incorrect because there are no mandatory words of trust intent. If, however, the court found that John did intend to create a trust, this would be the proper remedy. Choice **B** is incorrect; a resulting trust arises where a trust fails, in whole or in part. Here, there was *no* intent to create a trust (the language was only precatory), so it is not a failed trust. Choice **C** is incorrect; there is no equitable reason to impose a trust in favor of Bill.

68. **B** The interest of a beneficiary that is subject to the discretion of the trustee may not be subjected to the claims of his or her creditors,

until that discretion has been exercised. The creditor could levy upon Larry's remainder interest, because this interest is *not* subject to the trustee's discretion. However, a court would order that *no* amount be paid to the creditor until the last of Kathy's children died. Until that time, it would not be possible to determine Larry's *per capita* interest precisely. Choice **A** is incorrect. Larry's income interest is subject to the trustee's discretion (and therefore not attachable). Choice **C** is incorrect; it includes Larry's income interest, which is subject to the trustee's discretion and not subject to the creditor's claim. Choice **D** is incorrect because Larry's remainder interest may be attached by creditors, subject to the restriction discussed above.

69. C A trustor cannot create a spendthrift trust in favor of himself or herself. His or her interest is subject to the claims of creditors (present or prospective). Therefore, Ted may not create a spendthrift trust in favor of himself. Insofar as he retains an interest (*i.e.,* the income interest, in this case), it is subject to the claims of his creditors. Mae's interest, however, is not subject to the claims of Ted's creditors, unless the transfer constituted a fraud upon his creditors (*i.e.,* Ted was insolvent when the transfer of funds was *initially* made). Choices **A** and **B** are incorrect because Ted is not permitted to create a spendthrift trust in favor of himself. Choice **D** is incorrect because Mae's interest in the trust cannot be attached by Ted's creditors.

70. A A trust qualifies as a charitable trust as long as its purpose is charitable. Charitable purposes include: (1) the relief of poverty; (2) the advancement of education; (3) the advancement of religion; (4) the promotion of health; (5) governmental or municipal purposes; or (6) other purposes the accomplishment of which is beneficial to the community. Moreover, a charitable trust must benefit either society as a whole or a substantial segment of the community. If the purpose is a valid charitable purpose, and a broad segment of the community benefits (either directly or indirectly), the trust is usually a valid charitable trust, even though the trust funds may be distributed to only a limited number of recipients. The benefits of a charitable trust are that (1) the beneficiaries do not have to be ascertainable (and in fact should not be because it is to benefit a large segment of society), and (2) the trust is not subject to the Rule Against Perpetuities. Here, because the purpose of the trust is to discover a cure for cancer, and the benefits of this accomplishment will be shared by a large segment of society, the trust, most likely, is a valid charitable trust. Choice **B** is incorrect because a large segment of society will benefit indirectly and that is good enough for a charitable trust. Choices **C** and **D** are incorrect because charitable trusts are not subject to the Rule Against Perpetuities.

71. **D** Courts have enforced trusts "for charitable purposes" even though the trustee was authorized to select any charitable purpose. The trustee can probably use the money for any purpose that comes within the definition of "charitable" as that term is defined under the applicable law. Choice **A** is incorrect because the beneficiaries need not be ascertainable as long as the trust qualifies as a charitable trust. In addition, the courts have held that a trust for "charitable purposes" authorizes the trustee to select a particular charitable purpose and is a valid charitable trust. Choice **B** is incorrect because charitable trusts are exempt from the Rule Against Perpetuities. Choice **C** is incorrect; the trustee is not limited in his choices but may utilize the trust res for any charitable purpose.

72. **D** When the purpose of a trust is to encourage illegal activity, the trust is invalid. A trust created for the purpose of rewarding persons who have broken the law is invalid. Many people believe with Lynn that the drug laws are too punitive and restrictive. But they may not commit their funds to encourage violation of the law as long as it remains the law. It would be proper for Lynn to campaign politically to change the law, but not to reward violators of the law. The trust will fail and the trust res will pass to Max under intestacy principles. Choices **A** and **B** are incorrect because the primary purpose of the trust is to reward persons who have broken the law, and thus the trust does not have a valid charitable trust purpose. Choice **C** is incorrect; there is no presently cognizable general charitable purpose for this trust. The only persons receiving a benefit are those who have engaged in activity that is defined as illegal.

73. **D** A charitable trust cannot benefit a profit-making organization. Although International University is an educational institution, it is described as a profit-making organization. It is, therefore, disqualified as a valid charitable beneficiary. Choice **A** is incorrect; even though the purpose of the trust is education, it may not benefit a profit-making organization. Choice **B** is incorrect; the trust fails because the beneficiary of the trust is a profit-making entity. Choice **C** is incorrect; although the students may be indigent, the beneficiary is a profit-making organization.

74. B When the particular charitable purpose specified by a trustor has become impossible, or impracticable to accomplish, and it is determined that the trustor had a general charitable intent, a court may modify the trust so as to carry out the trustor's purpose to the extent that it is possible to do so. The theory permitting such modification is called the *cy pres* doctrine. Although Terry's alma mater was chosen as the recipient of the gift, it may be argued that Terry's primary purpose was to benefit "worthy students from Arizona." Thus, the *cy pres* doctrine should be used to allow the gift to be given to another charitable institution whose primary purpose is education and whose students include students from Arizona. Choice **A** is incorrect in that a charitable gift cannot be made to a profit-making organization. Choice **C** is correct only if the charitable gift is held to fail. In this instance, the broader purpose of educating Arizona students can be carried out without destroying the trust. Choice **D** is incorrect because *cy pres* should be applied before the trust is deemed to fail; and even if the trust were to fail, a resulting trust would be imposed and the money would go to the residuary clause where it would pass to Terry's parents.

75. B/C This is a very difficult question, probably better suited for an essay question rather than for a multiple choice question. There has been much litigation over whether a gift that contains provisions that discriminate on the basis of race and/or gender constitutes illegal discrimination. Here, there are no public entities involved in the immediate administration of the trust, but if Delphi balks at applying the terms of the trust and is sued, there would be an issue as to whether the court's enforcement of the original terms constitutes impermissible state action. The problem is that Delphi cannot accept the gift as intended, so the trust purpose has become impossible/impractical. From a doctrinal perspective, the general rule is that where the problem can be solved using administrative deviation, administrative deviation is preferred to cy pres because the former retains the settlor's original intent as to the trust's core, dispositive provisions. That would support the position that Choice **B** is correct because it solves the trust problem by changing the administrative provisions — substituting another institution that can adhere to the settlor's original restrictions. On the other hand, many courts find such discriminatory restrictions abhorrent, if not illegal, and to avoid issues of state action, apply cy pres to strike the offending provision. That would support the position that Choice **C** is correct because it solves the trust problem by striking the discriminatory provision and permitting Delphi to continue to administer the trust. On the other hand, some courts, though probably a minority, are reluctant to apply cy pres to such discriminatory restrictions and prefer simply to terminate the trust — although this is counter to the strong public policy in favor of sustaining charitable gifts whenever possible. That reasoning would support Choice **D**. But while Choice **D** is defensible, it arguably is incorrect in light of the call of the question, which asked what a court would "probably" do and this is a minority approach. Choice **A** is incorrect because the settlor clearly expressed strong feelings against using the funds for the education of atheists, which does not raise the same constitutional and statutory concerns as discrimination based on race and gender, and it would be inconsistent with his charitable intent to repudiate this constraint.

76. **B** A trustee is ordinarily prohibited from any type of self-dealing, which constitutes a breach of fiduciary duty, and under the "no further inquiry rule" the trustee's good faith and/or the reasonableness of the transaction is irrelevant. See also UTC §802(b). The trustee cannot personally purchase trust property even for its fair market value. (Restatement 3d. of Trusts, §78, Comment b [tentative draft 2005]). Although Edward had an implied right to sell the trust asset, the sale of trust property *to himself* was prohibited. Choice **A** is incorrect because, although Edward had an implied power to sell the trust assets under these circumstances, he did not have the right to sell them to himself. Choice **C** is incorrect because under the "no further inquiry" rule, where the trustee breaches the no self-dealing rule, the reasonableness of the transaction is irrelevant. Choice **D** is incorrect because absent express authorization by the settlor or consent by all the beneficiaries following full disclosure, a fiduciary cannot engage in self-dealing. (The newly adopted Uniform Trust Code adopts an exception to this traditional approach, but that exception is beyond the scope of this question.)

77. **A** Under traditional trust principles, a trustee has no implied power to *borrow funds* or to encumber trust property. A trustee cannot ordinarily borrow funds against trust assets or against the general credit of the trust, unless he has been specifically granted that power. Choice **B** is incorrect. Edward violated his duty whether

or not the net income was reduced. Choice **C** is incorrect; a trustee has no implied power to borrow funds against trust property. He or she must have the express authority to borrow. Choice **D** is legally incorrect. Edward did breach his fiduciary duty by exercising a power which he did not possess.

[Under the Uniform Trust Code, a trustee is granted broad powers over the trust property. The Code expressly grants each trustee "all powers over the trust property which an unmarried competent owner has over individually owned property;" and "any other powers appropriate to achieve the property investment, management, and distribution of the trust property . . . ." (UTC §815 (a)(2)(A) and (B)). The code goes on to expressly grant each trustee the power to "borrow money, with or without security, and mortgage or pledge trust property . . . ." (UTC §816(5)). The call of the question, however, expressly asked how the fact pattern would be resolved under traditional trust principles.]

78. C A trustee must act within the bounds of reasonable judgment in carrying out the purpose of the trust. (Restatement 3d of Trusts, §87 Comment d [tentative draft 2005]; UTC §814(a)). The grant of sole, absolute, or uncontrolled discretion does not completely insulate the trustee from judicial review. Even though "sole, absolute, and uncontrolled" discretion was granted to the trustee, she was required to carry out the purpose of the trust in a good faith, non-arbitrary manner. The favoring of one beneficiary over another without reason would be arbitrary, and an abuse of discretion, for which the court could impose liability. Choices **A** and **B** are incorrect in that the court does have the power to review the decisions of the trustee in these circumstances (*i.e.*, making income payments only to the oldest child, who might be the least needy); and there is no presumption that the trustee has acted reasonably when the facts (preferring one child to the others) would support a contrary presumption. Choice **D** is incorrect in that the court is not permitted to substitute its own judgment, but may impose liability for actions that are so unreasonable as to amount to an abuse of discretion by the trustee.

79. D Because real property values historically fluctuate greatly, a trustee is generally not authorized to invest in *unimproved land* for resale or appreciation. However, a trust instrument may specifically authorize the trustee to make such an investment. Here, Ted had no such authority. Choice **A** is incorrect; although a trustee is governed by

the prudent investor rule, investment in unimproved land for appreciation or resale is generally deemed imprudent by its very nature. Even under the modern portfolio approach, absent special
circumstances investment of *all* of the trust's assets in one parcel
of unimproved real estate is probably too risky and inconsistent
with the settlor's intent. Choice **B** is incorrect in that the applicable
rule is not mitigated by an appraisal that happens to support the
trustee's judgment. Choice **C** is incorrect; an otherwise improper
investment may be specifically authorized by the trust instrument.

80. **C** At common law and under earlier versions of the Restatement of
Trusts, cotrustees were required to exercise their trust powers joint-
ly, and the exercise normally required unanimity. (Restatement 2d
of Trusts, §194). The modern trend, as evidenced by the Restatement Third of Trusts and the Uniform Trust Code is to authorize
cotrustees who are unable to reach a unanimous decision to act by
majority decision — but if there are only two, their powers may be
exercised only by concurrence of both. (Restatement 3d of Trusts,
§39; UTC §703 (a)). Here there are only two trustees and the decision of one is insufficient even under the modern trend. If there is
an emergency or a cotrustee is unavailable to perform his or her
duties, the remaining cotrustee may act for the trust. (Restatement
3d of Trusts, §39; UTC §703 (d)). But this is not an emergency and
Baker is not "unavailable" to perform his duties, he simply does not
agree that an appeal is in the best interests of the trust. Able could try
to seek a court order dispensing with the need for Baker's consent
and cooperation in the appeal. But without the order, Able cannot
act alone. Choice **A** is incorrect because Able may not appeal the
judgment unilaterally. If he proceeds with the appeal anyway in
good faith, he may be entitled to reimbursement for the costs.
Choice **B** is incorrect because of the requirement of unanimity.
Choice **D** is incorrect. So long as Baker acts with reasonable business
judgment and in good faith, he may refuse to join in the appeal.

81. **D** Historically, once a trustee accepted the position, he or she could
not resign without court approval. Under the Uniform Trust Code,
the trustee can resign (1) with court approval, or (2) by notice to the
beneficiaries, settlor (if living), and all cotrustees. (UTC §705 (a)).
Here, Karl has done none of the above — though he arguably is not
"resigning" but only delegating his responsibilities while tempo-
rarily away. But the law is equally demanding with respect to a
trustee's ability to delegate his or her powers. At common law,

a trustee could only delegate ministerial powers at best, not discretionary powers. Here, Karl has purported to delegate all powers and duties — a clear breach of his common law duties as trustee. Under the Uniform Trust Code, a trustee is given greater authority to delegate powers and duties, but even then the trustee must exercise reasonable care (1) in selecting the agent, (2) in establishing the scope and terms of the delegation, and (3) in periodically reviewing the agent's actions. (UTC §807 (a)). There is no evidence here that Karl has exercised reasonable care in selecting Edward, and more importantly, there is no evidence that Karl has exercised reasonable care in establishing the scope and terms of the delegation and/or in monitoring Edward. Under both the traditional approach and the modern-trend approach, Karl has breached his fiduciary duty. Choice **A** is incorrect because Karl is not permitted under these facts to relieve himself of his duties as trustee during the year and would be liable for any resulting damages. Choice **B** is incorrect because Karl has not properly delegated his powers under either the traditional approach or the modern trend. Choice **C** is incorrect under the traditional approach because the trustee could delegate ministerial duties and powers, but not discretionary duties and powers; and it is incorrect under the modern trend because while it may be permissible to delegate discretionary duties and powers under the modern trend, it is permissible only under limited conditions that Karl has not established here.

82. **B** Under traditional trust principles, a trustee may employ agents to perform services for the trust, so long as the trustee exercises the care of a reasonably prudent person in selecting the agents and continues to oversee the performance of their assigned services. The duty to make investment decisions is not *totally* delegable. Karl was required to inquire of Edward his reasons for investing in particular stocks and the likelihood of their financial success. After these inquiries, Karl was required to make the investment decision himself. If Karl failed in either duty, he would be strictly liable for any loss (even if a reasonably prudent investor might have made the same investment decision as Edward). Choice **A** is incorrect; Karl is liable even if the stock would have been purchased by the prudent investor. Choice **C** is incorrect in that Karl was obliged to oversee, inquire into, and approve Edward's decisions. Choice **D** is incorrect; even if Karl exercised reasonable care in selecting Edward, he was still obliged to "supervise" and review all of Edward's investment recommendations.

[Under the Uniform Trust Code, a trustee is granted greater authority to delegate powers over the trust property as long as the trustee exercises reasonable care (1) in selecting the agent, (2) in establishing the scope and terms of the delegation, and (3) in periodically reviewing the agent's actions. (UTC §807 (a)). It is a closer call whether Karl has breached his duty under the Uniform Trust Code, but a strong argument can be made that Karl has not periodically reviewed the agent's actions in order to monitor the agent's performance. The call of the question, however, expressly asked how the fact pattern would be resolved under traditional trust principles so this latter discussion is moot.]

83. **B** Absent authorization in the terms of the trust, it is a breach of a trustee's fiduciary duty to borrow funds from the trust for his or her personal use. (Restatement 3d of Trusts, §78, Comment d [tentative draft 2005]). In addition to repaying the principal and interest of the loan, Karl must forfeit all profits that he made as a consequence of his loans from the trust. (Restatement 3d of Trusts — Prudent Investor Rule, §§205-06). Choice **A** is incorrect; Karl is legally obliged to remit any profits to the trust. It is immaterial to the central issue of trust that no damage occurred. Choices **C** and **D** are incorrect. It's plain and simple — Karl has breached his fiduciary duty to the trust. It was improper for him to borrow funds from the trust under any circumstances and he is liable whether or not the trust suffered any losses and whether or not he repaid his loans.

84. **D** A valid exculpatory clause in a trust is sufficient to excuse ordinary negligence; as a matter of public policy, however, it is not ordinarily construed as relieving a trustee for losses resulting from bad faith, intentional wrongs, or *gross* negligence. (Section §1008(a) of the Uniform Trust Code provides that despite a valid exculpatory clause a trustee remains liable for breaches committed in bad faith or "with reckless indifference to the purposes of the trust or the interests of the beneficiaries" — reckless indifference arguably includes intentional wrongs and gross negligence). The exculpatory clause here would therefore be sufficient to excuse Amy from liability based upon ordinary negligence, but not gross negligence. Choice **A** is incorrect in that Amy would be liable for the consequences of her gross negligence — that is, if she had invested in the new business without conducting any investigation at all. Choice **B** is incorrect in that if Amy were liable at all, the loss of income resulting from her negligence might affect the other beneficiaries

of the trust as well as Amy herself (Amy was entitled only to that portion of income necessary for her own support, maintenance, and education). Choice **C** is incorrect; if Amy's omission constituted gross negligence, she would be liable to the other beneficiaries for lost principal.

85. A Under traditional trust principles, a trustee is ordinarily *personally liable* for breach of contract regarding trust assets. Under the traditional approach, a trustee held liable for breach of contract has a right of indemnification from the trust, so long as he or she acted in good faith. Although Laura is personally liable as trustee under the traditional approach, she has a right to indemnification, assuming she acted in good faith and assuming there are sufficient assets. Choice **B** is incorrect; Laura is personally liable under the traditional approach. Choice **C** is incorrect; Laura probably has a right to indemnification under the traditional approach because she appears to have acted in good faith. Choice **D** is incorrect; Laura has a right of indemnification whether or not the trust document contains an exculpatory clause.

[It should be noted that the modern trend is that the trustee is **not** personally liable on contracts properly entered into in his or her fiduciary capacity in the course of trust administration as long as the trustee discloses his or her representative capacity and the identity of the trust. (UPC §7-306; UTC §1010 requires only disclosure acting in representative capacity).]

86. C Under traditional trust principles, a trustee is ordinarily personally liable for all torts he or she commits during his or her administration of the trust, whether or not he or she is personally at fault. Furthermore, a trustee cannot obtain *indemnity* from the trust when he or she is personally at fault. Because Bill was personally at fault (*i.e.*, he was driving negligently), he may *not* receive indemnity from the trust estate. The fact that Bill was arguably acting in the course of administering the trust is irrelevant. Choice **A** is incorrect because Bill may not indemnify himself under these circumstances under the traditional approach. Choice **B** is incorrect because Bill is personally liable under the traditional approach. Choice **D** is incorrect because an exculpatory clause ordinarily insulates a trustee from responsibility to reimburse a trust for diminishing its assets by his or her errors in judgment—it does not authorize indemnity for the personal negligence of the trustee in causing injury to third parties. (It should be mentioned that the trust assets are ordinarily not available to pay claims for torts personally committed by the trustee in the course of administering the trust. Even if Bill is judgment proof, Phyllis will probably not be able to recover against the trust's assets.)

[It should be noted that the modern trend is that the trustee is personally liable for torts committed in the course of trust administration only if the trustee is personally at fault. (UPC §7-306(b); UTC §1010(b)).]

87. **B** Under traditional trust principles, a trustee is ordinarily personally liable for all torts committed by employees of the trust while acting within the scope of their employment. The trustee is, in fact and in law, the employer. The trustee is ordinarily entitled to indemnity under traditional trust principles as long as he or she was not personally at fault. Bill is personally liable under the principle of respondeat superior; but because he was not personally at fault he may seek indemnity from the trust property. Bill's recovery, however, is limited to the trust assets; he cannot seek indemnity from the trust beneficiaries themselves. In this case, he must personally pay the excess damages ($100,000). Choice **A** is incorrect; a trustee may *not* ordinarily seek indemnity from the beneficiaries individually. Choices **C** and **D** are incorrect in at least one respect — Bill is personally liable under traditional trust principles.

[It should be noted that the modern trend is that the trustee is personally liable for torts committed in the course of trust administration only if the trustee is personally at fault. (UPC §7-306(b); UTC §1010(b)).]

88. **A** Under traditional trust principles, in most states, *stock dividends* are always treated as principal, and thus allocated to the *corpus* of a trust. Choices **B**, **C**, and **D** are all incorrect because stock dividends are usually allocated exclusively and entirely to the corpus of a trust.

[It should be noted that the modern trend is to adopt the portfolio approach to trust investments, which favors overall trust return as opposed to specific classification of the return as income or principal. Under the 1997 Principal and Income Act, §104, the trustee is granted the power of equitable distribution to reallocate the total return between the income and principal beneficiaries to ensure that the two groups are treated fairly while paying particular attention to the larger rate of return regardless of how the return is classified (income vs. principal).]

89. **D** When there is an income interest in a trust separate from the principal interest, the trustee is generally obligated to *sell unproductive property* within a reasonable time period. (Restatement 3d of Trusts, §240). (This rule also applies to "under-productive" assets, *i.e.*, those that produce so little current income, compared with what could be earned from an alternative investment having the same principal value, that it is unfair to the income beneficiary to keep the low-income assets.) Under the modern trend, the trustee has an obligation to apportion the proceeds between the income beneficiaries and the principal where the sale is delayed. The facts here imply that the trustee did not immediately sell the unproductive parcels of land. Therefore the trustee has a duty to sell the property within a reasonable period of time, and, in light of the delay in selling the parcels of land, to apportion some of the sale proceeds to the income beneficiaries. Choice **A** is incorrect because it does not acknowledge the trustee's duty to sell under these circumstances and it incorrectly allocates all of the sale proceeds to the principal. Choice **B** is incorrect because it fails to acknowledge the trustee's duty to sell under these circumstances. Choice **C** is incorrect because it fails to acknowledge the trustee's duty to apportion some of the sale proceeds to the income beneficiaries.

90. **D** Under traditional trust principles, *maintenance, taxes,* and *insurance* pertaining to trust assets are paid, in the first instance, *from income* (even though these expenditures protect both income and remainder interests). Under the traditional approach, all three expenditures are charged to the income beneficiaries. Choice **A** is incorrect in that taxes and insurance are also charged against trust income. Choice **B** is incorrect in that insurance is also charged against trust income. Choice **C** is incorrect in that the maintenance of trust assets is also charged against income.

91. **D** Under traditional trust principles (and still the Restatement 3d of Trusts approach, §63) the settlor has the power to revoke or modify a trust only to the extent the terms of the trust so provide. Because the facts indicate that Ellen did not expressly retain a power to revoke or modify, she can do neither. Choices **A, B,** and **C** are incorrect because Ellen did not explicitly retain the power to modify or revoke the trust.

[It should be noted that the Uniform Trust Code provides that a settlor retains the power to revoke or modify the trust unless the trust expressly provides otherwise. (UTC §602).]

Table of References to the Uniform Probate Code (UPC)

Table of References to the Uniform Trust Code

Table of References to the Restatement (2d) of Trusts

Table of References to the Restatement (3d) of Trusts

Revisions to Uniform Law Charts

I. Essay Questions

Q2:   Uniform Probate Code
        §2-202 added
Q7:   Uniform Trust Code
        §802(b) added
Q8:   Uniform Trust Code
        §402 added
        Uniform Probate Code
        §2-707 added
        Uniform Probate Code
        §2-603(b)(2) deleted
Q9:   Uniform Probate Code
        §1-201(11) added
Q10:   Uniform Probate Code
        §2-503 added
        Uniform Probate Code
        §1-201(24) deleted and
        §1-201(23) added
Q12:   Uniform Probate Code
        §2-106(b) added
        Uniform Probate Code
        §6-101 added
Q14:   Uniform Probate Code
        §2-507(a)(1) deleted and
        §2-507(a)(2) added
        Restatement 3d of Trusts,
        §8 added
Q21:   Uniform Probate Code
        §2-503 added
        Uniform Probate Code
        §2-104 added
Q22:   Uniform Probate Code
        §1-106 added
Q23:   Uniform Probate Code
        §2-512 added
        Uniform Probate Code
        §2-708 added
        Uniform Probate Code
        §2-709 added
        Uniform Probate Code
        §2-711 added
Q24:   Uniform Trust Code
        §602(a) added

Uniform Trust Code
§602(c) added
Uniform Trust Code
§503 added
Uniform Trust Code
§411 added
Uniform Trust Code
§411(c) added
Rest. 3d of Trusts,
§65 added
Rest. 3d of Trusts,
§63, Comment h added
Rest. 3d of Trusts,
§63, Comment i added

II. Multiple Choice Questions

Q11:   Uniform Probate Code
        §2-606(a)(5) added
Q12:   Uniform Probate Code
        §1-201(19) deleted and
        §1-201(18) added
Q15:   Uniform Probate Code
        §2-509(a) added
        Uniform Probate Code
        §2-502(b) added
        Uniform Probate Code
        §2-503 added
Q18:   Uniform Probate Code
        §2-801(a) deleted and
        §2-1105 added
Q22:   Uniform Probate Code
        §1-201(33) deleted and
        §1-201(32) added
Q26:   Uniform Probate Code
        §2-502(b) added
Q32:   Uniform Probate Code
        §2-901(a) added
Q37:   Uniform Probate Code
        §1-201(56) deleted and
        §1-201(55) added
Q42:   Uniform Probate Code
        §2-603(b)(1) added

Q43:   Uniform Probate Code
        §2-604(b) added
Q50:   Restatement 2d of Trusts,
        §24, Comment b
        deleted and Restatement 3d
        of Trusts,
        §13, Comment b added
Q51:   Restatement 2d of Trusts,
        §26 deleted and Restate-
        ment 3d of Trusts,
        §15, Comment b added
Q53:   Restatement 2d of Trusts,
        §122 deleted and Restate-
        ment 3d of Trusts,
        §46 added
Q56:   Restatement 3d of Trusts,
        §47 added
Q57:   Restatement 2d of Trusts,
        §62, Comment h deleted
        and Restatement 3d
        of Trusts,
        §29, Comment j added
        Restatement 2d of Trusts,
        §65 deleted and Restate-
        ment 3d of Trusts,
        §29, Comment i added
Q63:   Restatement 3d of Trusts,
        §54 added
Q65:   Uniform Trust Code
        §502 added
Q66:   Uniform Trust Code
        §503(b)(3) added
Q76:   Uniform Trust Code
        §802(b) added
        Restatement 2d of Trusts,
        §170, Comment b deleted
        and Restatement 3d of
        Trusts,
        §78, Comment b added
Q77:   Uniform Trust Code
        §815(a)(2)(A) added
        Uniform Trust Code
        §816(5) added
Q78:   Restatement 2d of Trusts,
        §187 deleted and
        Restatement 3d of Trusts,
        §87, Comment d added
        Uniform Trust Code
        §814(a) added

Q80:   Restatement 2d of Trusts,
        §170 deleted and
        Restatement 3d of Trusts,
        §78, Comment d added
        Restatement 3d of Trusts,
        §39 added
        Uniform Trust Code
        §703(a) added
        Uniform Trust Code
        §703(d) added
Q81:   Uniform Trust Code
        §705(a) added
        Uniform Trust Code
        §807(a) added
Q82:   Uniform Trust Code
        §807(a) added
Q83:   Restatement 2d of Trusts,
        §170, Comment l
        deleted and Restatement
        3d of Trusts,
        §78, Comment c(2) added
        Restatement 2d of Trusts,
        §206, Illustration 8 deleted
        and Restatement 3d
        of Trusts — Prudent
        Investor Rule,
        §§205–206 added
Q85:   Uniform Probate Code
        §7-306(a) deleted and
        Uniform Probate Code
        §7-306 added
        Uniform Trust Code
        §1010 added
Q86:   Uniform Trust Code
        §1010(b) added
Q88:   1997 Principal and
        Income Act
        §104 added
Q89:   Restatement 2d of Trusts,
        §240 deleted and Restate-
        ment 3d of Trusts,
        §240 added
Q91:   Restatement 2d of Trusts,
        §§330, 331 deleted and
        Restatement 3d of Trusts,
        §63 added
        Uniform Trust Code
        §602 added

Index

References are to the number of the question raising the issue. "E" indicates an Essay Question; "M" indicates a Multiple-Choice Question.